Dissident Gut

# Gender and the Body in Literature and Culture
Series editors: Ruth Heholt and Joanne Parsons

**Recent books in the series:**
*Consuming Female Beauty: British Literature and Periodicals, 1840–1914*
Michelle J. Smith

*Dissident Gut: Technologies of Regularity, Politics of Revolt*
Jean Walton

**Forthcoming**
*Vladimir Mayakovsky, Poetics of Virility and Masculine Style*
Connor Doak

*The Drunkard in Victorian Fiction and Culture: From Conviviality to Cursed Thirst*
Pam Lock

*Medicine and Women's Fiction: Hysteria, Bodies and Narratives, 1850s to 1930s*
Louise Benson James

*Trans Narrators: First-Person Form and the Gendered Body After 1990*
Chiara Pellegrini

# Dissident Gut

Technologies of Regularity, Politics of Revolt

Jean Walton

EDINBURGH
University Press

Edinburgh University Press is one of the leading university presses in the UK. We publish academic books and journals in our selected subject areas across the humanities and social sciences, combining cutting-edge scholarship with high editorial and production values to produce academic works of lasting importance. For more information visit our website: edinburghuniversitypress.com

© Jean Walton, 2024, 2025

Edinburgh University Press Ltd
13 Infirmary Street
Edinburgh EH1 1LT

First published in hardback by Edinburgh University Press 2024

Typeset in 11/13 Adobe Sabon by
by Cheshire Typesetting Ltd, Cuddington, Cheshire

A CIP record for this book is available from the British Library

ISBN 978 1 3995 3292 1 (hardback)
ISBN 978 1 3995 3293 8 (paperback)
ISBN 978 1 3995 3294 5 (webready PDF)
ISBN 978 1 3995 3295 2 (epub)

The right of Jean Walton to be identified as the author of this work has been asserted in accordance with the Copyright, Designs and Patents Act 1988, and the Copyright and Related Rights Regulations 2003 (SI No. 2498).

# Contents

| | |
|---|---|
| Acknowledgements | vi |
| Series Preface | ix |
| Introduction: The Biopolitics of Metabolic Disturbance | 1 |

### Part I: Macro-Peristalsis
1. Metabolic Rift and the Remedy of Faecal Recycling — 25
2. Faecal Habitus — 45
3. Marx's Regulation of Metabolism — 58
4. The Second Brain — 80

### Part II: Micro-Peristalsis
5. Unkinking, Streamlining and the Household Engineer — 109
6. The Peristaltic Desiring-Machine of Miss Louise — 129
7. The Creative Devolution of Reverse Peristalsis — 146
8. Peristaltic Politics of a Suffragette — 187
   Conclusion: Faecal Biopolitics in the Twenty-First Century — 231

| | |
|---|---|
| Bibliography | 262 |
| Index | 275 |

# Acknowledgements

I like to think that this project began almost a lifetime ago when, as a college student, I noted in my daily journal a curious quirk in my own peristaltic system: if I didn't spend some time writing each day, I mean seriously writing, I did not feel the urge to go. Writing thus became the key to my own regularity, and was crucial to what I later came to understand as my faecal habitus. Fast forward to conversations with my sociologist friend Greta Gilbertson at Fordham University in the early 1990s, about the prevalence of constipation among female peers we knew, and how the stress of daily life seemed to work against daily evacuations. If only we could be more laid back about it, we thought, and joked that someone should write a book titled 'Zen and the Art of Peristalsis'.

Although I did not write *that* book, the present one began to emerge when, while researching my first book (*Fair Sex, Savage Dreams*), I discovered Stekel's chapter on Miss Louise, who had discovered her own methods for getting the inner sphincter to open without the use of medication. Soon thereafter, archivist extraordinaire Leslie Hall revealed to me the riches of the Parkes Weber collection at the Wellcome Library in London, thus opening up the vista of a second fascinating case study. Over the following twenty years, in between other projects, I was drawn back to the question of metabolism and peristaltic regularity, and thanks to the encouragement of many generous fellow scholars, friends and institutions, *Dissident Gut* finally took its ultimate shape.

I want to thank the University of Rhode Island, whose Dean of Arts and Sciences, Winnie Brownell, was supportive of this project from its inception, as well as the URI Center for Humanities, whose $2,000 sabbatical research grant helped with travel to England.

# Acknowledgements

Thanks to colleagues in England for hosting presentations of chapters from the book; this includes Rob Kirk, Duncan Wilson and Ana Carden-Coyne at the University of Manchester's Centre for the History of Science Technology and Medicine (CHSTM) seminar series; Jackie Stacey, Monica Pearl and Daniela Caselli, at the University of Manchester's Summer Sexuality School; and Laura Salisbury at the University of London, Birkbeck, who generously hosted me, and whose brilliant work on Beckett, psychoanalysis and the gut inspired and encouraged me to press forward with my own research on the topic.

Periodic meetings over the years with Karl Schoonover, my divine companion in waste, toxins and cinematic detritus of all kinds, helped me to work out some of the subtler connections among the materials I was dealing with. And I would be nowhere without the constant friendship, intellectual exchange and glorious walks in the Lake District with my friend Laura Doan and her partner Marlene Mussell. Laura has long been my most relentless coach and drillmaster, insisting that I metabolise all the hoardings of my research into published products, and showing the way forward when I had seemed to reach a dead end.

The American Academy in Berlin, whose generous hospitality extends to partners of fellows, provided me with the space, library resources and a lively intellectual environment in 2015, while I composed the metabolic rift aspects of the book.

As I was completing final chapters, I benefitted from feedback and inspiration from colleagues at the 2017 Princeton Psychoanalysis and Postcolonialism workshop, namely Zahid Chaudhary, Dagmar Herzog, Ankhi Mukherjee, Joan Scott, Robyn Wiegman, Camille Robcis, Ranji Khanna and David Eng.

Maria Tumarkin and Melinda Harvey joined Mary Cappello and myself for a collaborative panel at the Essay Conference in Malta in 2019, where I felt encouraged to extend my academic work on peristalsis into the world of literary non-fiction.

I am deeply grateful to Manon Mathias, Elsa Richardson and Kevin Leomo for hosting me in Glasgow as their Keynote Speaker at the Modernity and the Gut Symposium, just as I was putting the final touches on this book. The community of biologists, historians, medical anthropologists, literary scholars and filmmakers that convened for this fabulous event made me feel at home, indeed.

The production team at Edinburgh University Press has been a dream to work with. This includes members of the editorial team:

Emily Sharp, Elizabeth Fraser, Series Editors Ruth Heholt and Joanne Ella Parsons, Desk Editor Joannah Duncan, Copy-editor Neil Burkey and, for the fabulous cover, Senior Design Controller Bekah Dey and Designer/Illustrator Emily Benton. On a more personal level, I enjoyed long-term intellectual colloquy with friends Karen Carr and Russell Potter, who have been my closest writing companions over the years, as well as Arthur Riss, who gave last-minute generous feedback.

I'm eternally indebted to Randi Wirth, Expert Physick of the first brain, for helping me to forge my way forward.

My brother Jack Walton, through his wry observations, my sister-in-law Kim Hardy, who agreed to be interviewed by me in the early phases of the book, and my sister Nancy Walton, who sent me the perspicacious gift of a Squatty Potty, showed that family can, indeed, get on board with even the most obscure academic projects.

And as always, I owe to my partner Mary Cappello, and in particular to the example of her gorgeously wrought books, the reminder that lucid and shimmering prose is indispensable in any sort of compositional projet; her dedication to the life of writing, despite the manifold obstacles thrown in our paths, inspires and sustains me beyond measure.

Previously published material:
An earlier version of chapters 5 and 6 appeared as 'Female Peristalsis' in *differences: A Journal of Feminist Cultural Studies*, 13.2 (2002): 57–89.

Chapter 4 is a revision of material included in 'Modernity and the Peristaltic Subject' in *Neurology and Modernity: A Cultural History of Nervous Systems, 1800–1950*, Laura Salisbury and Andrew Shail, eds. London: Palgrave Macmillan, 2010: 245–66.

# Series Preface

This series has a dedicated focus on gender and the body. With pressing questions about embodiment, gender identity, race, the Anthropocene and the post-human being played out in academia and wider society, this series provides space for full and detailed scholarly discussions in the form of collections and monographs. Encouraging interdisciplinarity and crossovers in subjects, time periods and genres, the series challenges and expands discussions around LGTBQI embodiments, race and racialisation, and the changing nature of masculinity, as well as opening up old and new debates around femininity and feminism. Looking at narratives from different periods and cultures, the series is committed to publishing pioneering research that will enhance many disciplines.

Series Editors: Ruth Heholt and Joanne Ella Parsons

# Introduction: The Biopolitics of Metabolic Disturbance

### Border metabolism

I begin with a contemporary scenario of state-sanctioned interference in the bodily functions of a population reduced to what Giorgio Agamben has called 'bare life', a population deemed to be undeserving not just of the basic necessities for survival, but of the definition of the human. This could refer to any number of global and American crises in recent years, but the one I am about to describe will, I think, suffice as an instance of what this book, in the broadest terms, is about: metabolic disturbance within the context of biopolitics, and the dissident gut that responds to it.

In the summer of 2019, Americans attempted to take in daily reports of a catastrophe that seemed at once impossible to assimilate and, to the average person, difficult to remedy. At the US/Mexico border, large populations of desperate people fleeing life-threatening situations in their countries of origin had been corralled into holding facilities, separated from their family members, subjected to intolerable living conditions and held for days, weeks, even months beyond what any person would imagine bearable. Although the depredations visited on these migrants at the border were manifold, I wish to stress in particular a direct attack on their metabolic systems: with what they were (or were not) fed; whether the food they received left them hungry, made them sick or gave them constipation or diarrhoea; with the conditions in which they were expected to digest and excrete; with the lack of safe and sanitary provisions for the elimination of waste; and indeed, with the conventions that would normally characterise their eating habits, the disruption of the very routines of ordinary childcare practices, the training of toddlers in the rudiments of their own bodily needs, or even the consistent human touch and care in early childhood development that makes it possible to experience a sense of self. In this respect, they were subjected to a wilful and sustained programme of metabolic disturbance, designed to administer discipline at the level of the autonomic nervous system, and to punish them for having attempted to enter a geopolitical metabolic system that sought to refuse them, by transforming them into 'refuse'.

By metabolic disturbance I mean wilful meddling, but also systemic intersection, with all aspects of the human alimentary tract, with how one eats, digests, eliminates waste, not only as a matter of essential survival, but as a matter of cultural and social thriving. Eating and excreting is a biological function, but it is also always a mode of living, a shared set of conventions, a disciplinary routine that can be taken for granted as a minor aspect of life, or must be vigorously attended to depending on one's geopolitical locale and one's access to or lack of resources for sustenance and hygiene. The peristaltic systems of individuals are always connected up with local, national and global circuits of food security, supply chains, agricultural practices, public and private plumbing arrangements, sewer and septic infrastructure or agreed upon places where you can relieve yourself, wastewater treatment plants, polluted waterways, fertilisation projects, and tensions between urban and rural locales. Small and large intestinal motility depends on the labour of food production, transportation, distribution and preparation, as well as the labour of waste management from the domestic to the global level.

There is no non-mediated mode of peristaltic function; the smoothness or disruption of motion in one segment of the grand scheme of a metabolic world has a relation to the smoothness or disruption of the well-being of any given human. If this is the case, then the question of 'metabolic disturbance' and a 'dissident gut' can never be a simple matter of a natural process that has been damaged or deranged. It is, rather, about a condition of being in the world (as opposed to 'in nature'), a world in which modern politics consists of a set of interventions for maximising the bio-functions of some, at the expense of the bio-functions of others, and where the bodily processing of this world is simultaneously a biological, affective and cognitive imperative. And so, with these broad strokes in mind of what might be meant by a disruption of metabolic life, I turn now to my opening scenario.

## The Biopolitics of Metabolic Disturbance 3

At US border detention centres, holding cells were filled so far beyond capacity that there was standing room only for days and nights on end, making it impossible to lie down or sleep. Inadequate showers or washing facilities, no soap or toothpaste, no changes of clothes and oppressive temperatures meant that detainees were denied the basics of what is considered necessary for routine hygiene. These facilities were meant only for a few hours' detention, so food supplies had to be supplemented by civilian employees who used their government credit cards to go grocery shopping; but they weren't able to get the most nourishing, appropriate or sufficient supplies.[1]

Infants, toddlers, children of all ages had been separated from adult family members, and were being held in overcrowded facilities with little or no childcare, no diapers, no fresh clothes, no showers – the younger kids handed over to older kids expected to look after them. Again there was insufficient food (children were hungry), and little or no medical attention (some children died).[2]

This news hit the US public at gut level. Some rationalised the situation, trusting the judgement of authorities; others deplored it, but felt helpless to do anything; still others mobilised by volunteering at shelters for undocumented immigrants or migrants who had been released from detention centres, or by contributing money to such centres, or by demonstrating in the streets, or by boycotting companies somehow implicated in the policy of inhumane conditions, or by litigating against the government to ameliorate conditions, or by calling on politicians to put pressure on the current White House administration. Certainly, images and stories of atrocities committed by our own government against vulnerable populations provoked visceral reactions in anyone who received the news. No one wanted to be responsible for such treatment, but it was a challenge to force those who had the power to stop it to act fast enough. We were sickened by what was happening.

To be sure, anyone who has read Agamben's characterisation of the concentration camp as the paradigm of the biopolitical nature of power in the modern age sees its obvious relevance to what was going on at the US/Mexico border. Aspects of the camps of the Third Reich were uncontestably true for US detention facilities: that the Nazi 'juridical basis for internment was not common law but . . . protective custody', also understood as a 'preventative police measure insofar as it allowed individuals to be "taken into custody" independently of any criminal behavior, solely to avoid danger to the security of the state' (Agamben 167); that those detained were 'stripped of every political status and wholly reduced to bare life', making the camp 'the most absolute biopolitical space ever to have been realised, in which power confronts nothing but pure life, without any mediation' (Agamben 171).

This is what characterises 'absolute biopolitical space', which is to say, the political space we inhabit in modernity. It must be understood, too, that the operation of reducing migrant bodies to 'bare life' in this scenario at the same time produces bodies of the American citizen, deserving of political status. As Agamben puts it, the modern emergence of the camp foregrounds how politics is now about a bifurcated 'biopolitical body' that appears on the one side as the 'Jewish' (or migrant) body and on the other as the 'German' (or American) body, 'as life unworthy of being lived' so that a 'full life' may be enjoyed.

Let's look a little more carefully at this notion of being 'stripped of every political status' (and give consideration to one particular element that is stripped away), of being 'reduced to bare life' (a life that is bare of the thing stripped from one), and of a life whose definition of 'pure' hinges on being 'without any mediation'.

Assuredly, we are in the presence of a camp insofar as individuals have been herded into an enclosed space where 'the normal order is *de facto* suspended and in which whether or not atrocities are committed depends not only on law but on the civility and ethical sense of the police who temporarily act as sovereign', in other words, those well-meaning government employees shopping for food with their state-issued credit cards (Agamben 174). The 'normal order' of things in the space of the detention camp was suspended, because the people detained there were deemed ineligible for the rights and conditions US citizens enjoy, so we had to trust that the border guards in charge had the 'civility and ethical sense' not to harm their captives. This is what it means to be 'stripped of every political status', to be reduced to the 'bare life' that contrasts with what makes the rest of us feel ourselves to be 'human'.

*Dissident Gut* shares this notion of the biopolitical nature of power, but it puts specific emphasis on one overarching aspect of the 'bare life' to which one may at any moment be reduced: the metabolic aspect. Our own gut reaction to daily reports of atrocities at the border is, I would argue, the nodal point at which we are implicated in a complex metabolic system operating at multiple scales and through diverse modalities. The scales range from individual peristaltic organisms to global agricultural networks, and the modalities through which they are implicated range from perceived threats to the metabolic integrity of the 'nation state' to the actual threatened bodies of migrants, from disrupted potty training to the transformation of humans into biohazards, from forced rechannelling of refugees into lethal escape routes (the too dry desert, the too wet river), to the clogging of toilets as a form of protest. Metabolic health and vitality was directly targeted in the border facilities, and the targeting of migrants' enteric systems was a way to deprive individuals and populations of the baseline of what allows one to feel human, of what makes it possible for one to be included in a 'world' of humans.

Agamben writes that the correct question to pose about this kind of concentration camp scenario is not how such crimes could be committed against human beings, but rather, what are the 'juridical procedures and deployments of power by which human beings could be so completely deprived of their rights and prerogatives that no act committed against them could appear any longer as a crime?' (Agamben 171). I'm going to lay stress here on the 'rights and prerogatives' of human beings as a matter of their peristaltic vitality, their metabolic health as it relates to the consequential metabolic systems through which they move. Do we have 'rights and prerogatives' that are not, in some way, defined by how we are caught up in material, economic, biological and social networks of metabolic transformation and peristaltic movement? As one writer puts it,

> bare life is only apprehensible in contrast to the plenitude of ways in which human beings really live, namely within and through one or another ensemble of social relations. Bare life is, then, a conceptual foil for all the historically specific and socially particular forms in which human ('biological') life is qualified by its inscription within one or another sociopolitical order. (De Genova 2016, 128)

There are innumerable ways in which our sense of ourselves as human depends on the taken-for-grantedness of our biological life, on the ways our bodies are inscribed in our sociopolitical order. The aim of *Dissident Gut* is to explore the theoretical, historical and political shape taken by just one of these ways during a consequential moment of capitalist domination: how we came to be, and continue to exist, as modern peristaltic subjects in a world that can be understood as a complex system of metabolic relations.

Seen through this particular biopolitical model, we can understand the exodus of people from Guatemala, El Salvador and Honduras as in part a result of what Marxist environmentalists are calling the 'metabolic rift' in the relation of humans to the earth that sustains their life processes – a rift involving the supplanting of traditional, bio-diverse agriculture with capitalist-driven monoculture, displaced rural populations forced to move to urban industrial areas in search of work, depletion of soil quality in the fields and overabundance of waste in the cities (Foster, 1999). To be sure, it is hunger, lack of a means to sustain oneself and immediate violence, often aimed at women and children, that motivates people to migrate north and present 'credible fear' for their lives as they petition for asylum. But the underlying cause of the major disruption to food security (and bodily security) in the global South is arguably an aspect of a global rift in what Marx called 'the metabolic interaction between man and the earth' (Marx 1976, 637).

At the same time, we can see the conditions within the holding cells in terms of how sovereign power (in the form of border agents) intrudes into the metabolic processes of captives, reducing them to 'bare life'. Insufficient food slows down the peristaltic system until children complain of hunger, their defences against infection compromised until they get sick.[3] Inappropriate food for adults (a steady diet of bologna sandwiches) interferes with intestinal motility until constipation sets in, and medical attention is required (Bier 2019). The crowding is so severe that people have to stand on toilets just in order to breathe.[4] This limits toilet accessibility, but when forced to make a choice, respiration comes first, elimination after. In dire circumstances, one is forced to prioritise one bodily need over another.

The *New York Times* reports that 'children as young as 7 and 8, many of them wearing clothes caked with snot and tears, are caring for infants they've just met... Toddlers without diapers are relieving themselves in their pants. Teenage mothers are wearing clothes stained with breast milk' (Dickerson 2019). The Office of Inspector General finds that things are 'chaotic' in these facilities, but let's be clear: it is a very specific form of 'order' that has been disrupted.[5] Where adults normally attend to the metabolic needs of their children, here children are expected to tend to the needs of other children who are strangers to them. Where normally a lactating mother may direct the flow of her breast milk to her infant's lips, here the milk leaks onto her clothes and is left to dry. Where normally one changes the diapers of infants and toddlers, here, there don't seem to be any diapers; the babies excrete onto their clothes and carry it around with them. The very distinction between adult and child is muddled insofar as mothers are included in the mix since they are too young to be detained with adults, yet old enough that they have children themselves, as indicated by the breast milk leaking onto their clothes. In fact, substances produced by the body, its snot, its tears, its milk, its urine and faeces – all of it seems to end up on the body, absorbed into clothing that never changes, and is never cleaned. This is the chaos of Mary Douglas's dirt defined as 'matter out of place', the purity of the nation threatened by the danger of filthy migrant bodies, the safety of the guards threatened by the polluting bodies of their captives. Denied the means of practising the standards of hygiene enjoyed by the rest of us, the people in the holding cells have been transformed into toxic waste. As 'biohazards', they pose a threat, so the guards arm themselves not only with facemasks (and this pre-dates the Covid-19 pandemic), but with guns as well.[6]

But there is another form of chaos as well that pertains to the order that usually reigns in the realm of early child development. To be sure, we can predict that separation from their parents will leave psychological scars on these kids for life. But in addition to that, to the extent that one of the ways 'human ("biological") life is qualified' includes metabolic regulation in the form of early toilet training, even this childcare routine is denied and suspended during these long periods of detention. There is no toilet training for these toddlers, who are expected just to relieve themselves in their pants. Metabolic sustenance is thus disrupted on both a material and a psychosocial register.

But what is the purpose of all this state-authorised intervention into the metabolism of captive bodies? An observation from Border Control management (as quoted in an Office of Inspector General report) offers an answer: they recognise that to detain migrants for so long creates a 'humanitarian issue', but they believe that 'if they do not have a consequence delivery system, either prosecution or ICE detention, the flow will increase' (OIG 2019b, 7).

Some clarification is necessary here: 'Consequence Delivery System' (or CDS) is the term given to a border security strategy worked out under the Obama administration during the

Department of Homeland Security's shift from a 'resource-based' to a 'risk-based' approach to its enforcement mission (*2012–2016 Border Patrol Strategic Plan* 7). As a Congressional Research Service Report put it, the CDS was designed 'to uniquely evaluate each subject [who is apprehended crossing the border] and identify the ideal consequences to deliver to impede and deter further illegal activity' (CRSR 2019). To do this, border patrol agents use 'laminated cards with matrices describing the range of enforcement actions available for a particular migrant' to ensure that 'everyone who is apprehended faces "some type of consequence" other than voluntary return' (CRSR 2019). The consequences entail various forms of removal from the United States, either through 'fast-tracked' or 'Streamlined' prosecution, repatriation, transfer to Mexico, or other forms of 'expedited removal' (Boyce 2014).

What is notable about the remark of the Border Control management (that a CDS is needed to decrease the flow of migrants) is that the creation of the 'humanitarian issue' in the process of 'ICE detention' is clearly understood to be a 'Consequence Delivery System' designed to counter illegal border crossing – despite the fact that inhumane living conditions were not officially listed among the original 'consequences' when the policy was put in place.

Moreover, it would appear that the 2019 iteration of the CDS no longer treats border-crossers as discrete subjects to be interviewed and individualised, but rather as a mass of alien bodies whose enclosure and enforced proximity to each other is both the 'consequence' delivered to them and the condition that transforms them into a dangerous mob *deserving* of consequences. The crowding, the inappropriate or insufficient food, the denial of hygienic resources, the degradation of metabolic processes on every level, delivered *en masse* to thousands of people, whether under the official orders of Homeland Security or not (because we are talking about the 'police who temporarily act as sovereign' here), are *de facto* being justified as a deterrence to the flow of migrants across the US border.

We can add to this that the language typically used by observers reporting on the crisis reflects a tacit understanding of the practices at the border as also an attempt to regulate the metabolic system of the nation state. In reference to the channelling of children from one agency to another, Human Rights Watch researcher

Clara Long describes them as being moved among an 'extremely bloated set of detention centers and shelters' (Long 2019). The prolonged 'extended lengths of stay' under the Trump administration has 'really slowed down the process to reunify children with family members in the US' (Long 2019). We can understand this as a matter of deliberately decreased motility within the channels through which the nation state absorbs and processes the bodies taken into its system; if there had previously been some regularity in the progress of people moving through the bureaucratic and material conduits of the United States immigration system, in 2019, there were massive blockages in the flow, creating 'bloating' in the peristaltic chambers of the Department of Homeland Security.

Given the metabolic nature of all this, and especially of the 'consequences' being meted out to those reduced to the conditions of 'bare life', perhaps it is no surprise that captives protested the targeting of their peristaltic systems by stopping up the metabolic system of the detention centres themselves: an Office of Inspector General memo reports that 'there had already been security incidents among adult males at multiple facilities. These included detainees clogging toilets with Mylar blankets and socks in order to be released from their cells during maintenance' (Costello 2019, 7). But more seriously, revolt took the form of hunger strikes, as migrants stopped their own metabolic systems in hopes of putting into motion the channels of amelioration outside the confines of the detention centres (Montes 2019). In response, officials fed their prisoners by force, in a mechanical attempt to start the peristaltic system back up again. The refusal to take food as a means of protest under incarceration, followed by the insertion of rubber tubes into the bodies of the offenders, dates back to the radical activism of the suffragettes a hundred years ago. Hunger strikes and subsequent forcible feedings, as we will see, are at the heart, or more precisely perhaps, at the fundament of the dissident gut.

## Regulating regularity

This recasting of the 2019 migrant crisis at the US border in terms of its metabolic aspects models the sort of extended feminist, Marxist and biopolitical analysis for which I hope this book lays the foundations. *Dissident Gut* brings together Marxist economics and environmentalism, sociological theory of bodily habitus, medical accounts of the peristaltic system, neurogastroenterology, childcare manuals, the history of sanitary reform, psychoanalytic treatments of the hysteric and activist memoirs to investigate the macro and micro workings of metabolic life as it emerged in the early twentieth century. One of the premises of the book is that peristaltic processes, far from being uncomplicated, natural and untouched by social, political, affective and environmental surrounds, are as deeply mediated as any other aspect of modern life. It is a commonplace to strive for 'regularity' in our bowel habits; but by focusing on the metabolic aspect of biopolitics, we will see that this simple matter of 'regularity' is deeply implicated in a complex system of cycles, circuits, spirals, movement and transformation, of transfers of power and capital, of the natural resources that sustain life, of the cultural routines that define it, of the desires and disgusts that motivate human action, and the calibrations that allow us to experience a comforting consistency, predictability and balance in our day-to-day living. In the name of maximising life, global and national biopolitics sustains the metabolic health of some populations, while damaging that of others. And too often, these 'others' are those who have been relegated to the feminised labour of dealing with waste, which has the simultaneous effect of transforming them into 'waste' themselves.

Marx's deployment of a metabolic model of movement and transformation, his remarks on the necessity to control and mediate our metabolic relation to nature, and environmentalist articulations of his theory of 'metabolic rift' provide a major part of the theoretical underpinnings of this book insofar as it seeks to understand human regulatory interventions into our peristaltic processes. But even as I frame this project as a matter of humans regulating metabolism, I am also alert to the 'mindedness' of metabolic processes themselves, or of what Elizabeth Wilson calls the dynamicism of biology as it, in turn, defines and shapes our social lives, with politicised implications. In this respect, the book is indebted to two sometimes contradictory traditions of thought: that which studies the political and regulatory effects of systemic arrangements on human life, as in Marxism or Bourdieu-inflected sociological thought; but also that which draws out the ways an unconscious (whether construed as ideational or biological) speaks back to, resists or even reconfigures regulatory regimes, as in feminist appropriations of psychoanalytic theory, or in Foucauldian understandings of the play of power and desire, or in new materialist construals of the agency of matter.

While I've opened this book with a contemporary American scenario to dramatise what I mean by the metabolic – and thus peristaltic – aspect of people's lives, in the chapters that follow, I will be focusing more particularly on the late nineteenth and early twentieth century in England and Europe, tracing out the emergence of metabolic thinking as it relates to capitalism in the industrialised locales of the West and global North. I've divided this investigation into two parts. Part I covers what I call 'Macro-peristalsis', in which each chapter lays out a theoretical approach to the systemic shape taken by metabolic life as it emerged at the turn of the twentieth century. These chapters include Marx's theory of metabolic rift and his understanding of the workings of labour and capital as a metabolic process, a sociological theory of modern 'faecal habitus', biomedical theory of the workings of the alimentary system and a Foucauldian meditation on toilet-training as a disciplinary capitalisation of time in the body. Part II, 'Micro-Peristalsis', consists of three case studies of white, British and European women in the early twentieth century. These women's deviant peristaltic systems were subjected to medical intervention, producing, through their own or their doctors' discourse, a way to reconstruct the felt bodily and psychic experience in a specific corner of modern peristaltic life. Each 'doctor-patient' pairing, at once gendered, raced and classed, yields a close-up, more detailed analysis of how particular instances of the dissident gut play out for women expected to take up the labour of peristaltic regulation and hygiene in a domestic context. As with any case study, they are specific to their time and place, and yet are, I hope, transferable to other contexts, other populations, other deployments of critical thought as it is brought to bear on the biopower of metabolic life.

## Theoretical affinities

Before I lay out the ensuing chapters in more detail, I'd like to say a few words here about existing research that overlaps with, but does not share quite the same interdisciplinary or aspirational territory as *Dissident Gut*. Popular books like Mary Roach's *Gulp* (2014) and Giulia Enders's *Gut* (2015) have delighted the general reader who wishes to know the latest scientific research on all things related to the alimentary tract, from input to output, though without digging deep for a sustained cultural analysis of how 'the' peristaltic system hooks up to the other systemic circuits of recent history. Sociologist David Inglis's book and essays (2001) on what he calls the 'modern faecal habitus' usefully characterises the history of Western bowel habits as a kind of technology for class distinction, laying some groundwork for my own exploration of how the human gut nevertheless exceeds its socialisation. Much has recently been published on the history and (geo)politics of human waste, including the work of Rose George (2008); Erland Marald (2002); Gay Hawkins and Stephen Muecke (2003); and Dana Simmons (2006), though these studies of waste (and its management) are rarely tied in to questions of faecal habitus, or the way our bowel habits are regulated. Many scholars have been working on the culture or history of metabolism, from a variety of different angles. Parama Roy (2010) and Solomon Harris (2016) perform sustained examinations of metabolic living in a (post)colonial context; a host of environmentalists have been following the lead of John Bellamy Foster (1999, 2000) in tracing out the implications of Marx's theory of 'metabolic rift'; others, like Swyngedouw et al. (2006), take metabolic approaches to the workings of urban systems. Varied feminist investigations have directed renewed attention to biology, affect and the body, moving out from a strict focus on sexual difference to consider gendered experience in relation to metabolic concerns. This includes Myra Hird's reflections on metabolism and sexual difference (2012); studies of eating practices in the work of Elizabeth Grosz, Elspeth Probyn, Susan Bordo and others; and the work of science-based gender research by scholars such as Elizabeth Wilson, Evelyn Fox Keller, Stacy Alaimo, Anne Fausto-Sterling, Donna Haraway, Karen Barad and Brian Massumi (2002), who have for some time been advocating (in different ways) for more sustained attention to biology in studies of the gendered body, or for a new kind of feminist materialist approach to embodiments of the psyche, or for cultural analysis of affect and the gut.

Hannah Landecker's groundbreaking research on the changing model of metabolism in medical discourse over the past two centuries comes perhaps closest to the sort of history of peristalsis I'm aiming for. In a series of articles, she traces an important shift in the understanding of human metabolism, moving from a one-way process in which the body (like a factory) transforms ingested material into energy, to a two-way process in which both body and ingested material act to transform each other simultaneously (Landecker 2013, 217). Metabolism today may be seen as 'post-industrial', she writes, in part because it post-dates industrialisation, but also because of 'what industrialization has done to the body' (Landecker 2011, 173). If the biomedical study of metabolism had previously been more concerned with 'manufacture' (our bodies converting nutrients to cells, for example), today it pertains more to regulation (Landecker 2011, 173). In her focus on the contemporary scene, the zone of regulation Landecker analyses extends into the molecular dynamics of body and environment, and is primarily the domain of the medical researcher and policy-maker. *Dissident Gut* also concerns itself with 'regulation', though less with metabolism as a *zone* of regulation, and more with the role played by systems and individuals expected to 'regulate' their metabolism at the level of peristaltic motility and consistency, even as their biology asserts an agency of its own. While Landecker briefly touches on the role of Marx in our understanding of metabolism, *Dissident Gut* lingers with the concept of metabolism in Marx, focusing on regularity as it is tied with temporal cycles or pulsions of movement, and with how, as Marx puts it, man 'mediates, regulates, and controls [*vermittelt, regelt und kontrolliert*] the metabolism between himself and nature' (Marx 1867/1976, 283). This drilling down on metabolism in Marx is necessary for a sustained exploration of the disciplinary implications of the question of how 'man' regulates metabolism, and I mean disciplinary in two senses: how peristaltic regulation enters discourse in different intersecting investigational disciplines; and how a disciplining of the viscera became compulsory at the turn of the twentieth century.

This book also has affinities with Elizabeth Wilson's focus, in *Gut Feminism*, on how the peristaltic system is a matter of both the psyche and the flesh. Her engagement with psychoanalysis, in its recognition of the 'mindedness' of the viscera, is closest perhaps to the kinds of questions I am asking in the case studies I'm examining (particularly in Chapter 6). But in *Dissident Gut*, I seek to juxtapose these psycho-biological questions of gut-consciousness with larger questions of economic and political organisation, particularly with regard to human intervention into the material, natural world. In the context of the rise of capitalism in the Western world, I place pressure on the fact that in domestic contexts, a lot of the labour accorded to women was about dealing with household waste, even as they were expected to regulate their own excremental output. If the broad movements of industrial capitalism consist of production, consumption and waste, not enough attention has been paid to the implication of women in this question of waste management, with the exception of the work of some materialist or Marxist feminists, like Vandana Shiva, Ariel Salleh, Timothée Haug and Silvia Federici. Where feminist critique is concerned, there is still very little overlap between psychoanalytic itineraries like Wilson's on the one hand, and Marxist on the other. Part of the project of *Dissident Gut* is to bring these two often conflicting modes of focusing on female subjectivity into the same framework.

## Chapter layout: from macro to micro-peristalsis

### Part I: Macro-Peristalsis

In Chapter 1, I introduce how the concept of 'metabolic rift' has become the basis of a Marxist environmentalism, led by sociologist John Bellamy Foster, and taken up by a growing array of scholars wanting to think through the global repercussions of industrialism under capitalist and socialist systems alike. At the centre of the theory of metabolic rift is the story of a pre-capitalist era, when humans ate the food produced in nearby fields and gardens, then returned their excrement back to the soil, in an unbroken cycle of production, consumption, fertilisation and production. Centuries of disenfranchisement of small farming communities, the enclosures system that drove farmers off the land and transformed them into labourers with nothing to sell but their labour, and subsequent concentration of these populations in industrialised cities disrupted this cycle, depleting soil of its nutrients and polluting urban areas. The idea of a rift in man's metabolism with nature encompasses an infinite array of material debts and excrescences (deforestation; ruination of natural habitats; extinctions of mammals, insects, birds, fish; water and air pollution; melting of polar ice caps – all of the effects that add up to global climate change in the Anthropocene). But in Marx's narration of the problem, the central animating story is that of the farmer whose excrement had once replenished his fields, but who was now forced to shit in the city, thus robbing the soil of important nutrients, and polluting urban waterways. It is this excremental nexus at the core of metabolic analysis that I want to examine more closely, as I ask what the implications were for women in particular, in this period when the concentration of labourers in industrialised cities was coming to a crisis.

This includes a meditation on how 'metabolism' has extended beyond its application to single organisms and come to serve as a model for systems in general. I look, for instance, at how metabolism has proven useful to analyse the workings of the city, or of the interface between humans, fat and city infrastructure. With this focus on fat (as a correlate to faecal matter) I consider how metabolic thinking entails a reconsideration of what constitutes 'waste' in the first place, especially in the context of the history of faecal recycling, where human excrement is treated not as waste, but as a resource.

In Chapter 2, I note that none of this 'metabolic rift-based' ecological research has overlapped with another branch of sociology devoting itself to a Bourdieu-inspired analysis of what David Inglis has termed our 'faecal habitus'. Inglis traces the historical emergence of a modern faecal habitus back to the end of the nineteenth century in England and Europe, examining the ways bodily rites of elimination are tied in with class-based systems of distinction. These two chapters thus bring together metabolic rift with Inglis's insights about the bourgeois faecal habitus to understand why water-based flush systems took over as the primary means of dealing with human excrement, and gestures toward a Foucauldian recognition of the relation between faecal 'regularity' and regulatory regimes.

In Chapter 3, I return for a more sustained look at Marx's concept of 'metabolism' as labour, embedded in nature, and leading out through all social and economic relations. This entails a close reading of how Marx deploys a metabolic model for his understanding of economic circulation and exchange, of products transforming into commodities, and of social relations among humans, a 'social metabolism' modelled on and extending from what he understands as our metabolic relation to nature. But I also draw out some implications of Hannah Arendt's observation (in *The Human Condition*) that Marx neglected to make a distinction between 'labour' and 'work', that is between human activity within the realm of 'metabolism with nature' and that belonging to the realm of world-making. Although Arendt depicts 'Man' as engaged in both labour and work, I emphasise the need to acknowledge that, historically speaking, there has been a gendered division of labour: women perform most of the metabolic activity, and men, the work of world-making. If among white women of the metropole, there is a marked division whereby metabolic labour has been feminised and denigrated, and the work of world-making the provenance of white men, how might we bring into view the metabolic *value* generated by the organs of regularity as they are deployed by women as meta-industrial labourers in the metropole?

My consideration of Marx's emphasis on the regulation of our metabolism with nature lays the groundwork for an elaboration, in Chapter 4, of the neurological model of the workings of the digestive system, or the autonomic nervous system, as it was understood in the early twentieth century. We find here a model of the human as a tube for processing the world, entailing evolutionary, developmental and quotidian registers of temporality. Insofar as the gut is figured in its capacity to think, a sort of 'second brain', a series of questions are raised about the neurological ambiguity of peristaltic agency. We contemplate what 'thinking' actually is, especially if we allow that it is not always conscious or rational, but cross-cut or underwritten by obscure desires and ambivalences occurring at the level of the large intestine.

Chapter 4 also makes a foray into the discourse of regularity in childcare manuals, where toilet training emerges as a matter of female labour involved in the disciplining of the viscera, of what Foucault calls the accumulation and capitalisation of time in the body. We come to understand the peristaltic system as what Brian Massumi has called the 'interoceptive perceptual apparatus' – that is, a visceral mode of perception that encounters the world and makes decisions about it, independently of our cortical nervous system, and thus accounts in part for 'autonomy of affect'. This chapter teases out the question of how toilet training plays a role in the regulation of this internal perceptual and affective system.

### Part II: Micro-Peristalsis

The intestinal systems of women in particular were targeted for the most sustained intervention in early twentieth-century campaigns for regularity, as can be seen in Chapter 5, where I open with an account of Sir Arbuthnot Lane's aggressive surgeries to straighten the 'kinked' bowels of his mostly female patients, whom he deemed to suffer from intestinal stasis. To that, I correlate the emphasis on the rationalisation of housework in this same period, as female 'domestic engineers' were encouraged to eliminate wasteful gestures as they moved through their kitchens, and to attend to their metabolic health once a year by checking into a sanitarium for fine-tuning. I then turn, in Chapter 6, to the case study that became the generative kernel from which this book sprang, the 1920s psychoanalytic account by Wilhelm Stekel of a woman whose peristaltic system, and her bowel habits, were intimately bound up with her sexual and affective life.

This is the first of three chapters, each presenting the case study of a British or European woman whose peristaltic system – that is, her experience of ingestion, digestion and excretion – became in some way remarkable, and thus remarked upon in psychoanalytic, medical and political writing. As I will have noted already in Chapter 3, women are among the class of labourers who take care of the 'meta-industrial labor of mediating the humanity-nature interface' (or what Marx calls man's metabolism with nature) (Salleh 2010, 207). In the global North, where my study focuses, this labour takes the form of unremunerated housework and childcare, where toilet training, the management of household waste, and the regulation of flows into and out of the domicile are relegated, for the most part, to women. For this reason, I zero in on cases where women were producing discourse (either through the agency of a medical practitioner, or through their own writing) about what Salleh calls the 'ecosystem' of their own bodies, with implications for the larger metabolic systems that surrounded them (Salleh 2010, 211).[7]

In Chapter 8, I move from psychoanalysis on the continent to general medicine in England, to consider a London physician obsessed with whether his patient's topsy-turvy peristaltic system was caused by an organic or a psychogenic lesion. While London politicians debated whether public toilets for women should be built in the city's busiest thoroughfares, this prominent doctor began a decades-long investigation of a woman whose faecal vomiting seemed to suggest that the entire human enteric system could function in reverse. The subsequent 'partnership' of patient and doctor in the interest of knowledge production resulted in a series of publications on the borderline between biology and psychology, between hysteria and malingering, between the dissident gut and 'tertiary sex characteristics'.

And in Chapter 8, I turn to the rise of the militant phase of the female suffrage movement, to examine a tale of political revolt, narrated by the peristaltic subject herself: an Englishwoman who, by joining with imprisoned hunger strikers, wilfully subtracts her own metabolic system from that of the British Empire, and explicitly defines this subtraction as a form of political discourse. In this case, I count the hunger strike of the incarcerated suffragette as a form of activist intervention into the biopolitical dimension of electoral politics, and the practice of 'forcible feeding' as the sovereign's metabolic retaliation.

Whatever conventions define the modern faecal habitus for a given population in this era, in these three cases, we witness disruption, discomposure, cessation, even reversal of peristaltic norms. This throws into relief, at a micro-level, the function of the viscera as a site of communication, as a metabolic transfer point where autonomic processes intersect with voluntary choice, where felt bodily duration is at odds with, or must be regulated by, the abstract time of industrial and domestic production, the domestic time of heteronormativity, the clinical time of science, and the historical time of political change. The narrow focus on female peristaltic subjects allows us, too, to complement Inglis's observations about the role of class difference in the formation of a modern faecal habitus, by further investigating the role gender plays in the deployment of peristaltic practices.

Since moving one's bowels is only in part an autonomic function, entailing a combination of conscious choice and unwilled activity, and since the accounts of these women's experiences are quite explicit, at a micro-level of intimacy, they offer opportunities for asking questions about agency within regulatory regimes that extend into the very viscera of human experience. Moreover, since peristalsis is a temporal function of the body, involving flows and pauses, appropriately scheduled actions, periods of inactivity followed by crises of urgency, it allows examination of felt duration, of the phenomenological experience of time.

The close readings of these case studies are interspersed with an array of related contextual material: the ubiquity of medical and hygienic discourse emphasising bowel regularity and linking it to good citizenship, productivity, marriageability, moral development and the like; rationalisation of industrial and domestic production; an emphasis on streamlining in architectural design and product packaging; a debate about the feasibility of installing public conveniences for women in a heavily travelled commercial neighbourhood in London; medical and psychoanalytic attempts to parse out the exact border where the organic leaves off and the psychological begins; and child-rearing manuals emphasising the importance of good toilet training. While I can't say that these women typify deviations from a peristaltic norm (thus confirming the contours of that norm), it is my hope that by entering as far as possible into the biopolitical logic of how their experiences were 'put into discourse', I might draw out clues as to the state of what Harris Solomon calls 'metabolic living' in the early twentieth century in England and Europe.

In Chapter 8, I move outward from these case studies to consider how the metabolic strategies of incarcerated suffragettes were observed and incorporated by a consequential visitor to London from the Indian subcontinent by way of South Africa. I'm referring to Mahatma Gandhi, who adopted the hunger strike as part of the newly emerging practice of what he called 'Satyagraha', a nonviolent political movement that he saw as having been modelled by suffragette 'satyagrahis'. And in my conclusion, I shift from the early twentieth to the twenty-first century and from the global North to South Asia, where global 'security' plays out in the form of sanitation campaigns premised on, but not necessarily in the spirit of, Gandhi's dream of *Swaraj*, or self-determination at every level of the metabolic system, from the human body to the nation-state. I examine two approaches to the management of human excrement, contrasting a bourgeois state-promoted clean-up campaign with a grass-roots activist-led movement where a 'people's science' does really seem to prevail among the 'meta-industrial' labourers living as pavement dwellers in Mumbai.

But lest we think the question of faeces in the open air is only a problem in countries like India, I close with consideration of another metabolic crisis on American soil (literally on its soil, in fact): in rural areas with inadequate tax bases (inhabited, in other words, by the rural poor), we find once again that the modern faecal habitus is impossible to maintain when the septic systems into which human excrement is deposited are doomed to failure, spewing faecal matter onto surrounding yards and ditches.

In this book, shitting is not a metaphor for other forms of production, nor is the human as tube through which the world passes merely a fanciful image for the other ways we exert change in our environment, nor is the relation between the alimentary canal and the modern sewage system merely an analogous one. Rather, as we shall see, the metaphorical, the imagistic, the analogical give way to the co-extensive and the systemic; our peristaltic systems revealed as hooked up with and materially implicated in a plethora of other networks, with the result that it is often hard to tell what is internal or external to our 'selves', or where agency of one sort trails off, and is taken up by agency of another, or whether we are talking on a biological or a psychic level. A metabolic politics of transformation moves from the dissident gut outwards into every social, political and global domain.

### Notes

1. 'Right now the food for over a thousand detainees a day is being paid for by two civilian staff on credit cards, and they're spending $10,000 a day on cards not designed for that purpose' (OIG 2019b, 7–8).
2. 'And after going there and talking to these kids, it's very easy to see why those conditions can easily become life-threatening, particularly because of the infectious disease risks, the lack of hygiene, and the fact that when people – when children are coming down with the flu or getting sick, the care plan appears to be to put them in a quarantine cell alone with no real child care. I mean, it sounds like someone's coming in twice a day to give some medication, but no one is really taking care of them. And so, it's very easy to see why those conditions are giving rise to death after death after death' (Long 2019, quoted on *Democracy Now*).
3. 'The children told the lawyers they were given the same meals every day – instant oats for breakfast, instant noodles for lunch, a frozen burrito for dinner, along with a few cookies and juice packets – which many said was not enough. "Nearly every child I spoke with said that they were hungry", Ms. Mukherjee said' (Dickerson 2019).
4. 'Maintaining hygienic conditions at this facility is a challenge for Border Patrol. In many cells, we observed aliens standing on toilets because of the overcrowding to make room and gain breathing space (consequently, limiting access to sinks/toilets)' (OIG 2019a, 3).
5. 'Border Patrol management described Paso Del Norte Bridge Border Patrol Station (PDT) as "chaos"' (OIG 2019b, 7).
6. 'Ms. Mukherjee said children were being overseen by guards for Customs and Border Protection, which declined to comment for this story. She and her colleagues observed the guards wearing full

uniforms – including weapons – as well as face masks to protect themselves from the unsanitary conditions' (Dickerson 2019).
7  'The Eurocentric dissociation of humans from nature is an old cultural contradiction, often called on to justify the capitalist domination of class, race, sex-gender, and species others. It would be more accurate to say that people themselves are ecosystems, in humanly embodied form. Meanwhile, caregivers, peasants, and foragers, are the indispensable intermediaries of ecosystemic flows and human aspirations' (Salleh 2010, 211).

# Part I: Macro-Peristalsis

# 1

# Metabolic Rift and the Remedy of Faecal Recycling

A passage from Victor Hugo's *Les Misérables* brings together three of the elements that describe the shape and extent of what I think of as metabolism in this book:

> Paris casts twenty-five millions yearly into the water. And this without metaphors. How, and in what manner? Day and night. With what object? With no object. With what intention? With no intention. Why? For no reason. By means of what organ? By means of its intestine. What is its intestine? The sewer. (quoted in Marald 2002, 66)

In this rant on the spewing of human excrement into the Seine, Hugo references the human peristaltic system ('intestine'); the city infrastructure, and by extension, the environment in general ('sewer'); and economics ('twenty-five millions'). The first two seem self-evident and unremarkable: Hugo thinks of the sewer system as the peristaltic system of Paris. If we think of the city as like a body, we can also think of it as shitting its waste out into the Seine. But this is not just a metaphor for bad hygienic practices; insofar as the sewer is the 'organ' by which Paris eliminates its waste, we will come to see that there is an organic continuity between human and urban infrastructure. The same substances flow through both, insofar as they are connected to each other.

Moreover, the economic aspect is not in this quote alone self-evident: why would the casting of human waste into the water be formulated in terms of 'millions' (i.e. millions of francs)? What is so valuable about all that shit that flows away? What we discover is that shit equals money, not in Freud's sense of the equation, but insofar as it is a valuable commodity whose worth has not been properly recognised. It has been mis-channelled. Hugo shares with his contemporary Karl Marx an understanding of the metabolic rift between nature and man, and both the economic and environmental cost thereof.

In this chapter, I take up this concept of 'metabolic rift' as it has been revitalised for a twenty-first-century Marxist environmentalism that brings together the metabolism of nature with that of economics. Marx and Engels drew from agricultural chemist Justus von Liebig to account for how industrialisation resulted in the linked depletion of soil in rural areas and the pollution of urban living space. Capacious enough to span the scale from the molecular to the global, and the spectrum of registers from the natural to the manmade, metabolism came to be the perfect model for thinking through the relationship of organic with artificial systems in cities that are now cut off from the agricultural fields that provision them. Urban Studies has adopted the model of metabolism to understand the complex workings of the city, and to trace, for example, the metabolic movement of material substances (like fat and faeces) through its infrastructure. Ultimately, this chapter thinks through the very definition of 'waste', raising the idea that it is only context that makes us think of excrement as waste. This becomes evident when we examine the history of faecal recycling in England and Europe. Utopian agriculturalists, engineers and urban planners were adept at fashioning recycling schemes as the solution to the rift between (urban-dwelling) humans and the nature that provisioned them, but the scaled-up, automated systems for accomplishing this did not seem to account for a class of labourers, women in particular, whose role it was, and still is, to mediate the metabolism between 'man' and nature.

## Metabolic rift

In the opening chapters of the first volume of *Capital*, Karl Marx relies on a metabolic model to describe how, according to traditional economics, commodities seem to assert a value of their own, after which he begins to dialectically travel outward toward the role of labour in the formation of value. I will be examining this deployment of metabolism to understand the workings of capitalism in a subsequent chapter. But before I turn to Marx's reliance on metabolism as an explanatory system, I want to lay out the nineteenth-century agricultural science that drew Marx's attention in the first place to a consequential gap between human bodies and food-producing soil. It is this gap, which came to be called 'metabolic rift', that led Marx to use the concept of metabolism as a dialectical tool throughout his investigation of the workings of capital. The deployment of Marx's concept of metabolic rift is responsible for having reframed questions of excrement, waste and environment in explicitly metabolic terms, and thus central to an investigation of how human peristaltic behaviour, down to a granular level, hooks up with the circuits of modern capitalist systems.

The story of metabolic rift presupposes, above all, the assertion of a prelapsarian world in which small-scale agriculture served the needs of humans living nearby the fields, the idea of a charmed circuit, an unbroken, perfect rhythm of compatibility with an ever-sustaining earth. It's not just the truism I'm thinking of here, that from dust we come and to dust we shall return, which seems to emphasise mortality rather than vitality. I have in mind, rather, images of the farmer, before large-scale disenfranchisement, tilling the land with an ox, drawing from it beans, potatoes, wheat and all the other comestibles that find their way onto the cottage table, and onto those of his village neighbours. A small group of people, living in proximity to the modest plots of land that they have themselves farmed, consume the fruit of their labour and their bodies are sustained and invigorated by the nutrients in their fresh or preserved vegetables and fruit, or the bread made from the flour ground from their grain. What does not get absorbed into their bodies finds its way out again, back into the soil, replenishing it with essential organic compounds, so that from season to season, year to year, new crops can be brought forth, and the cycle of sowing, reaping, eating, excreting can begin again.

If a symbiotic relation between human and earth is imagined here, it has to do with how each becomes the locus of transformation for the other; the soil hosts the metamorphosis of seed into plant, of potential into consumable. The human body, on the other side, hosts the processing of ripened crops back into precious nitrogen, phosphorus and other micro-organisms necessary to the fertility of agricultural soil. Matter travels from earth to human body and back to earth again, but can only move through the circuit if it is converted along the way, through the exertion of human labour, into a form compatible with each hosting receptacle. The receptacles are not, in turn, merely holding places, but machines for necessary conversion. Part of the conversion process involves preparation of food to make it edible by the human side of the equation, as well as proper channelling of the excremental by-product of human consumption, so that it can replenish the earth.

This perfect metabolic *perpetuum mobile* did not come to be fully appreciated until developments in the chemistry of agricultural science, and in particular the insights of German chemist Justus von Liebig, had begun to delineate a serious break that had occurred in the natural rhythms of human body with the earth that sustained it. Karl Marx called this a 'rift' in the human-earth metabolism, which contemporary Marxist environmentalists today refer to as 'metabolic rift'.[1] In an essay arguing for the importance of Marx's writings for environmental studies, John Bellamy Foster succinctly recounts the developments that led to a dawning realisation of the 'metabolic rift' that had occurred as a result of industrialisation in the eighteenth and nineteenth centuries. In the mid-nineteenth century, during the second agricultural revolution, it became apparent that, far from offering an endless capacity for production, agricultural soil contained elements that had to be replenished if it was to transfer those elements to the plant life that emerged from it (Foster 1999, 376). In 1840, Liebig published 'the first convincing explanation of the role of soil nutrients, such as nitrogen, phosphorous, and potassium, in the growth of plants' and argued for the urgency of replenishing what was systematically taken out of the soil by intensive agricultural activity (Foster 1999, 376). Despite the importation of vast quantities of nutrient-rich bird guano from Peru, as well as efforts to produce fertiliser synthetically, England continued to come up short on its supply of nitrogen, thus raising serious concerns about soil fertility under capitalism (Foster 1999, 376–7).

It was becoming obvious that what underlay the problem, at the most basic level, was the forced migration over time of human populations from less intensively settled areas dispersed across England, Europe and the United States, to increasingly densely populated cities. This meant that products grown in agricultural areas had to be transported greater and greater distances, and in more massive quantities, away from their point of origin to service the human organisms that now lived crowded together in the metropolis, but that had (in earlier generations) resided near the origin of their food resources. In the face of this system of 'spoliation', Liebig argued for a 'rationalised' agriculture based on a 'principle of restitution; by giving back to the fields the conditions of their fertility, the farmer insures the permanence of the latter' (quoted in Foster 1999, 378). The idea of a rift was conceived, in this respect, as a matter of spatial distance, of a geographical expanse across which essential connections could no longer be made.

As the soil was being robbed of its fertility, the cities themselves were being over-laden with the very elements that would be beneficial, were they not hundreds of miles away from the place where they could have a positive effect. Liebig elegantly summarised the situation by expressing a wish that, for me, encapsulates the peristaltic utopia that informs this book:

> If it were practicable to collect, with the least loss, all the solid and fluid excrements of the inhabitants of the town, and return to each farmer the portion arising from produce originally supplied by him to the town, the productiveness of the land might be maintained almost unimpaired for ages to come, and the existing store of mineral elements in every fertile field would be amply sufficient for the wants of increasing populations. (Liebig, 1863, 274)

Liebig was drawing attention to the irony in the fact that, because of the concentration of human populations in cities located at great distances from agricultural fields, bird guano, or even bones from European battlefields, had to be expensively transported over vast distances to replace what had been robbed from the soil. Meanwhile, agricultural products travelled to urban areas, where they were only partly absorbed into the bodies of the human inhabitants there; what was not absorbed then made its way as excrement into the latrines, water closets, sewer systems and eventually the natural waterways that ran through these cities, thus polluting the environment within which these populations lived.

The seemingly far-fetched fantasy of 'collecting' urban excrements and returning to each farmer 'the portion arising from produce originally supplied by him to the town' was in fact the basis of a serious recycling proposal on Liebig's part: in his 1865 'Letters on the Subject of the Utilization of the Municipal Sewage' he argued, 'basing his analysis on the condition of the Thames – that organic recycling that would return the nutrients contained in sewage to the soil was an indispensable part of a rational urban-agricultural system' (Foster 1999, 378).

Karl Marx, in turn, drew from Liebig's work to elaborate his theories of labour exploitation alongside the simultaneous exploitation of the land. As Foster has demonstrated, Marx put the case in terms that were explicitly framed by the model and metaphor of metabolism. 'Large landed property,' Marx wrote in *Capital*, Volume 3,

> reduces the agricultural population to an ever decreasing minimum and confronts it with an ever growing industrial population crammed together in large towns; in this way it produces conditions that provoke an *irreparable rift* in the *interdependent process of the social metabolism*, a metabolism *prescribed by the natural laws of life itself*. The result of this is a squandering of the vitality of the soil, which is carried by trade far beyond the bounds of a single country. (Marx 1981, 949, my italics)

And elsewhere, in *Capital*, Volume 1:

> Capitalist production collects the population together in great centres, and causes the urban population to achieve an ever-growing preponderance. This has two results. On the one hand it concentrates the historical motive force of society; on the other hand, it *disturbs the metabolic interaction between man and the earth,* i.e. it prevents the return to the soil of its constituent elements consumed by man in the form of food and clothing; hence it hinders the operation of the eternal natural condition for the lasting fertility of the soil. Thus it destroys at the same time the physical health of the urban worker and the intellectual life of the rural worker. (Marx 1976, 637)

Foster makes an intricate and compelling case for the rootedness of modern environmentalist theory in Marx's writings on metabolic rift, and for the usefulness of metabolic models in general. The term 'metabolism', he reminds us, after being used by German physiologists in the 1830s and 1840s 'to refer to material exchanges within the body, related to respiration', grew to have a broader meaning when taken over by Liebig in his *Animal Chemistry*, and then eventually 'emerged as one of the key concepts, applicable both at the cellular level and in the analysis of entire organisms, in the development of biochemistry' (Foster 1999, 382). Even today, it is 'used as a central category in the systems-theory approach to the relation of organisms to their environments' (Foster 1999, 382).

In this respect, metabolism began to be used, certainly in the hands of Liebig, Marx and Engels, as a model for understanding not just purely 'natural' or 'organic' processes, but those entities created by human intervention into and manipulation of these processes – ranging from the workings of agriculture, to the functioning of urban space, to the economic transactions of capital itself. Or, more to the point we are tracing here, it became the model that linked the 'natural' domain of plant, animal and human growth to the 'artificial' domain of the commoditisation of human labour, and systems of incorporation, growth, production and waste. It now covers everything from the single cell to the human body to global ecosystems, including every aspect of those systems as they have been constructed through human agency (Foster 1999, 382). We will examine Marx's metabolically inflected concept of labour as the means by which man's metabolism with nature is 'regulated' in Chapter 3. But here, I would like to focus on the implications of a 'rift' in a metabolism figured specifically in agricultural terms, and what it means for metabolic models of urban systems of exchange and transformation.

Foster lays out the groundwork to be found in Marx for a project of sustainability, premised on the urgency to address what he had identified as the rift – caused as much by industrialised agricultural practices as by the mechanised production of commodities in the cities – in the metabolic circuit that had originally prevailed between man and nature. This circuit had been ruptured precisely by the vicissitudes of capitalist exploitation – of the land as much as of the workers. Liebig's dream of returning urban excrement to its rightful domain in the faraway fields of the farmer was echoed by Marx in his acknowledgement that 'the failure to recycle nutrients to the soil had its counterpart in the pollution of the cities and the irrationality of modern sewage systems'. London was a prime example of this, Marx wrote, given that its inhabitants 'can do nothing better with the excrement produced by 4.5 million people than pollute the Thames with it, at monstrous expense' (Marx 1981, 195). Engels agreed, writing that: 'in London alone a greater quantity of manure than is produced by the whole kingdom of Saxony is poured away every day into the sea with an expenditure of enormous sums', and that we needed to re-establish an 'intimate connection between industrial and agricultural production', along with 'as uniform a distribution as possible of the population over the whole country' (Engels 1935, 95). In this Marxian account, the 'excrement produced by man's natural metabolism' as well as industrial waste needed to be recycled back into production to complete the metabolic cycle (Foster 1999, 383).

## Urban metabolism

In 'Metabolic Urbanization: The Making of Cyborg Cities', Erik Swyngedouw argues for the superiority of the concept of 'metabolism' (and its attendant term, 'circulation') over other recent metaphors 'that attempt to fuse together heterogeneous entities – like networks, assemblages, rhizomes, imbroglios, collectives'. That 'metabolism' is superior as a model for the social world in all of its material and immaterial, organic and inorganic aspects is attributable to two important features: that it is a dynamic model (of movement and change) rather than a static one; and that it encourages us to envision elements not only different from each other, but belonging to completely disparate orders (language and food, for example, or bodily sensation and porcelain) as hooking up with each other precisely for the purpose of their mutual transformation. Put in Marxist terms, Swyngedouw writes, any 'environmental "production" process' is necessarily a metabolic process, 'energized through the fusion of the physical properties and creative capacities of humans with those of non-humans' (Swyngedouw 2006, 23).

An urban environment, for example, is not only connected to, but has a metabolic relationship with an infinite array of other entities: the goods, fuel, commodities, vehicles, people, water, information, electrical impulses and all the other things that flow into and within it, the products, detritus, waste, information, people and all the other things that flow out of it, all of it transformed by the workings of the inner-connected urban structures and processes themselves. Those same humans who enter, circulate within and leave the city are themselves the site of metabolism, taking in foodstuffs that are transformed by the digestive system into usable nutrient molecules, or that are expelled in the form of excrement, which in turn finds its way into the water that has entered the city, and that will then make its way to another metabolic site where further transformations will occur. Meanwhile, through the circulation of ballots (whether they be electronically or manually passed along), human individuals travel into legislative spaces for the purpose of generating agential discourses that, in turn, will determine things like where and when the waste produced by the city's inhabitants will be collected, transformed and eliminated. Being part social, part natural and deeply historical, the subjects of any urban system can be thought of as hybrid 'intermediaries'. Insofar as they 'embody and express nature and society and weave networks of infinite liminal spaces', they are 'simultaneously real, like nature; narrated, like discourse; and collective, like society' (Swyngedouw 2006, 24).

One of the chapters in *In the Nature of Cities* demonstrates how metabolism works as a model for movement and transformation in an urban system, while at the same time offering an analogy for understanding the peristaltic movement of food through the human body, and onward as excrement, into and through the city infrastructure that houses it. Simon Marvin and Will Medd trace how a massive weight-loss campaign proceeded by way of 'real, narrated, and collective' elements as residents, businesses and whole cities were deployed to mobilise their fat and keep it on the move. Human bodies and sewer systems were understood to be co-extensive in that they were susceptible to the detrimental effects of excessive fat deposits, targets of intervention where fat is concerned, and functioned as metabolic systems – indeed, together they comprised the over-arching metabolic system for the city's fat.

At the level of discourse, *Men's Fitness* magazine galvanised national attention by ranking cities (collectives) according to their obesity level, with the result that local governments invested resources into aggressive fitness campaigns. Philadelphia, for instance, announced its goal to lose 76 tons of weight in 76 days (in tribute to the city's basketball team, the 76ers). As a giant avatar for its inhabitants the city became a focal point for identification as individuals ('real' as in natural organisms) voluntarily enrolled in schemes for removing their body fat, in an attempt to slim down their 'fat-city' reputation. The symbolic concept of the 'fat city' literally remobilised fat to 'reshape the metabolism of bodies and the city' (Marvin and Medd 2006, 141). Sewers, like bodies, were also targets of slimming campaigns, as 'lean sewer' ordinances and brochures promoting 'fat-free sewers' attempted (with limited results) to dissuade households and restaurants from sending grease down the drain (Marvin and Medd 2006, 143).

Understanding the connections among fat in individual human bodies, fat at the level of city identity, and fat flowing through fast food preparation into the infrastructure itself (the sewage network) required thinking of the city as a site of multiply connected metabolisms (Marvin and Medd 2006, 143).

Fat had to be kept on the move, mobilised in its liquid state, rather than allowed to harden into a solid that would stop up and paralyse bodies and sewer systems alike. The aim was to avoid stasis at all costs, and to promote motility at all levels:

> just as bodies trying to lose fat require the enrolment of a wide set of networked relations from food supply chains to transport infrastructures that become *mobilized* through the city collective, so too we find that strategies of removal of fat in sewers involves a vast array of food supply chains and *transport* infrastructures that include the local configuration of waste management to the global markets for oils. (Marvin and Medd 2006, 145, my italics)

I summarise Marvin and Medd's study here to extend our understanding of mobility beyond the human and organic to include the non-human and inorganic. They set up a model for following just one element of the material world, fat, as it moves through and among interdependent metabolic systems, reliant not only on physiological, mechanical and technological, but also symbolic, discursive and disciplinary systems of propulsion (the magazine *Men's Fitness* as a 'stimulant' to the mobilisation of fitness and weight-loss schemes, for instance). An element in both human and infrastructural metabolisms (people, sewers), passing between the two, fat functions as actant and as material that is acted upon; it is the perfect substance for the discursive elaboration of a metabolic model of social systems.[2] Moreover, because of its shifting value (as beneficial for insulation, energy, the formation of cell membranes, but dangerous when allowed to accumulate beyond a desirable amount) fat offers an opportunity to build a definitional model of waste and its elimination.

This account of the mobilisation of fat through interlocking metabolic systems is in some ways a revival of a model already dominant in the early twentieth century – the era of this book's primary focus. I'm thinking here of the observations of Dr H. Des Voeux, famous for coining and popularising the term 'smog' in 1911 when he delivered a paper on the shocking number of deaths due to industrial smoke at the Manchester Conference of the Smoke Abatement League of Great Britain. Circulation of air in cities and human bodies was not the only aspect of human/urban metabolism that concerned Des Voeux.[3] In a 1924 paper on constipation he wrote:

> Personally, I hold the belief that people can eat as much as they wish provided that the food passes through quick enough, and that all residuum is cleared daily – in fact, so long as the main drain of the body functions properly. In other words, it is not so much what we admit that does the harm, but the refuse which we do not expel, for what we retain unduly becomes a prey to putrefactions of all sorts and the results are dire. It is a constant mystery to me how much time, attention and money the modern English will expend on the main drain of their houses and how little they will expend on their own drain, which after all is but the commencement of the house drain – unfortunately disconnected. (Des Voeux 1924, 43)

Marvin and Medd's disquisition on the necessity to keep fat on the move has its antecedent, as we shall see, in early twentieth-century anxiety about (and concerted efforts to remedy) the malady of constipation and 'intestinal stasis'. Our common-sense assumption that faeces can simply be categorised as waste must be modified to include the question of location and movement; 'waste' is not only about particular substances, but about where a substance is located, and whether it is beneficial to or undermines metabolic transformations.

We take for granted, for instance, that the product of our defecation is to be flushed away and removed through an efficient water-borne sewage system, and that it should not come back to haunt us with its unpleasant appearance, odour or disease-producing bacteria. It is 'waste' in the sense that it apparently has no function in our everyday lives, and thus must be removed from the system in which we live. But as the discussion of 'fat' suggests, particularly when it is put into the same frame of reference as Liebig and Marx's theory of a 'metabolic rift' between the agricultural field and the faraway mouths it must feed, waste might be more accurately defined not simply as a by-product that emerges from the human body when the work of metabolism has converted foodstuffs into cells that are beneficial for life, but rather as what *fails* to leave the body, but is stored as a material substance that is detrimental to life. That is, 'waste' is not what is expelled from the body, but rather, what is unusable, but still contained by the body (and by the city-as-body, when considered in terms of its infrastructure). If 'mobilisation' is prized above all elements in the metabolic model, then excrement, particularly when it regularly emerges from human bodies, is by definition a *useful* aspect of the metabolic system, not a waste product. Comparable to Mary Douglas's idea that dirt is 'matter out of place', unwanted deposits of fat, whether in bodies or in the sewer system, are more amenable to the definition of 'waste'.[4]

Moreover, the process of 'elimination' where waste is concerned is also defined along the lines of the rationalisation of industrial and domestic production. In that context, the elimination of waste is not so much about the removal of matter, but rather the cessation of useless motions, and the maintenance of useful ones. Waste is 'eliminated' by its subtraction from a routine of movements that do not contribute to the aim of the routine, or that expend more energy than is necessary for its accomplishment. Like preventing the deposition of fat in the first place, to eliminate waste in the factory system requires reconfiguring the methods by which a product is assembled. As long as excrement is understood to be a crucial ingredient in the replenishing of agricultural soil, then it becomes 'wasteful' to treat the by-products of human metabolism as something to be eliminated, rather than something meant to continue its journey along the complete cycle of growth, harvest, consumption, fertilisation and back to growth again.

## The rise and fall of faecal recycling

Given that even as early as Liebig there was some consensus about the desirableness of returning human excrement back to the soil, one of the conundrums facing historians of agricultural development and urban infrastructure is why the impulse to repair metabolic rift through the recycling of human waste was eclipsed by the rise of the modern water-borne sewer system, with its polluted outflows into nearby bodies of fresh and salt water, such as the Thames, the Seine, the Spree and the ocean. Many schemes for faecal recycling (in addition to Liebig's own) were put forward in England and Europe, and even temporarily implemented, throughout the nineteenth century.

In 'Everything Circulates', Erland Marald quotes the passage from Hugo's 1862 *Les Misérables* that I opened with at the beginning of this chapter. Influenced by Liebig's account of metabolic rift, Hugo spins out a fifty-page rant on the failure of Paris to make better use of its ordure, setting up a one-way sewer system that spews valuable matter into the river, with two results: 'the land impoverished, and the water tainted. Hunger arising from the furrow, and disease from the stream' (quoted in Marald 2002, 66). Living in exile in England, Hugo praised the recycling systems he observed in some English towns, which 'had constructed a double tubular apparatus, which functioned like "the lungs of a man"', and which transported fresh water to the cities and sewage back to the fields (Marald 2002, 66). Although it appears that Hugo anthropomorphises the technology of the city infrastructure (depicted as intestines and lungs), he also stresses that the valuable matter being spewed by Paris into the water is 'without metaphors'. It would seem as though this model of human metabolism implicated in city metabolism is not a matter of analogical thinking so much as the spectacle of an inter-connected series of tubes and pumping systems traversing organic and non-organic alike.

Meanwhile, German chemist Alexander Müller devoted himself to plans for the recycling of 'night-soil and city waste' in Stockholm, where he had been instated at the Royal Swedish Academy of Agriculture (Marald 2002, 75). Again, adhering to the principle of indestructible matter following unlimited cycles, Müller sought to find the most advantageous way to make faecal matter viable as a fertiliser, by patenting an earth-closet in which solid excrement would be separated from urine, making it easier to 'dry and concentrate' faeces in poudrette factories (Marald 2002, 77). Müller travelled to Berlin (where authorities had purportedly rejected a water-based system), so that he could observe their barrel collection system (Marald 2002, 77). In the introduction to a report issued by the German Society of Agriculture ('The Utilisation of Urban Faeces'), Müller stressed the entirely subjective concept of 'waste' and 'filth', pointing out that night-soil might be classified as a 'resource from another angle' (Marald 2002, 78). The report put forward a recycling model that dispensed with the barrels in favour of a comprehensive system of interconnected pipes leading from each household to a central pump station. In this manner, 'excrement was sucked from the whole city and gathered in one place. From there the faeces could be sold directly to the farmers, be composted or be industrially processed for manure powder' (Marald 2002, 79). The authors were particularly enthusiastic about this dry pneumatic system, given its potential to keep water free from faecal contamination even as excrement was directed where it could be most useful. 'All the links in the chain between individual urban dweller, via the manure industry, to the individual farmer, would then be automatic and effective' (Marald 2002, 80). It was a perfect utopian model of an interconnected human, city, infrastructure metabolism, reinstating the cycle that had been disrupted by the rift of industrial capitalism, though it neglected to acknowledge one important 'link' in the chain from farmer to urban dweller, namely, the female intermediary who prepared the food and cleaned up after domestic excreters. I'll come back to this shortly.

In England, many efforts were made in the realm of human waste recycling, by private and public concerns. As Christopher Hamlin points out, 'Until about 1880 most sanitarians, whatever their view of the chemical mechanisms of natural cycles, agreed that the way to prevent zymotic disease and to maintain agricultural productivity was to insure that all organic wastes were returned to arable land' (Hamlin 1985, 392–3). But city officials were beset by technological challenges as to the best way to recycle human waste, since none of the three main methods seemed entirely successful, affordable or practicable. Irrigation projects (simply spraying raw sewage over nearby agricultural fields) failed from 'too heavy application of sewage. It was reported that photographs of British sewage farms were repeatedly mistaken for pictures of the ocean, so heavily were they irrigated' (Hamlin 1985, 394). Precipitation processes, in which attempts were made to draw usable sludge to the bottom of settling tanks, also failed. And conservancy systems, i.e. dry methods by which faecal matter was collected by 'municipal or company employees' encountered administrative problems (Hamlin 1985, 394).

Perhaps the most utopian, or certainly the most thoroughly ideologically elaborated of such schemes was that developed by French chemists Jean-Baptiste Dumas and Jean-Baptiste Boussingault, involving a 'holistic theory of circulation between animals, plants, and the atmosphere' and for whom 'dung lay at the center of all earthly exchange' (Simmons 2006, 75–6). Dumas built up a chemical cosmology of life, a 'recycling universe' in which the earth was 'in eternal circulation, its life sustained by the efficient use and reuse of food and waste' (Simmons 2006, 82). Merely 'way-stations' in 'nature's vast movement', humans and animals (or the poor conceived as mere animals) had little active role in this model. Or rather, their labour was not needed to produce and reproduce life – only their bodies as places where food would be transformed, through metabolism, into the necessary components for replenishing the soil.

The principles of Dumas and Boussingault's self-perpetuating cycle of life were implemented in an experimental farming colony led by printer Pierre Leroux in a settlement near rural Creuse. Here, colonists published political tracts, and lived off vegetables fertilised by their own excrement according to the theological-scientific principle of what they called the 'circulus'. They 'gathered their daily secretions and recycled an admixture of human waste as garden fertilizer', seeking to demonstrate that 'every man is the producer – and even, precisely, the reproducer – of his own consumption' (quoted in Simmons 2006, 87).

'The human body,' as Simmons puts it, 'that perfect and complete machine in nature, would replace the enslaved and emaciated body of the factory worker' (Simmons 2006, 87). In Leroux's words, 'when you penetrate to the very foundation of your means of production ... industry refers you to agriculture, and that sends you back to your manure' (quoted in Simmons 2006, 87). There was no need to exploit the work of labourers, require them to exchange their physical motions for minimal wages, since the 'work' of transforming the world was always already being performed by one's digestive system. You had merely to reinvest properly the product of that intestinal labour – i.e. manure – and humans and earth would be mutually sustaining.

This physiocratic discourse of the 'circulus' included a racialised component insofar as it conjured a figure responsible for blocking an otherwise continuous motility: finance capital was depicted as the engorged Jew, 'retaining matter within himself, even as it pops out in the form of malevolent warts', his 'grotesqueness' coming from 'the ill effects of a kind of constipation' (Simmons 2006, 91). Thus, the antisemitic figure of the 'constipated capitalist stood against the excreting man of nature' in Leroux's vision of 'corporeal economy' (Simmons 2006, 91).

Meanwhile, although the point of this physiocratic model for subsistence was to eliminate the need for exploited labour under industrial capitalism, in practice, 'man's' body did not just accomplish survival through its automatic consumption of food and production of fertiliser. Some labour, after all, *was* required between the coming ripe of the fruits of the field, and its appearance on the dinner table. Leroux's instalment of self-sufficient man to replace the exploited labourer in the factory merely subtracts the labour from 'man's' body without acknowledging that other labourer who makes it possible for nature's raw products to be consumed, whether it be in the domestic space of urban industrialism or bucolic experimentalism: the female meta-industrial labourer who cleans, chops, boils, fries, bakes, mashes and fricassees, not to mention lays the table, then clears and cleans after the event of consumption. It is possible that men and women both collected and distributed their bodies' 'products' back over nature's fields and gardens; but in any case, no mention was made of a gendered division of labour, or more properly, of the human body's autonomous labour of metabolic transformation as opposed to the labour of the domestic cooker and cleaner.

While these faecal recycling schemes may have offered a more environmentally sound means of repairing metabolic rift, the utopian fantasy of automation they engaged in seemed blind to the role of meta-industrial labourers working at the interface between nature and the world, a blindness that we find in Marx's work as well. To articulate what precisely is missing from these discourses of metabolism, I turn to Ariel Salleh's eco-feminist Marxism. As Salleh puts it, 'most women across the world are socially positioned as labour right at the base of the accumulation hierarchy', where they carry out what she calls the 'meta-industrial labor of mediating the humanity-nature interface' (Salleh 2010, 207). Meta-industrial labourers are those workers 'nominally outside of capitalism, whose labour catalyses metabolic transformations – be they peasants, gatherers, or parents' (she also includes indigenous peoples, houseworkers, migrants and, most often, women) (Salleh 2010, 212).[5] In her analysis of lacunae in Marx's metabolic model of labour, Salleh aggregates the theoretical interventions made by materialist feminists in several overlapping areas: those who focus on wages for housework and the valorisation of domestic labour; those who stress how women's reproductive labour contributes to the maintenance of capital; and environmental and ecological feminists who draw parallels between housework in industrialised countries and subsistence activities in postcolonial contexts to show how 'theorization of labor based exclusively on the experience of working *men* is seriously deficient' (Salleh 2010, 208–9, my italics). Like other Marxist feminist work, Salleh's argument acts as a corrective to the minimal attention to gender in Marx's writings; but in her case, she directly engages the discourse of metabolism in Marx in order to emphasise the relation between the environmental extractivism of capitalism ('robbing the soil', or the earth in general) and the exploitation of unpaid women's labour. Her contribution to materialist feminism is to re-frame what has been called 'reproductive labour' in terms of how it mediates metabolic cycles on the one hand and industrial capitalism on the other (including industrialised agriculture), by renaming it 'meta-industrial labour'. The 'meta' serves the dual purpose of situating this form of labour as intimately responsive to humans' '*meta*bolism with nature', and as distinct from, alongside and transformative of the productivism of capitalism. 'The nonmonetized but regenerative activities of this unnamed class are not only essential to sustaining everyday life,' Salleh writes, 'in many so-called developing regions, this labour materially resources capitalist markets as well' (Salleh 2010, 208). Shifting attention away from the male factory worker who is the paradigm of capitalist exploitation in Marx, Salleh focuses instead on the 'meta-industrial' labourer presumed to be external to industrial production, and engages Marx's language of metabolism to do so.

In the global North (where our attention is focused in *Dissident Gut*) 'the usual site of meta-industrial labour is the nonmonetized domestic sphere', or in other words, the private domicile where women engage in unpaid housework and childcare. Salleh argues that women are not simply victimised by their relegation to the unremunerated reproductive labour that undergirds capitalist production outside the home, but they are also producers of 'metabolic *value*', that is, a form of value that is catalysed by their labours, and without which there would be no exchange or use value (Salleh 2010, 207). She argues, moreover, that their meta-industrial labour has resulted, over time, in the production of knowledge, and that women, along with indigenous and peasant labourers, are practitioners of a 'people's science' (Salleh 2010, 207), one that supports ecological integrity through work that is 'relational, flow oriented, and regenerative of biotic chains' rather than reliant entirely on extractivism in the interest of capitalist exchange value (Salleh 2010, 212). We might imagine, thus, that the labour of meta-industrials, those preparers of foodstuffs, cleaners of domestic space and collectors of human excrement at the 'base of the accumulation hierarchy' was crucial to the success or failure of any master plan to return precious faecal matter to the fields.

In any case, by the late nineteenth century, all these recycling schemes fell into decline and were entirely overshadowed by water-based sewer systems whose sole purpose was to eliminate the offending matter, with no efforts to return it where it might do some ecological good. As Marald puts it, 'from the 1870s onwards, the discussion about recycling instead concerned technological, sanitary and economic problems', while at the same time, the development of 'new mineral and nitrogenous fertilisers' seemed to have solved the shortage of nutrients needed to replenish the soil. Theories of zymotic decomposition and then of bacterial transmission, both of which seemed beneficial when applied to soil, but dangerous when considered in relation to human bodies, reached a tipping point whereby only the negative aspects of decomposing matter were emphasised. Since there was 'no place for any kind of filth in a modern city', an 'increasing skepticism towards the use of human excrement as fertilizer grew' (Marald 2002, 81). And finally, the very 'chemico-theological outlook' that had underlain many of the recycling schemes, with their emphasis on an explicit or implied cosmos in which all was interconnected in a 'circulus' of life-force, was undermined by modern bacteriology.

> When the recycling discourse was discarded, so were efforts to create an interdependence between the cities and the countryside and agrarian and sanitary interests, which had been emphasized in the mid-nineteenth century. With the rejection of the chemico-theological idea, the connection between recycling, wealth and the survival of society as a whole disappeared. (Marald 2002, 81)

Christopher Hamlin echoes this account of the waning of recycling models:

> By the late 1870s ... [t]he new bacteriology, and especially its emphasis on bacterial toxins as the proximate causes of pathological effects, obscured the clarity and explanatory power of the zymotic analogy. There was less mention of the deplorable waste of the nation's fertilizer, not because any technical solution to the fertilizer problem had been found, but owing to a growing acceptance that sewage recycling was rarely profitable, and that agricultural and sanitary reforms were

not as beautifully intertwined as the principles of sanitary science suggested they ought to be. (Hamlin 1985, 409)

The recycling principle survived only in the form of a weak rationalisation for what had become the dominant sanitarian solution: 'Recognizing that pouring sewage into the sea was the simplest way of getting rid of it,' Hamlin wryly observes, 'some sanitarians began to point out that sewage would still be recycled, only through the commercial fisheries rather than through agriculture' (Hamlin 1985, 409).

I will have more to say about the manifold recycling projects that came to preoccupy sanitarians, agriculturalists and even the general reading public in England, but I want now to make a foray into another perspective on the management of faecal matter, at its 'point of origin', that is, where each individual subject was depositing his or her waste into whatever receptacle had been deemed most appropriate and advantageous.

### Notes

1 See Foster, 1999. Also: Saito, 2017. The importance of the concept of metabolic rift as central to Marxist environmentalism is signaled by a comprehensive bibliography published in *Monthly Review*, and updated as recently as July 2020. See Wishart, Jonna et. al., 'Metabolic Rift: A Selected Bibliography', *Monthly Review*, https://monthlyreview.org/commentary/metabolic-rift/.

2 Marvin and Medd's metabolic model for the movement of fat in human bodies, the city and city infrastructure is in keeping with what Hannah Landecker has termed an industrial rather than a postindustrial model of how metabolism is understood. Landecker's 'Postindustrial Metabolism: Fat Knowledge', *Public Culture*, 25:3, 2013 offers a complementary analysis of how metabolism is thought outside the limits of a strictly biological model. The focus in her article is, as she puts it, 'the relationship between food, time, and biology with the shift from metabolism as factory to metabolism as iteratively generated interface, which is also a shift from the time of energetics to the time of information' (Landecker 2013, 499).

3 'Smog', Encyclopedia Britannica.com. https://www.britannica.com/science/smog#ref16457 (Accessed 4/16/2018)

4 'Night soil and other kinds of city waste were not "dirt" from the outset; instead they became it when one went against the order of

nature. Dirt could therefore be transformed into a valuable resource if brought back to the "right place"' (Marald 2002, 71).
5  As Salleh explains, 'because this kind of work [self-sufficient provisioning] mostly takes place at the unmechanised margins of neoliberal growth economies, in households, in rural areas where small farmers still operate, and in indigenous hunter gathering communities, I prefer to replace the term reproductive labour (which it certainly is) with the broader expression – meta-industrial labour' (Salleh 2004, 8).

2

# Faecal Habitus

### Excretory dirt as symbolic capital

In the previous chapter, it seems that a combination of economic, technical, scientific and medico-hygienic forces conspired to ensure that the modern flush toilet, hooked up to a vast water-borne sewer system, would become the optimal site even to this day for the evacuation of our bowels (in the industrial and then post-industrial Western world, in any case). But these forces do not entirely account for why flushing faeces into a sewer system came to supplant faecal recycling schemes. The story of metabolic rift and its (thus far failed) remedies exists alongside another account of our modern peristaltic habits, one that emerges from sociological theory rather than from the histories of sanitation, agricultural science and Marxist environmentalism.

In *A Sociological History of Excretory Experience*, David Inglis argues that, while medical and scientific discoveries were important in the state construction of water-based sewer systems, we can only gain a full understanding of the situation by focusing on 'the conjunction of socially-produced evaluations of excreta as morally dirty, contained in the classificatory schema of the bourgeois faecal habitus' (Inglis 2001, 213). Any history of modern human bowel habits must be broadened beyond scientific and public health issues to include consideration of the 'socio-historical factors' (Inglis 2001, 15).

> [I]f it is accepted that excreta and excretion are – at least in part – subject to socio-historical mediation, then it becomes possible to claim that a historiography of excreta and excretion in modernity that was

focused *solely* on medical and natural scientific knowledges, would be far too narrow an approach. This is so because there are other, non-medico-scientific, *socio-historical factors* which are involved in such a history. (Inglis, 2001, 14–15)

By 'socio-historical factors' Inglis is referring to the development of what Bourdieu has termed a class habitus, that is to say, 'comprehension of the ways in which the bodies and bodily practices of . . . individuals are "shaped" by their class position' (Inglis 2001, 15). The habitus of a social class 'involves a symbolic classificatory system which in turn generates characteristic bodily practices, which are engaged in by the class member on an autonomous level, unconsciously,' Inglis reminds us. 'It includes things like [as Bourdieu puts it] "the most automatic gestures or the most apparently insignificant techniques of the body – ways of walking or blowing one's nose, ways of eating or talking"' (quoted in Inglis 2001, 33). Even more importantly, every bodily habit or gesture, every practice or ritual, is motivated by the necessity of distinguishing oneself as a member of a class from those of subordinate classes. Thus: 'The symbolic classifications of the dominant will seek to denigrate the dominated, for classifications are "not so much means of knowledge as means of power, harnessed to social functions and overtly or covertly aimed at satisfying the interests of a group"' (quoted in Inglis 2001, 36).

Inglis traces a history of faecal distinction back to the medieval period and leading up to the nineteenth and twentieth century, shifting along the way from the aristocracy's use of faecal habitus to distinguish itself from subordinated classes, to what became the predominant focus of the eighteenth and nineteenth century: the efforts of the bourgeoisie to maintain dominance over the working class. The way the bourgeoisie excreted was determined in large part by the extent to which its 'faecal habitus' could be deployed to distinguish it from the proletariat. As symbolic capital, excretory dirt was 'an important element in distinguishing refined bourgeois bodies from unrefined and filthy proletarian flesh' (Inglis 2001, 51).

Inglis structures his discussion of the bourgeois faecal habitus almost entirely around a clean/dirty binary, with all elements of the bourgeois habitus aiming to keep the bourgeois body on the clean side of the binary, and the proletariat body on the side of filth. The bourgeois faecal habitus is thus comprised of 'a symbolic-classificatory schema, which contains characteristic evaluative symbolisations of the qualities of excreta; and a set of excretory practices, which are peculiar to that habitus, and which are generated by its schema' (Inglis 2001, 42). The classificatory schema thus represents the bourgeois body as devoid of excreta, and generates excretory practices that would help the bourgeois subject deny his body's production of excremental waste (Inglis 2001, 43). To borrow from Bakhtin, the bourgeois faecal habitus portrayed the bourgeois body as 'strictly completed, finished . . . isolated, alone', with no 'apertures by which organic processes may occur or through which effluvia could leak' (quoted in Inglis 2001, 50–1).

Faced with the obdurate fact of a body that does, after all, defecate, the bourgeoisie had to develop excretory practices that would help to maintain at least the fiction of a non-excreting body. It is to this class-based social necessity that Inglis attributes the rise of the water-borne sewer system, a technology that accomplished a number of goals at once, and that (at first) could be made accessible to some (the bourgeoisie) and denied to others (the proletariat). The water-closet in the private home ensured, first of all, that defecation could be hidden from public view, and even from the view of the members of one's household. Excreting into a water-filled vessel that could then be flushed enabled the individual who defecated not to see the evidence of his own body's capacity to produce filth. Once flushed away, even incriminating odour could be minimised or eliminated. Inglis cites a French source from 1880 to illustrate how 'water flushing was expected to protect the excreting person from the noxious entity his or her own body had produced, and thus to deny as far as possible that it had ever existed':

> City dwellers must be carefully protected from their excretions from the moment they are produced. The waste outlet, normally kept sealed, should be opened briefly, and waste should be forcefully expelled from the residence by a powerful stream of water. (quoted in Inglis 2001, 262)

The assurance that a scientific sewer system would then deal with the evidence that had been flushed, rendering it inoffensive, served to complete the process of denial that the bourgeois body defecated. The faecal habitus also entailed the use of indirect and increasingly euphemistic language whenever referring to defecatory matters, thus removing the bourgeois subject even further from the domain of the filthy (Inglis 2001, 205–85).

But with increased population density in urban areas, forcing more proximity among bourgeois and proletarian citizens, it became less and less feasible to maintain a class-based clean/filthy dichotomy. The stability of the bourgeois faecal habitus, as a guarantor of bourgeois hegemony, was undermined by threats of disease, contagion, moral decay and political insurrection. As the nineteenth century reached its closing decades, instead of 'operating unproblematically as a means of retaining bourgeois symbolic superiority ... the excretory filth of the proletariat served instead to push that class outside the confines of bourgeois symbolic regulation' (Inglis 2001, 218). As Inglis puts it:

> The excreting proletarian produced forms of hygienic dirt which produced miasmas (and later germs), which in turn cut down the laboring capacities of his or her fellow proletarians, and threatened the health of the bourgeois master. Moreover, endowed with such rampant and uncontrolled excretory capacities, the proletarian created a morally filthy environment for herself and her cohorts, an environment that seemed to be under no form of discipline whatsoever. (Inglis 2001, 219)

The bourgeoisie was faced with a difficult choice: they could either retain cleanliness as a form of distinction (between themselves and the proletariat class), thus exacerbating the crisis of filth in the urban environment, or they could relinquish the monopoly on cleanliness by extending their own habitus to the working class, rendering them, too, faecally cleanly. This could only be accomplished by recasting how excreta would be dealt with in all urban areas (Inglis 2001, 219). Thus, through state-administered hygiene measures extending water-based sewering and private water-closets to everyone across the board (albeit in uneven waves), regardless of social class, what had been the bourgeois faecal habitus now became what Inglis calls the *modern* faecal habitus. 'As proletarian areas were sewered, and as the proletariat began to operate within the conditions of the sanitary governance of the bourgeois State, their bodies slowly began to be reshaped in bourgeois perception. The nature of proletarian corporeality was increasingly less thought of as unconditionally filthy, a source of both disease and disorder' (Inglis 2001, 239). All of the elements of refinement and cleanliness previously reserved for the bourgeoisie eventually became universalised in the modern industrialised world, with the repercussion that faecal habits could no longer be deployed as a tool for social distinction.[1]

In Inglis's analytical focus on *class*-based social distinction, it seems that gender and race-based distinction cannot be integrated into *A Sociological History of Excretory Experience*. His account of how 'city dwellers' relied on water-closets to 'be carefully protected from their excretions from the moment they are produced' makes no mention of the women whose labour ensured that the 'waste outlet' in question remained free of residual matter, for instance. And his discussion of 'refined bourgeois bodies' as distinguished from 'filthy proletarian flesh' leaves out that it is almost always women whose job it is to give that illusion of refinement, and that in the realm of the proletariat, the female body is considered doubly filthy, by virtue of a presumed intermixing of the sexual with the excretory organs. It would thus seem that at least one significant sector of the population, those engaged in the human labour still necessary to remove faecal matter at the interface between the bourgeois bottom and his scientifically engineered flushing systems (not to mention all those dirty nappies produced by middle-class infants that don't just automatically wash themselves) might find the fiction of bourgeois faecal cleanliness implausible, to say the least.

Inglis does register the gendering of faecal habitus through a symptomatic gesture in a passage I've just quoted, in which he describes the conditions under which the bourgeoisie was compelled to give up its monopoly on faecal cleanliness and extend it to the working classes, i.e. the production of miasmas and germs that diminished the labouring capacities of the proletariat, thus threatening the 'health of the bourgeois master'. Here, Inglis writes, the 'rampant and uncontrolled excretory capacities' of the proletarian 'created a morally filthy environment for *herself* and *her* cohorts' which seemed to be 'under no form of discipline whatsoever' (Inglis 2001, 219, italics mine). I suspect that the use of '*herself*' for the proletarian in this passage is just a randomly chosen textual moment to vary pronouns, so as not to keep using he/him/his as the default universal. But this switch to the female pronoun at precisely this juncture is also indicative of Inglis's intuited sense that the proletariat is *de facto* gendered female to the extent that their environment is perceived to be under 'no form of discipline' and thus in need of the (male) disciplinary techniques of the 'bourgeois master'. It is only in his co-authored article with Mary Holmes that Inglis *directly* addresses the gendering of faecal habitus.[2]

In 'Toiletry Time: Defecation, Temporal Strategies and the Dilemmas of Modernity', the temporality of the defecating body is examined in relation to the rise of rationalised industrial practices of capitalist economic systems. Here, Inglis and Holmes conceive modernity as, by turns, 'civilised', 'capitalist', 'instrumentally rational' and 'patriarchal' – each in terms of how bodies become more and more constrained over time to excrete in a manner that is both temporally and spatially at odds with 'natural' urges. In a section titled: 'The Feminine Fecal and Temporal Constraint', they point out that women do most of the cleaning up of faecal matter, as well as the training of the child 'into the habits of the "civilised" community'. Thus: 'toiletry time, especially that of females, is not confined to the periods when individuals void their own wastes, but also encompasses the time those individuals spend on regulating and collecting the wastes of other people' (236). They focus on the fact that most toilet training of infants, disposal of domestic waste in the household, as well as in institutional settings (emptying of bedpans in hospitals, for instance), is accorded to women, at the same time that men have greater access to public bathrooms than women do. Moreover, 'the chronological control of an infant's defecation is one aspect of a whole set of cadences that women seek to impose on the household in which they work, and which are at the same time imposed on women by the patriarchal logic of the role of housewife' (Inglis and Holmes 2000, 237). Though they don't call it that, it is Ariel Salleh's 'meta-industrial labour' that Inglis and Holmes are referring to in their observation that the patriarchal logic of capitalism requires women to impose 'a whole set of cadences' on their household. In this respect, they lay the groundwork for the more sustained examination of the history of toilet training as the place where meta-industrial labour overlaps with the gendering of faecal habitus in Chapter 4.

## Faecal habitus in the wake of metabolic rift

I'd like to step back for a moment now and consider the insights of David Inglis and John Bellamy Foster within the same framework.

To begin with, it is striking to me that there is no overlap in Inglis's work on faecal habitus and Foster's discussion of Liebig, Marx and Engels on metabolic rift – neither makes reference to, or seems aware of, the other's forays into the modern history of human excreta in the Western world. I am compelled, then, to argue for how these two perspectives on the peristaltic aspect of metabolic systems might be productively thought together.

Both Inglis, in his socio-historical account of modern-day conventions of excretion, and Foster, in his attempt to reanimate Marx's insight about metabolic rift for present-day environmentalism, make their case in terms of class antagonism and class struggle. For Inglis, social rituals around defecation are a means by which one class distinguishes itself as 'superior' to an 'inferior' class. Habitus (as in Bourdieu) is the unconsciously inherited set of practices by which class distinction is maintained, but which breaks down (as a means of class distinction) when proximity of the proletariat to the bourgeois citizen (in the crowded city) presents a hygienic threat, and so the worker must be extended the same privileges that had been reserved for the bourgeoisie itself.

In Foster's account, class is the category used to highlight who gains and who pays in any change to the metabolic relation between humans and the natural environment, or (*pace* Liebig), between humans and the (agriculturally productive) soil. Foster does not concern himself with 'faecal habitus' per se (that is, the conventions around one's bowel habits) except insofar as a huge percentage of the population after a certain historical moment are now defecating in the city, far from the place where the food they had eaten was grown. This has the effect of depleting the agricultural soil that would otherwise have been enriched by human faeces in earlier generations, and of polluting any nearby waterway into which the sanitation system empties, as human excrement, now highly concentrated in the city, presents as a toxic substance to be eliminated rather than as fertiliser with an explicit use-value.

The question that might be posed to the work of Inglis, then, is how would a 'metabolic model' for thinking about excreting humans enrich the sociological understanding of faecal habitus that he has elaborated? And on the other side, the question for Foster is, how would the concept of 'faecal habitus' contribute to a more detailed sense of the metabolic model by which 'man's needs' within 'nature' are regulated and rationalised? For Marx, a disrupted metabolism between 'man' and 'nature' is the basis for understanding how exploited labour within capitalism functions; but the concept of 'faecal habitus' can enrich this with a consideration of the relation between labour and the elimination of waste – also within a metabolic model of humans in their natural, built, industrialised and domestic environment.

Inglis's discussion of the bourgeois (and eventually, of the modern) faecal habitus is invaluable as a context for understanding the social dimensions of modern sanitary reform, and a crucial element in the elaboration of how bodily habits are routinely deployed within hegemonic or disciplinary power arrangements. But in light of the discovery of metabolic rift, and nineteenth-century efforts to address it precisely through broad-based schemes for the massive redirection of human faecal matter from its source at the human body to its rightful destination in the agricultural field, I would suggest that the clean/dirty binary that Inglis posits as the controlling model for the bourgeois faecal habitus could be usefully modified to account for what must have been just as important to the bourgeois sense of bodily integrity – its disciplinary training as a functional component in larger peristaltic or metabolic systems.

We must engage a *metabolic* rather than a *binary* model for understanding the perspective taken by the bourgeoisie on its own body, especially given that women's labour is a crucial component in maintaining and regulating peristaltic health and consistency. Given that modern faecal discourse of the period focused as much on the ecological necessity to replenish the soil as it did on the dangers of urban filth, it is more accurate to say that rather than a blanket of silence or euphemism around faecal matters, there was an imperative to speak freely about the fate of one's waste, that is, to ensure its proper insertion into a metabolic model of mobility (on the model of Marvin and Medd's discussion of keeping 'fat' on the move). As Christopher Hamlin demonstrates, the urgency of mending the metabolic rift was debated not only within scientific circles, but in highly public venues; this meant that anyone who happened to read the daily news or attend public lectures would have felt themselves to be addressed by pressing questions as to the best way to coordinate their most intimate habits with the city's infrastructural needs:

> The importance of recycling urban wastes, not just as a legal, political, and medical matter, but if Liebig were right, also a matter of

human survival, together with the inability of experts to reach consensus about how to recycle them, made sewage treatment and associated issues prime subjects for lengthy and acrimonious discussion in a broad range of forums and formats: in newspapers such as *The Times*, in numerous parliamentary papers and on the floor of the House of Commons, in political speeches, literary reviews, engineering or architectural journals like *The Engineer and the Builder*, and sporting journals like *The Field*, as well as in medical and public health periodicals and in numerous pamphlets. Papers on sewage recycling were heard at the Institution of Civil Engineers, the Chemical Society, the British Association for the Advancement of Science (which between 1869 and 1876 had a standing committee to investigate sewage recycling), the Royal Society of Arts (which in the late 1870s held annual conferences on the 'Health and Sewage of Towns'), the Royal Agricultural Society (which gave prizes to the best sewage farms), and even by groups as ostensibly uninvolved with sanitary matters as the Balloon Society of Great Britain and the Jewish Working Men's Club. Protracted debate often followed these papers: discussion of C.N. Bazalgette's paper on 'The Sewage Question' occupied the next five meetings of the Institution of Civil Engineers. Even *Punch* treated recycling with respect. (Hamlin 1985, 394–5)

Anyone who kept up with current affairs would have been familiar with the notion that failure to recycle human waste could lead to the fall of great civilisations (Hamlin 1985, 399); that China, by contrast, could show how 'strict attention to keeping cycles of matter intact could sustain a large population' (Hamlin 1985, 399); that 'sewage was a "treasure," an untapped "mine of gold," and the mysterious soil processes that converted it into plant life [according to an 1865 editorial in *Builder*] a "transformative miracle by which the foetid refuse of the population, the excrementitious offscourings of man and beast, the poisonous causes of diseases and death in town, can become a source of life, of vigour, of fertility, and of beauty in the country, making the herb more grateful to the cattle, the flower more fragrant, and fruit more delicate and more rich"' while 'failure to recycle ... caused ... immorality, drunkenness, war, starvation, and revolution' (quoted in Hamlin 1985, 399).

Even if all this rhetoric was so much hype, designed to sell one's particular recycling system, still, it underlined the importance of recycling *tout court*. In some formulations, defecation was not a function to be denied, hidden, consigned to silence, but rather to be practised in abundance: in sewage recycling 'lay the answer to Malthus, for sewage was the only fertiliser that increased in proportion to the population' according to social reformer Charles Kingsley, who advocated in favour of a 'Chadwick-inspired venture which proposed to sell London sewage to Fulham market gardeners' (Hamlin 1985, 404). Thomas Hawksley, a London physician at the Margaret Street Infirmary for Diseases of the Chest, argued against the 'evil of water-carriage sewerage' in favour of 'the rightness and righteousness of earth closets' – through which matter would move in a 'round of obedient duty' in an 'efficiency and goodness' that would reveal 'the control of God' (Hamlin 1985, 404–5).

It may be the case that 'excretory dirt' was in fact the symbolic capital mobilised by the bourgeoisie to distinguish itself from the proletariat. But it was not as simple as imaging the bourgeois body as having no anus, no 'apertures by which organic processes may occur or through which effluvia could leak'. It wasn't so much that the bourgeois body had to be depicted as *that which did not excrete* over and against a proletariat body that did. It was more an issue of figuring the bourgeois body as the site of a problematised metabolic or peristaltic system.

If, as Foucault argues, the bourgeoisie thought of their sex, for instance, as 'a fragile treasure, a secret that had to be discovered at all costs' (Foucault 1980, 121); if the 'deployment of sexuality' was something that the bourgeoisie 'tried on themselves' before extending it, with transformations, to a subordinate class (Foucault 1980, 122), then the same is true of the bourgeoisie's sense of its peristaltic self. We could say that bourgeois 'regularity', as much as its sexuality, was a matter of 'an intensification of the body, a problematization of health and its operational terms: it was a question of techniques for maximizing life' (Foucault 1980, 123).

While it is true to say, as Inglis does, that faecal habitus had everything to do with the peristaltic habits of the bourgeoisie, and little to do with those of the working class, it is not that the bourgeoisie sought to 'repress' the peristaltic habits of the 'classes to be exploited' – but neither did they exactly repress their own habits of defecation. Faecal habitus was more about the 'self-affirmation of one class rather than the enslavement of another: a defense, a protection, a strengthening, and an exaltation that were eventually extended to others – at the cost of different transformations – as a means of social control and political subjugation' (Foucault 1980, 123). And why not borrow Foucault wholesale here? 'With this investment of its own [bowel habits] by a technology of power and knowledge which it had itself invented, the bourgeoisie underscored the high political price of its body, sensations, and pleasures, its well-being and survival' (Foucault 1985, 123; my substitution). The bourgeoisie 'provided itself with a body to be cared for, protected, cultivated, and preserved from the many dangers and contacts, to be isolated from others so that it would retain its differential value; and this, by equipping itself with – among other resources – a technology of [regularity]' (Foucault 1980, 123). In this substitution of 'regularity' for Foucault's sexuality, there emerges, not a denial, but a sensitisation of the anus, the sphincter and the large bowel, as the point of egress for a carefully calibrated processing of the world through the bourgeois intestinal system; not the sealing off of the body to potential forces of defilement, but an attunement of the excreting body with the other metabolic systems through which it passed, and which passed through it; not a silence or even a disguising of discourse around all matters excretory, in an effort to censor and deny its existence, but an imperative to examine one's excretory experience, and to determine whether it was of the most advantageous regularity, of the healthiest consistency, proper colour, neither too abundant nor too meagre; that it be produced through artificial aids to regularity, or that it be produced only through the most natural of methods; that one voids only at one optimally prescribed time of day, or that one be free to excrete whenever necessity requires; in other words, discursivity was essential to ensure that the defecating body was functioning at its ideal capacity.

Inglis is correct in arguing that defecation and faecal matter are both forms of social capital, ready to be used as a mode of distinction to assert the superiority of one class over a subordinated class, and thereby to maintain hegemony within a given field of power. As Foucault says about sexuality along these same lines: 'This process . . . was linked to the movement by which it asserted its distinctiveness and its hegemony. There is little question that one of the primordial forms of class consciousness is the affirmation of the body' (Foucault 1985, 126). Foucault's account of the eventual extension of the bourgeois habitus to the working class is true on both counts of sexuality and regularity – with a slight adjustment we see how Foucault's observations mirror those of Bourdieu and Inglis: 'The living conditions that were dealt to the proletariat, particularly in the first half of the nineteenth century, show there was anything but concern for its body and [regularity]: it was of little importance whether those people lived or died, [were constipated or diarrhoeal], since their [peristaltic system] was something that took care of itself in any case. Conflicts were necessary (in particular conflicts over urban space: cohabitation, proximity, contamination, epidemics, such as the cholera outbreak of 1832 . . .) in order for the proletariat to be granted a body and a [regularity] . . . there had to be established a whole technology of control which made it possible to keep that body and [regularity], finally conceded to them, under surveillance (schooling, the politics of housing, public hygiene, institutions of relief and insurance, the general medicalization of the population), in short, an entire administrative and technical machinery made it possible to safely import the deployment of [regularity] into the exploited class' (Foucault 1985, 126).

Modifying Inglis's concept of faecal habitus as a matter of perfecting regularity, rather than separating the clean from the filthy, is, I would argue, an important step in moving from Marx's concept of metabolic rift to a fully articulated theory of metabolic biopolitics. To this end, we will delve, in the next two chapters, into a more fully articulated understanding of Marx's metabolic model of labour and the transformations of capital, and follow that up with the biomedical model of the human enteric system that emerged at the turn of the twentieth century.

## Notes

1 For an interesting follow up to Inglis's work on the modern faecal habitus, see Weinberg and Williams (2005), who studied contemporary university students to show how gender and sexuality affect whether an individual is more or less likely to be constrained by conventions surrounding what they call 'faecal events'.
2 And elsewhere, Inglis broadens the parameters of faecal habitus to examine how 'dominant groups in colonial and post-colonial contexts' assert the '"inferiority" of subaltern groups', by representing them in terms of their faecal waste (Inglis, 2002, 208). The previous distinction between bourgeois and proletariat consists today of a distinction between the 'white' English and the postcolonial (or

immigrant of color). 'If we are truly to understand the ways in which contemporary racist discourse works, we must interrogate the constellation of material and symbolic factors which are the conditions of possibility for the mobilisation of resources of faecal and other forms of corporeal symbolism by one group against another' (Inglis, 2002, 219).

# 3

# Marx's Regulation of Metabolism

### Regulating metabolism

In 'Karl Marx and the Tradition of Western Political Thought', Hannah Arendt remarks that, according to Marx,

> what made socialism scientific and distinguished it from that of his predecessors, the 'utopian socialists', was not an economic theory with its scientific insights as well as its errors, but the discovery of a law of movement that ruled matter and, at the same time, showed itself in the reasoning capacity of man as 'consciousness', either of the self or of a class (Arendt, 2018, 34)

In the next two chapters, I will examine more minutely the metabolic strands in Marx's *law of movement* that rules *matter* and *consciousness*, and then turn to a sustained exploration of the physiology of the human peristaltic system understood as a 'second brain', or a brain in the gut. I thus read together a theory of movement within two concomitant discourses: Marx's analysis of a capitalist economic system in which labour was rationalised along metabolic lines, and physiologist J.N. Langley's turn-of-the-century description of the human enteric system. Both entail a temporality of development; in Marx it is historical, in Langley it is evolutionary. While it might seem more logical to begin with the physiological workings of peristalsis in the body before moving on to the presumed metaphorical use of it in economic theory, I argue that economic movement as conceived by Marx is coterminous with Langley's account of the physiological movement of bodily metabolism. Thus, I begin dialectically with the macro movements of capital before considering the emergence of a medical account of the 'second brain' within that system of circulation, and its requirement of human mediation.

Marx lays importance not on the fact of 'having' a metabolism, nor that we are implicated in nature 'by' a metabolism, nor even that social relations, as vectors of power, repression, resistance and revolutions are metabolic in nature. What he comes back to most insistently is that wherever metabolism can be found, it seems that its absorptions and incorporations, its transformations and metamorphoses, its residues, ejections and excrescences – indeed, its very mode of production – cannot be accomplished without some inevitable mediation. And humans are the mediators. Moreover, as we will see, neither Marx nor one of the closest readers of his metabolic model, Hannah Arendt, accounts for the fact that this 'mediation' of metabolism, in the global North at any rate, is for the most part accomplished by the meta-industrial exertions of women.

Let's return to Marx's concept of metabolism in his story of a damaging rift in the symbiosis between humans and the arable land that sustains them. It will be instructive to see where, having discovered the rift between agricultural production and urban consumption, Marx relies on the model of metabolism to characterise human activity in general. As we recall from Chapter 1, Marx wrote that the collection of the population together in urban areas

> disturbs the metabolic interaction between man and the earth, i.e. it prevents the return to the soil of its constituent elements consumed by man in the form of food and clothing; hence it hinders the operation of the eternal natural condition for the lasting fertility of the soil. (Marx 1976, 637)

And in the third volume of *Capital*:

> Large landed property reduces the agricultural population to an ever decreasing minimum and confronts it with an ever growing industrial population crammed together in large towns; in this way it produces conditions that provoke an irreparable rift in the interdependent process of social metabolism, a metabolism *prescribed* by the natural laws of life itself. (Marx 1981, 949, my italics)

We have here the two registers of metabolism that characterise Marx's writings throughout: a primary, quite material, 'natural law of life itself' consisting of the 'metabolic interaction between man and the earth', which in turn 'prescribes' a secondary relation referred to as 'social metabolism'. But how is 'social metabolism ... *prescribed* by the natural laws of life itself'? At first, it might seem as though the term 'social metabolism' is merely a metaphor to describe the transformations of social relations in capitalism. But I would argue that Marx is here suggesting a material continuity of the 'natural' with the 'social' workings of metabolism. To understand this, let's first consider the meaning of man's metabolic relation to the earth.

In Marx, labour is defined above all as a process by which:

> man, through his own actions, mediates, regulates, and controls [*vermittelt, regelt und kontrolliert*] the metabolism between himself and nature. He confronts the materials of nature as a force of nature. He sets in motion the natural forces which belong to his own body, his arms, legs, head and hands, in order to appropriate the materials of nature in a form adapted to his own needs. Through this movement, he acts upon external nature and changes it, and in this way simultaneously changes his own nature. He develops the potentialities slumbering within nature, and subjects the play of its forces to his own sovereign power. (Marx 1976, 283)

To understand what is going on in this passage, we will begin with this ambiguous 'nature' that slides from an entity external to man, to an intrinsic property of man, and back again: if at first nature is separated from (and yet connected to) man by the term 'metabolism' (the metabolism between himself and nature; he confronts the materials of nature), it soon serves to characterise man himself as a force of nature. If man can be a force of nature it is because of the 'natural forces' of his body, arms, legs, head and hands. These he uses to appropriate what he needs from a nature that is separate from him again in the next sentence. By acting on this 'external nature', he changes it, but also his 'own nature'. If metabolism paradoxically marks both the gap and the continuity between 'man' and 'nature', it is in part because, through his labour, man 'mediates, regulates, and controls' it. Metabolism is both a process of transformation and an operation that requires human intervention and governance in the form of 'labour'.

### Grown-on and grown-in tools

But what precisely allows Marx to call man's bodily parts (arms, legs, head and hands) natural forces? To understand this, we turn to a text that predates Marx's reliance on the concept of metabolism, when he was thinking of the human/nature dyad in terms of the organic versus the inorganic. In *The Economic and Philosophical Manuscripts of 1844*, Marx writes that man, like any animal, depends on nature to live:

> The universality of man appears in practice precisely in the universality which makes all nature his inorganic body – both inasmuch as nature is (1) his direct means of life, and (2) the material, the object, and the instrument of his life activity. Nature is man's inorganic body – nature, that is, insofar as it is not itself human body. Man lives on nature – means that nature is his body, with which he must remain in continuous interchange if he is not to die. (Marx 1988, 31–2)

The characterisation of nature as 'inorganic' might come as a surprise to contemporary readers accustomed to associating the 'natural' with the 'organic' (for example, in discourses around the organic food industry). John Bellamy Foster and Paul Burkett offer some insight into this nineteenth-century usage of the terms organic/inorganic. According to the scientific vocabulary of the period, organic indicated that which pertained to bodily organs, whereas inorganic simply meant anything that was *un*related to bodily organs (Foster and Burkett 2000, 412). Marx inherits this sense of organic/inorganic from ancient Greek usage in which the term *organon* referred both to organs and tools; 'organs were initially viewed as "grown-on tools" of animals' in contrast to the artificially created tools of human beings. Both the organs of animals and tools fashioned by humans were understood to be a 'part of the general process of species adaptation to natural conditions' (Foster and Burkett 2000, 408).

Consider the hand, for instance. As Engels understood it, once the human became upright, the hand developed more rapidly than the brain, and only after did the two then develop 'through a complex, interactive set of relations now referred to by evolutionary biologists as gene-culture coevolution' (Foster and Burkett 2000, 414). This freed the hand, which 'could henceforth attain ever greater dexterity and skill, and the greater flexibility thus acquired was inherited and increased from generation to generation'. In this respect, the hand, as a grown-on tool, is at once the *organ* of labour but also the *product* of labour through a process of inheritance through generations of improvements (Foster and Burkett 2000, 414).

It was the assimilation of Liebig's agricultural science and Jacob Moleschott's materialist account of *stoffwechsel* in plants and animals (which, as Schmidt puts it, 'portrays nature, on the model of human physiology, as a vast process of transformation and metabolism'), that eventually motivated Marx's shift to a metabolic model in his later work (Foster and Burkett 2000, 418) – but the dialectic of organic/inorganic relations continued to persist in his writing as well.[1]

At a primary level, then, metabolism expresses the idea that man, as an organic creature fitted with organs as 'grown-on tools', is metabolically implicated in a larger system of nature that is at the same time transformed by it. To these external bodily organs, I will now add the '*grown-in* tools' of the stomach, bowels, sphincter and the other internal organs that perform their transformations of inorganic nature. As Alfred Schmidt puts it: 'Just as in living nature assimilation changes the inorganic into the organic, so man assimilates that "inorganic body" in his work and converts it in an ever-increasing measure into an "organic" part of himself' (Schmidt 1971, 80).

Put more insistently, we could say that if nature is man's *inorganic* body (might we even say a Deleuzian body-without-organs?), the corollary of this is that man is nature's *organic* body. Thus, when Marx says that 'man, through his own actions, *mediates, regulates, and controls* the metabolism between himself and nature' it means two things: first, that man depends on the stuff of nature to survive by transforming nature's non-organic material into objects with use-value (which he may then consume and transform in a metabolic process); and also, that in training the organs of his own body (which in effect is a form of sharpening or adapting his grown-on, or *grown-in*, tools), he is metabolically transforming nature as well, insofar as his body is the organic body of nature. This is the meaning of 'he transforms nature but he also transforms himself'. The organs of the hands are trained (through both evolutionary and generational time) for their functionality in labour; but, as the model of metabolism even more explicitly suggests, his internal organs are trained both to complement the labour his hands perform and to fashion products of their own by converting nature's inorganic materials into the usable energy and nutrients that keep alive nature's organic body (his own), as well as the excreted by-product that replenishes the inorganic nature that supplies the food man must eat. Metabolism in (man's) organic body of nature extends outward through exchange and transformation to include the inorganic nature that flows through this body; in this respect it 'makes' of nature its 'inorganic body' while at the same time serving as organic body to nature. To put man's relation to nature in terms of metabolism is to maintain continuity between man and nature even as they must seem to be opposed to each other; it is Marx's way of moving beyond a reductive duality of Man/Nature, and to figure it dialectically. Schmidt, in fact, characterises the very unfolding of history as a matter of nature's self-mediation through man:

> Nature attains self-consciousness in men, and amalgamates with itself by virtue of their theoretical-practical activity. Human participation in something alien and external to them appears at first to be something equally alien and external to nature; but in fact it proves to be a 'natural condition of human existence', which is itself a part of nature, and it therefore constitutes nature's self-movement. (Schmidt 1971, 79)

So we have arrived at this notion of a primary metabolism as nature dialectically mediating itself through man's organs, those grown-on, but more importantly, *grown-in* tools. But before we ask how this metabolic relation between man and nature 'prescribes' social metabolism, I want to consider an important modification Hannah Arendt makes to Marx's metabolic model of labour. Her work is especially significant in a context where we think of the 'world' as something that runs through us, even as we are positioned within worlds of metabolic movement.

### Labour versus work

As a reminder, all of this emphasis on organs as tools, on appropriation for transformation and consumption, on metabolism as the basis for survival, is Marx's discourse for the concept of labour. 'Mediation, regulation, and control' of a primary metabolism between man and nature is accomplished through a labour that defines the human as a species. This fundamental labour, necessary for survival, is understood to be a basic human characteristic, prior to its appropriation by specific historical formations – including agrarian, feudal and industrial societies. 'Labour,' Marx writes, 'as the creator of use-values, as useful labour, is a condition of human existence which is independent of all forms of society; it is an eternal natural necessity which mediates the metabolism between man and nature, and therefore human life itself' (Marx 1976, 133).

Arendt takes up precisely this metabolic definition of labour, only to point out that Marx has neglected to differentiate labour from another activity that defines our condition as humans: work. She agrees that labour is immersed in the 'metabolism between man and nature', but asserts that work (which Marx subsumed under the umbrella term of labour) rises above the repetitious cycles of pure survival. 'Labor is the activity,' Arendt writes, 'which corresponds to the biological process of the human body, whose spontaneous growth, metabolism, and eventual decay are bound to the vital necessities produced and fed into the life process' (Arendt 1998, 7). In this respect, labour is cyclical, never-ending, ensuring survival in a metabolic relation to nature through feeding and maintaining physiological existence. 'Work', on the other hand,

> is the activity which corresponds to the unnaturalness of human existence, which is not imbedded in, and whose mortality is not compensated by, the species' ever-recurring life cycle. Work provides an 'artificial' world of things, distinctly different from all natural surroundings. Within its borders each individual life is housed, while this world itself is meant to outlast and transcend them all.[2] (Arendt 1998, 7)

Unlike labour, which either services the human body or produces only consumable goods, work transforms material into durable objects, the chairs, tables, buildings, communications and transportation systems, art, music and literature, everything, in short, that make up the 'world' we live in. In terms of metabolic processes, the difference between labour and work is that labour returns its transformed materials back to nature almost immediately, whereas work prolongs this return over years, decades, centuries, even millennia. If the human condition of labour is 'life itself', the human condition of work is 'worldliness' (Arendt 1998, 7).

Much of *The Human Condition* concerns itself with demarcating the boundaries among four elements in a sort of give and take of influence and encroachment: labour, work, nature and world; this is where a productive, and gendered, ambivalence begins to emerge. Consider the following passage:

> While nature manifests *itself* in human existence through the circular movement of our bodily functions, *she* makes *her* presence felt in the *man-made* world through the constant threat of overgrowing or decaying it. The common characteristic of both, the biological process in *man* and the process of growth and decay in *the world*, is that they are part of the cyclical movement of nature and therefore endlessly repetitive; all human activities which arise out of the necessity to cope with them are bound to the recurring cycles of nature and have in themselves no beginning and no end, properly speaking. (Arendt 1998, 98, my italics)

The 'human activities' Arendt refers to here are those classed under the heading of 'labour', which (endlessly) takes place within the realm of metabolic nature, but also as a means of defending the world. It is interesting that, within the span of one sentence, nature is an 'it' when manifesting in our bodily functions, but is personified as 'she' and 'her' when threatening the integrity of the world with overgrowth and decay – as though the metabolic principle of change transforms even the nature of nature it/herself. Moreover, the world is itself specifically '*man*-made', as though to reinforce its masculine distinction from feminised nature. Likewise, 'man' and 'the world' are shown to share a commonality. The constant, and now *gendered*, threat of nature comes through in the second half of the sentence:

> unlike *working*, whose end has come when the object is finished, ready to be added to the common world of things, laboring always moves in the same circle, which is prescribed by the biological process of the living organism and the end of its 'toil and trouble' comes only with the death of this organism. (Arendt 1998, 98)

Arendt notes that when defining labour as 'man's metabolism with nature', Marx 'indicated clearly that he was "speaking physiologically" and that labour and consumption are but two stages of the ever-recurring cycle of biological life' (Arendt 1998, 99).

Whatever labour produces 'is meant to be fed into the human life process almost immediately, and this consumption, regenerating the life process, produces – or rather, reproduces – new "labor power", needed for the further sustenance of the body' (Arendt 1998, 99). From a feminist point of view, of course, Arendt is talking about the reproductive labour of unremunerated women's work – though she does not acknowledge it. Moreover, if the worker in some sense lives on through the world created by his durable objects, the labourer, as an organism, merely dies at the end of all her toil and trouble.

'Labor, when it incorporates, "gathers", and bodily "mixes with" the things provided by nature,' Arendt writes, 'does actively what *the body does even more intimately* when it consumes its nourishment. Both are devouring processes that seize and destroy matter' (Arendt 1998, 99–100, my italics). The intimate bodily process referenced here is clearly the metabolic digestive process, its 'physiology' both a model for and extension of 'labour'. The logic of Arendt's model is that as a devouring and destructive process, labour is unlike work, which has the distinction of (creatively) changing material into an enduring finished product.

Clearly Arendt wants to valorise work as a world-making activity, since our inhabitation of the (political) world is what defines us fully as humans. But at the same time, from the point of view of the environmentalist, 'work' itself introduces, or threatens to introduce, a metabolic rift insofar as it constantly disrupts the natural cycle of matter. Labour is itself in keeping with an uninterrupted metabolic cycle since resources are returned swiftly rather than indefinitely extracted from the earth, whereas work, insofar as it takes away material from nature in order to fashion it into objects for the world, creates a disruption or rift.

Though she does not use the discourse of 'metabolic rift', Arendt tacitly acknowledges that nature actively fights against the metabolic rift caused by world-making; it does this in the way it, or sometimes she, 'forever invades the human artifice, threatening the durability of the world and its fitness for human use', through 'processes of growth and decay'. Against these processes, it is the job of labour to launch an 'unending fight' (Arendt 1998, 100). 'The protection and preservation of the world against natural processes are among the toils which need the monotonous performance of daily repeated chores' (Arendt 1998, 100). If work designs and fashions the objects of the durable world, labour's most vigorous employment is to protect these objects, even as it paradoxically simultaneously tends to the bodily needs of world-making workers. 'This laboring fight [to protect the world],' Arendt writes, is 'distinguished from the essentially peaceful fulfillment in which labor obeys the orders of immediate bodily needs' (Arendt 1998, 100).

It now appears that to engage in labour (unlike work – whose loyalty is only to the world) is to be split between fealties, to nature on one side, to the world on the other. Does 'man' keep his own metabolic system tightly circuited into that of nature, consuming its material only to excrete it 'swiftly' back again as replenishing fertiliser? Or does he devote his attention to the unending fight against nature's incursions into the world, preserving the products fashioned through work, indeed, prolonging the time it will take for them to decompose and be returned back to nature? It's not as though engaging in this endless labour to shore up the human-built world will earn the kind of recognition or indeed, even immortality, that work garners.

> The daily fight in which the human body is engaged to keep the world clean and prevent its decay bears little resemblance to heroic deeds; the endurance it needs to repair every day anew the waste of yesterday is not courage, and what makes the effort painful is not danger but its relentless repetition. (Arendt 1998, 100)

After all, man's labour may resemble Hercules' great feat of cleaning the stables, 'but unfortunately it is only the mythological Augean stable that will *remain* clean once the effort is made and the task achieved' (Arendt 1998, 100–1, my italics).

Arendt expresses some anxiety that labour *as* metabolic process requires little or no human agency to accomplish its peaceful tasks of fulfilling bodily needs in a 'direct metabolism with nature'; it seems almost to require no effort at all, like what the 'body does even more intimately', when it consumes and metabolises its contents. Once labour is associated with and in fact located within our physiological metabolic systems, processing nature's material so that it can be returned as replenishing compost (as in a comprehensive faecal recycling system, for instance), does this mean that labour might, after all, entail no toil and trouble at all – especially given that so much of it has been automated through machine technology?

And might modern thought itself be somehow diminished by its funnelling through the concept of 'process'? 'Within the framework of experiences given to introspection,' Arendt writes, 'we know of no other process but the life process within our bodies, and the only activity into which we can translate it and which corresponds to it is labor' (Arendt 1998, 116). Clearly, it is the digestive and enteric process of biological consumption and excretion Arendt is talking about here when she refers to the 'life process within our bodies', i.e. our metabolic system. The coincidence of the discovery of 'processes' in the natural sciences and of 'introspection' in philosophy serves as grounds, in other words, for emphasising how metabolism becomes the 'model' for the philosophical concept of 'process' in general, for introspection, and for how Marx's theory of economics is organised around labour in particular.

Hannah Landecker also notes Arendt's observation here, and remarks that 'the metabolism of the nineteenth and twentieth centuries traced here was a very particular concept, and remarkably inward looking – for all the dynamism of metabolic process, it allows freedom from the world' (Landecker 2013, 224).[3] But in fact, Arendt faults Marx's metabolic model precisely because it has laid the groundwork for a Bergsonian theory of life that poses a threat to worldliness; it seems to have 'lost sight of the only activity necessary to sustain the life process', excludes 'that minimum of initiative present even in those activities which, like labouring and begetting are urged upon man by necessity' (Arendt 1998, 117). This loss corresponds 'to the factual historical development which made labor more effortless than ever before and therefore even more similar to the automatically functioning life process' (Arendt 1998, 117).

By 'factual historical development', Arendt means the technological automation and bureaucratisation that has rendered labour 'effortless', so that socialised men, freed from the necessity to labour, would 'spend their freedom . . . in those strictly private and essentially worldless activities we now call hobbies' (Arendt 1998, 116, 118). If Bergson's *elan vital* evinces a dynamism, it threatens to occlude and take the place of conscious 'initiative'. As a result, men don't 'work' anymore in the public sphere (where political activity can be engaged), and they don't even seem to 'labour' in the physiological sphere (since physiology dynamically takes care of itself *and* nature); rather they engage in 'hobbies' in the social sphere, which has nothing to do with the public sphere, and certainly doesn't seem to prepare them for political action. Or, as she says elsewhere, man has become a mere 'jobholder', his individual life 'submerged in the over-all life process of the species', as though the 'only active decision still required of the individual were to let go, so to speak, to abandon his individuality, the still individually sensed pain and trouble of living, and acquiesce in a dazed, "tranquilized", functional type of behavior' (Arendt 1998, 322).

And yet, in contrast to the worldlessness of passive labour, modern-day 'introspection', immersed as it is in a Bergsonian theory of life processes, is figured by Arendt as metabolically hooking us back up with the world: 'since this biological life, accessible in self-observation, is at the same time a metabolic process between man and nature, it is as though introspection no longer needs to get lost in the ramifications of a consciousness without reality, but has found within man – *not in his mind but in his bodily processes* – enough outside matter to connect him again with the outer world' (Arendt 1998, 312, my italics).

It is surprising that immersion in bodily processes connects us back to the outer *world*, since it would seem to contradict Arendt's earlier observation that (metabolic) labour is the only activity that 'corresponds strictly to the experience of *worldlessness*' (Arendt 1998, 115, my italics). In labouring, 'the human body, its activity notwithstanding, is ... thrown back upon itself, concentrates upon nothing but its own being alive, and remains imprisoned in its metabolism with nature without ever transcending or freeing itself from the recurring cycle of its own functioning' (Arendt 1998, 115). While 'labouring' is 'thrown back upon itself' and forced to concentrate 'upon nothing', thus trapped in 'worldlessness', introspection, on the other hand, finds within man the 'bodily processes' that (because metabolic) connect him back with 'the outer world'. There is, thus, a fundamental ambivalence about whether metabolism connects with or separates us from the world, an ambivalence that may be clarified if we bring into view the metabolic gendering of labour and introspection.

### The outsourcing of labour

Arendt maintains this discourse of 'man' as labouring, working, thinking, theorising, worlding and making history, reluctant all the while to acknowledge that the metabolically inflected forms of labour she discusses are carried out by women, or by populations feminised by their dissociation from the 'man' who works, thinks and makes the world. Indeed, when Arendt remarks on the difference between the cleaning of stables performed by Hercules and the cleaning performed by 'man' as mundane daily labour (the one heroic, requiring courage in the face of danger, the other merely painful by virtue of its constant repetition), it seems the perfect juncture to point out that it is not after all 'man' who carries out this daily cleaning, but rather the class of humans that have been accorded to Salleh's realm of meta-industrial labour. 'Man' has, it would appear, *outsourced* the care and maintenance of his metabolic self.

Maybe Arendt can't be blamed for not seeing this 'outsourcing' for what it is, since Marx's own theory doesn't make it visible. As Timothée Haug has put it (drawing from the work of Roswitha Scholz), 'waged work has to be considered as the one visible and acknowledged side of a split form of life. Meanwhile the other side remains excluded by the logic of valuation implemented under capitalism' (Haug 2018, 197). The split-off and invisible side 'encompasses all the activities that remain necessary to connect and mediate the purchase of commodities and the metabolic process of reproduction, e.g. the preparation and repairs of commodities for consumption, the maintenance of the household and the bearing and breeding of children' (Haug 2018, 197). This unpaid labour, like the continued extraction of resources from the earth, must be kept invisible *as* outsourcing in order to guarantee the accumulation of surplus value that makes capitalism work. Meta-industrial labour is only 'external' to capitalism in the sense that it is not waged labour, but it is 'internal' to capitalism in the sense that it lowers production costs (Haug 2018, 200). For this reason, Haug warns against assuming that unpaid women's labour, or subsistence economies at the margins of global capital, represent 'an economic and political autonomy from capitalist domination' (Haug 2018, 200). The spheres of unpaid women's labour and waged men's work are thus dialectically intertwined; and if women's reproductive activities seem 'close to nature' it's really as a result of their 'partial exclusion from the commodity-market' (Haug 2018, 200).

Arendt on some level recognises that this is the case, but follows out a different trajectory for locating the site of that outsourcing, attributing it to automation and bureaucratisation rather than to the division of humans into those who may engage in the heroic worlding satisfaction of work and introspection, and those who must endlessly clean out the stables of our daily existence.[4] Once we visualise the labouring bodies who do the cleaning, or indeed, all of the mediating, regulating and controlling of our metabolism with nature, it is impossible to see them as 'passive', or lacking in 'initiative'; we might even want to say they show 'courage' and a kind of 'heroism' after all, not only for persevering in their unending metabolic labours, but also for petitioning and even dying in history-making struggles to be adequately compensated for these labours.

To reiterate: Arendt's parsing of Marx's labour into metabolic labour on the one hand and world-making work on the other approaches the threshold where she might have recognised the distribution of labour and work across differentiated populations; but it was a threshold she did not cross. Instead, she faults her monadic universal 'man' for allowing automation to rob him of his initiative, to become a jobholder, indeed, to become passive and feminised. The criss-crossing of her arguments between nature versus world, passive versus active, nature versus history, devouring versus creating, consuming versus producing is laced through with gendered implications, whereby the feminine is invariably implicitly or explicitly on the nature, passive, devouring side of the binary, even as women per se are not named as engaged in either metabolic labour or world- and history-making work.

It may thus seem paradoxical to draw from Arendt's work here, since she has hardly been considered a feminist, not least because of her inability to acknowledge the value of unremunerated domestic work.[5] But her very immersion in Marx's metabolic model of labour, her disambiguation of labour and work, has made it possible to make visible what is obviously a male prerogative of world-making work and introspection.

## Social metabolism

It is precisely in the 'world' valorised by Arendt that Marx traces out the 'social metabolism' prescribed by man's metabolism with nature. Since we are about to examine the metabolic terms through which Marx explains the economic circulation of money and commodities, it will be instructive to consider that in at least one of the sources from which Marx derived his understanding of metabolism, the workings of the economic market were already being thought along the lines of metabolic transformations. In the midst of his account of a circuit of ingestion and transformation among nature's elements ('What man excretes nourishes the plant. The plant changes the air into solids and nourishes the animal, etc.'), Jacob Moleschott makes the following observation:

> The name 'metabolism' has been given to this exchange of material. We are right not to mention this word without a feeling of reverence. For just as *trade is the soul of commerce*, the eternal circulation of material is the soul of the world ... the quintessence of all activity on earth is the movement of the basic materials, combination and division, assimilation and excretion. (quoted in Schmidt 1971, 87, my italics)

So even as we consider Marx's sense of how natural metabolism 'prescribes' social metabolism, we must at the same time understand both the natural and the social, earth and world, as consistent with an overarching law of transformation and exchange, indeed of 'assimilation and excretion', that characterises all movement. An analogy such as this: 'In the same way as the continued existence of an individual is bound up with the functions of the body, society too must stand in an uninterrupted productive contact with nature' (Schmidt 1971, 89) is not to be understood as the 'existence of two levels of reality, accompanying each other without mediation' (Schmidt 1971, 90). Rather:

> In the direct labour-process, i.e. the metabolism between man and nature, the material side triumphs over the historically determined form; in the process of exchange, which depends on the labour-process, the historically determined form triumphs over the material side. (Schmidt 1971, 92)

Natural and social are co-extensive in these formulations.

The articulation of social relations as a matter of metabolism is no more evident than in the chapter of *Capital* titled: 'Money, or the circulation of Commodities' (Marx 1976, 188–244). Thought in terms of human physiology, the 'money' in this title relates to the 'circulation of commodities' along the same lines as 'fibre' might relate to the 'circulation of ingested matter'. Money is the fibre essential for metabolic motility, in the overall series of exchanges, transformations, velocities and stagnations that characterise the peristaltic movement of the economic system that defines social relations among humans.[6]

The chained transformations defining social metabolism are multiple, and take place along diverse registers, from constantly mutating commodities to the quality of labour itself (as it moves from private to social, from concrete to abstract), from the now crystal, now dissolving form of money, to the participants in the market who are buyers one minute, sellers the next, and back again. Indeed, we even witness 'the conversion of things into persons and the conversion of persons into things' (Marx 1976, 209). To trace out this phantasmagoria of transformations, we begin with the monotonous shape-shifting of commodities themselves.

The minute a product of basic labour finds its way onto a market, where it can be exchanged for another kind of product, it is transformed from a commodity with a use-value to a commodity with an exchange value. 'In so far as the process of exchange transfers commodities from hands in which they are non-use-values to hands in which they are use-values, it is a process of social metabolism. The product of one kind of useful labour replaces that of another' (Marx 1976, 198). Indeed, this entire chapter traces the 'change in form or the metamorphosis of commodities through which the social metabolism is mediated' (Marx 1976, 199).

In an advanced capitalist system, commodities are no longer directly exchanged (20 yards of linen for a family bible, for instance); rather their transformation, one into another, is accomplished through a mediating metamorphosis into money. The weaver thus exchanges his linen for £2, then in turn exchanges the £2 for the bible. 'The linen, for him a mere commodity, a bearer of value, is alienated in exchange for gold, which is the shape of the linen's value, then it is taken out of this shape and alienated again in exchange for another commodity, the bible, which is destined to enter the weaver's house as an object of utility' (Marx 1976, 199–200). In the first moment of this transaction, there is a 'leap taken by value from the body of the commodity into the body of the gold' (Marx 1976, 200). The completed transaction Marx abbreviates as C-M-C, or Commodity-Money-Commodity; but then he points out that where the material content of the movement is concerned, it could really be represented as C-C: 'the exchange of one commodity for another, the metabolic interaction of social labour, in whose result the process itself becomes extinguished' (Marx 1976, 200). By 'extinguished' Marx means that once purchased by the buyer, a commodity reverts back to its use-value (yet another transformation) through the action of being consumed, to satisfy the buyer's need. The exchange process is 'extinguished' as soon as the commodity disappears from the market and returns to the realm of needs satisfied by consumption. In this way, commodities appear and disappear from the market, as they shift from their use-value, to exchange-value, and back to use-value again when consumed by their buyers.

Marx is insistent about characterising each transformation in bodily terms, as though the grown-on and grown-in tools of primary metabolism are always still in play. If gold is a 'measure of value', for instance, it is because

> all commodities measured their values in it, and thus made it the imaginary opposite of their natural shape as objects of utility... [Gold] became real money because the commodities, through their complete alienation, suffered a divestiture or transformation of their real shapes as objects of utility, thus making it the real embodiment of their values. When they thus assume the shape of values, commodities strip off every trace of their natural and original use-value, and of the particular kind of useful labour to which they owe their creation, in order to pupate into the homogeneous social materialization of undifferentiated human labour. (Marx 1976, 204)

The human labour that has gone into the production of any product-turned-commodity is, through the process, 'undifferentiated' because 'in their money-form all commodities look alike. Hence money may be dirt, although dirt is not money' (Marx 1976, 204). The 'two golden coins in return for which our weaver has parted with his linen are the metamorphosed shape of a quarter of wheat', though the weaver has no way of knowing that the buyer of his linen had acquired his coins through the prior sale of his wheat. Money is thus 'the absolutely alienable commodity, because it is all other commodities divested of their shape' (Marx 1976, 205).

The way Marx emphasises this generalised alienation of money is in keeping with the bodily imagery throughout, or rather, is a tale of visceral bodies transforming into a substance dispossessed of carnal properties: 'Since every commodity disappears when it becomes money it is impossible to tell from the money itself how it got into the hands of its possessor, or what article has been changed into it. *Non olet*, from whatever source it may come' (Marx 1976, 205). A footnote explains the meaning of this classical allusion: 'It (money) has no smell', was apparently the reply given by Roman Emperor Vespasian to his son Titus, 'when the latter reproached him for obtaining money by taxing the public lavatories' (Marx 1976, 205, n.). Marx's laconic aside, *non olet*, enlarged upon in the translator's note, reminds us of the continuity between human metabolism and that of the social body, connected as they are where human excretion is permitted to enter the state-sanctioned public lavatory through the payment of a tax. Aside from illustrating how the odour of the body's most offensive product is eliminated through its transformation into 'money itself', this piquant aside, *non olet*, opens up an interesting take on the requirements of sovereign citizenship. I will return to the question of the public privy, but here I would just note that one's status as citizen would appear to rest on his very capacity to pay the tax necessary for the privilege of depositing his excrement in the state-prescribed receptacle, thus purchasing the safeguarding of his waste. In order to continue circulating as a politically recognised subject above ground, his shit must circulate as hygienically recognised waste in the underground.

Wheat becomes linen becomes bible becomes whisky in Marx's social metabolic system. But only because money, interposed between each commodity, 'breaks through all the individual and local limitations of the direct exchange of products, and develops the metabolic process of human labour' (Marx 1976, 207). And while commodities, once purchased, disappear from the market, to be consumed as use-value, money never vanishes: 'It always leaves behind a precipitate at a point in the arena of circulation vacated by the commodities... When one commodity replaces another, the money commodity always sticks to the hands of some third person. Circulation sweats money from every pore' (Marx 1976, 208). Commodities move in a circuit from their existence as use-value, to their exchange-value, metamorphosing into money, then back once more into a different commodity, disappearing again into the off-market space of consumption. Money, however, takes a path 'followed from the hands of one commodity-owner into those of another' in a 'circulation' or 'currency' (rather than a closed circuit) (Marx 1976, 210). It 'constantly removes commodities from the sphere of circulation, by constantly stepping in to their place in circulation, and in this way continually moving away from its own starting-point' (Marx 1976, 211). A precipitate that sticks to the hands, a bodily fluid sweated from pores, a constant usurper, stepping in to take over each commodity's place in circulation, money is always on the move, leaving unhygienic traces of itself on every point of human contact.

Inevitably, the question of speed arises in Marx's account of circuits enmeshed in circulation. Since the repeated money/commodity transformations follow in a 'temporal succession',

> It is segments of time therefore which form the measure of the duration of the process, in other words, the velocity of the circulation of money is measured by the number of times the same piece of money turns over within a given period. (Marx 1976, 215–16)

And thus we arrive at the peristaltic motility of social metabolism:

> The velocity of circulation of money is merely a reflection of the rapidity with which commodities change their forms, the continuous interlocking of the series of metamorphoses, the hurried nature of society's metabolic process, the quick disappearance of commodities from the sphere of circulation, and their equally quick replacement by fresh commodities. (Marx 1976, 217)

In this rapid velocity of circulation can be found the 'fluid unity' of the transformation of commodities from use-value to exchange-value and back again (Marx 1976, 217). But by the same token, 'when the circulation of money slows down, the two processes become separated, they assert their independence and mutual antagonism; stagnation occurs in the changes of form and hence in the metabolic process' (Marx 1976, 217). When 'hurried' velocity gives way to 'stagnation', when the 'perpetuum mobile of circulation' flags, it is a sign that the 'series of metamorphoses is interrupted' since 'sales are not supplemented by subsequent purchases', so that 'money is immobilized' (Marx 1976, 227). This occurs because, in some cases, there has developed 'the necessity and the passionate desire to hold fast to the product of the first metamorphosis', i.e. its 'gold chrysalis':

> Commodities are thus sold not in order to buy commodities, but in order to replace their commodity-form by their money-form. Instead of being merely a way of mediating the metabolic process [*Stoffwechsel*], this change of form becomes an end in itself... The money is petri-

fied into a hoard, and the seller of commodities becomes a hoarder of money. (Marx 1976, 228)

Metabolic motility, in other words, has slowed to a stop because what had served as the lubricating laxative of the system, money, is no longer allowed to function in its proper role. It is 'hoarded' with the result that peristaltic stasis, or a form of economic constipation, sets in. Marx differentiates between 'naïve forms of hoarding' (practised, for instance, by 'Asiatics, particularly the Indians' who have been known to 'bury their money' [Marx 1976, 228]) and hoarding in 'more developed commodity production', where, although sellers must also buy in order to keep money in circulation, there are those who find a way to sell more than they buy, so that 'hoards of gold and silver of the most various sizes are piled up at all the points of commercial intercourse' (Marx 1976, 229). Hoarding may also appear in its aesthetic form, where commodities made of gold and silver grow 'with the wealth of civil society' (Marx 1976, 231). And finally, there is the practical aspect of hoarding in an economy where 'metallic circulation prevails': since the 'quantity of money in circulation unceasingly ebbs and flows' and must be capable of 'expansion and contraction', hoarding creates reserves to 'serve as channels through which money may flow in and out of circulation, so that the circulation itself never overflows its banks' (Marx 1976, 231–2). The chapter ends with a footnote that makes explicit the catabolic function of money within social metabolism. Having just noted that failure to limit the 'hoards' in the strong-rooms of banks is an 'indication of stagnation in the circulation of commodities', Marx offers a quote from W. Petty's *Political Anatomy of Ireland*:

> 'Money is but the fat of the Body Politick, whereof too much doth as often hinder its agility, as too little makes it sick ... as fat lubricates the motion of the muscles, feeds in want of victuals, fills up the uneven cavities, and beautifies the body; so doth money in the state quicken its action, feeds from abroad in time of dearth at home; evens accounts ... and beautifies the whole; altho' more especially the particular persons that have it in plenty.' (quoted in Marx 1976, 244)

This extended image links us back up again with the ambiguity we encountered in the previous chapter about what constitutes waste where the metabolism of the human body is concerned. Is it what the body retains in the form of excess fat, a hindrance to bodily agility, an obstacle to desired motion? Or is it the undigested refuse excreted from the body, in need of a state-sanctioned receptacle? Or is it, as we shall see in the pages that follow, backed-up stool, hoarded for too long in the large intestine and thus a source of 'auto-intoxication'?

As we move from Marx's story of incessant transformations among nature, men and commodities to the prevailing medical and scientific accounts of metabolic health and functioning in the human body, we find a corporeal existence as much a target of 'mediation, regulation, and control' as Marx's metabolism between man and nature. And while surveillance of what we eat is surely a crucial aspect of the imperative to regulate our metabolism, I want to focus in the next chapter on the vicissitudes of what goes on at the 'output' end of the process. When we think of motility in the human body, we are evoking its peristaltic aspect in particular – not so much the autonomic metamorphoses at the molecular and chemical level but the movement through expanding and contracting visceral conveyances, a movement that is only partly autonomic. The rest of the time it is susceptible to our desires, our will, our affective states, our social relations – indeed, our implications, conscious and unconscious, in what Marx thought of as social metabolism. A look at the medical consensus of the early twentieth century suggests that it is not metabolism *tout court* that comes under our 'mediation, regulation, and control', but that aspect of it that involves peristaltic motion.

## Notes

1 Foster and Burkett's article on the organic/inorganic in Marx also kicks off an exchange with Ariel Salleh about whether the concept of nature as 'man's inorganic body' is to be dismissed as an instrumentalist or anthropocentric view. See Foster and Burkett (2000), Salleh (2001), and Foster and Burkett (2001).
2 The third activity in Arendt's tripartite model is 'Action'; it entails neither the 'matter' of labour, nor the 'things' of work, but goes on 'directly between men' and 'corresponds to the human condition of plurality, to the fact that men, not Man, live on the earth and inhabit the world'. While labour and work are somehow related to politics, the 'Action' necessitated by plurality is 'specifically the condition ... of all political life' (Arendt 1998, 7).

3 Landecker puts it like this: 'The particular outcome – for political theory in this instance – depended on the specificity of which "biological process within ourselves" provided the model, and in Marx's case it was the German tradition [Liebig, Moleschott] of total metabolism, which saw the body as a site of combustion and exchange, where what mattered was the generation of energy for labour power in the service of more life and more capital' (Landecker 2013, 223).
4 It is interesting that Hercules' solution to the cleaning of the Augean stables has more to do with his wits than his courage; by diverting the waters of a nearby river to flow through the stables, he devises a classic automated flush system, thus ensuring a permanent elimination of the abundant manure produced by the livestock.
5 Seyla Benhabib registers the tradition of feminist critique of Arendt when she points out that the emphasis in *The Human Condition* on the 'dignity of the political':

> may help explain the odd locutions in the first pages of the HC such as the 'shadowy interior of the household' and 'the light of the public sphere' (HC, 38); her unintelligible definition of society – *Gesellschaft* – 'as excluding the possibility of action' (HC, 40), which to our ears sound like an oxymoron! Are we faced here with a denigration of the private sphere, of the household and of woman's work? Many of us have interrogated these aspects of Arendt's work from a feminist perspective (Benhabib, 2020).

See also Bonnie Honig, ed. (1995).
6 Actually, it might be more precise to say that money is like shit – not in the sense that Freud means – but in the sense that what the body does not metabolise into nutrients is excreted, and (when not misdirected) returned to nature, recycled as nutrients to the soil and thus to food, which is then ingested again. The 'use-value' aspect of food is that which the body-as-buyer 'consumes'. But that nutritional value of food cannot travel by itself through the body – it must always be helped along by its fibrous or non-absorbable component – that aspect of it that has no 'use-value' in the sense of being extinguished by having been absorbed. If we were to conceptualise our bodies as like the marketplace, then they are both the locus where objects realise their use-value in consumption (as our bodies absorb them to renew their living labour capacities) and their exchange-value as non-consumable but always circulating commodity – that is, the commodity that represents all commodities: money-as-shit.

# 4

# The Second Brain

### The gut that thinks

I turn now to a neurological account of the human peristaltic system that dates back to about the same era when scientific managers applied time and motion studies to the labouring body, to increase efficiency and decrease waste in both industrial and domestic workplaces.[1] In this account, the peristaltic system is sometimes under the domain of the brain and central nervous system, but more often controlled by what has come to be termed 'the second brain', a division of the autonomic nervous system that completely escapes directives from the first brain, and yet which is responsive (and therefore susceptible) to the natural and cultural environment. In this account, our gut 'thinks by itself' insofar as it functions independently of our first brain; but at the same time, like the leg that marches, the arm that aims the rifle, the hand that practises perfect penmanship, it offers another target for the modern fashioning of what Foucault calls the 'docile body'. Mary Ann Doane has commented that modernity 'was characterized by the impulse to wear time, to append it to the body so that the watch became a kind of prosthetic device extending the capacity of the body to measure time' (Doane 2002, 4). I would argue, in fact, that the body itself became, and continues to function as, a kind of chronometer, its neurological capacities engaged for the purpose of gauging and modulating duration, thus making of itself a guarantor both of the regularity and the uni-directionality of time.

I will be considering two representative medical accounts of how digestion and excretion work, one by neurogastroenterologist Michael Gershon, whose 1998 book *The Second Brain* details the emergence of the enteric nervous system in early twentieth-century physiological science, the other by British medical practitioner Josiah Oldfield, whose 1943 article on constipation was typical of the discourse of regularity throughout the previous four decades. Read together, these texts offer a striking Darwinian account of the human body in an evolutionary context, and demonstrate that, while the neurological model of the 'second brain' was developed in the early twentieth century, when the discursive distinction between organic and psychological concepts of the 'nerve' had not yet solidified, it has since received renewed attention at the turn of the twenty-first century, allowing for a particularly labile approach both to the embodiedness of linguistic and cultural aspects of subjectivity and to the social aspects of embodiedness. As I will show, the modern concept of the 'nerve' and the persistent history of its ambiguity as at once a physiological, a psychological and a social phenomenon, especially with regard to its role in peristaltic processes, permits a promising approach to the question of the relationship between the subject and the social realm.

Gershon's model of the peristaltic system in some ways sidesteps the question of how metabolism *per se* functions, to focus more specifically on how non-assimilable substances travel from one end to the other of the body-as-tube. With him we ask, what is it that facilitates the motility of this channel, this 'grown-in tool' through which the world travels, and which functions as a thoroughfare through the human being – either as species being, or as alienated subject of capitalism?

Gershon's account begins with the conventional understanding that our bodies are, for the most part, structured hierarchically when it comes to nerves. We have a central nervous system, consisting of the brain and the spinal cord, and a peripheral nervous system, which takes orders from the central processing headquarters. In addition to this, the nerves which connect the brain and the spinal cord to the rest of the body, and which carry the commands sent out by the central controlling organs, may be classified under two broad categories: the skeletal motor system and the autonomic nervous system.[2] Generally (though there are exceptions to this rule), the skeletal nerves require our conscious attention to carry messages to our muscles (to set the table and salt our potatoes, for instance), while the autonomic nervous system is involuntary, carrying orders from our brain that escape our conscious attention, but which are essential to internal bodily functions. The autonomic nervous system can be further classed into two major subdivisions, depending on which aspects of the body are being serviced: the sympathetic division, which pertains to responses involving the entire body, such as heartbeat and blood pressure, and the parasympathetic division, which is restricted to single organs like the bladder or the pupils (Gershon 1998, 14).

Gershon does not depart from this conventional model of the human nervous system until he arrives at the scientific insight that provides the title for his book. Turning to a 1921 text titled *The Autonomic Nervous System*, he notes that most physicians (in the 1990s) seem unaware that its author, J.N. Langley, divided the autonomic system into not two (sympathetic and parasympathetic) but three categories. Western medicine seemed to have forgotten or ignored Langley's discovery of this third division of nerves since the publication of his book, at least until Gershon drew renewed attention to it in the late twentieth century. This emerging, disappearing and resurfacing division of nerves is of paramount importance for anyone interested in the vagaries of peristalsis, because its duties are entirely limited to the operation of the intestines, and for this reason, Langley dubbed it the 'enteric nervous system'.

What distinguishes the enteric nervous system from the other two divisions of the autonomic system is that it doesn't seem to be connected to the central nervous system at all. Whereas the sympathetic and parasympathetic nerves receive and act upon messages from the first brain, the enteric nervous system can make decisions all on its own, without taking orders from a higher authority. Indeed, Gershon describes the autonomy of the enteric nervous system in terms of contrasting systems of governmentality in the body. The central nervous system 'clearly outranks the peripheral nervous system', and thus gives the orders.

> Commands flow *from* the brain and spinal cord via the nerves of the peripheral nervous system *to* muscles and glands (the effectors of the body)... The brain is at the top, the effectors and sensory receptors are at the bottom. (Gershon 1998, 16–17, emphasis in original)

But in a section headed 'Rebellion in the Bowel: The Brain Below', Gershon announces an insurrection against this otherwise hierarchical arrangement. Since the enteric system can 'process data its sensory receptors pick up all by themselves, and . . . can act on the basis of those data to activate a set of effectors that it alone controls', it may be considered a kind of

> rebel, the only element of the peripheral nervous system that can elect *not* to do the bidding of the brain or spinal cord... The enteric nervous system is thus an independent site of neural integration and processing. This is what makes it the second brain. (Gershon 1998, 17, emphasis in original)

Unlike all the other organs in the body, whose reflex actions cease when their connections to the central nervous system are severed, the peristaltic reflex of the gut can function as though it has a brain of its own.

Moreover, it almost seems as though the enteric brain is 'second' only in the sense that its discovery followed that of the 'first' brain; in the final analysis, both brains are essential to the functioning not only of the body, but of culture in a larger sense. 'The enteric nervous system may never compose syllogisms, write poetry, or engage in Socratic dialogue,' Gershon comments, 'but it is a brain nevertheless' (Gershon 1998, 17). Another way to put this, perhaps, is to say that it is not the brain, but rather the mind, that engages in linguistic and cognitive activities, but that we risk losing the cerebral organ if our enteric brain functions badly. And yet, it is precisely on the slippage between 'mind' and 'brain' that Gershon relies to maintain the striking effect of his argument. While we think with our first brain, there is some more 'thinking' going on in our gut, a thinking of which we have not been aware. For Gershon, this unconscious thinking lies beyond the purview of the psychoanalyst, but is newly accessible to the biologist, armed with the 'chemical language' with which nerves 'talk' to each other (Gershon 1998, 25). Thus, to understand the enteric brain, one must understand the functioning of serotonin and its receptors since, as Gershon's research has proven, serotonin is one of the primary substances in this chemical language.

For Gershon, the use of terms like brain, language, talking, etc. is metaphorical, serving only to illustrate processes that are purely biological. He does not mean to imply that the gut can actually participate in a symbolic system of communication or thinking, in the way that the mind (as opposed to the brain) can. Indeed, his argument becomes most polemical when it counters the (then) widespread accepted wisdom among doctors and laity alike that so many enteric dysfunctions are 'psychological' in origin. The discovery of a virus as the cause of many ulcers, for instance, has revolutionised the cure for these ulcers, shifting attention from ineffective psychotherapeutic treatment of stress to pharmaceutical remedies that eliminate the ulcer's organic pathogen. But, as I will be suggesting, retaining a more material conception of there being a 'second brain' in the gut offers possibilities for understanding ways in which the gut communicates with the world, ways in which it is 'social' after all.[3]

Where peristalsis is concerned, what precisely are our two brains doing? To answer this question, we must understand how Gershon, and his predecessor Oldfield, conceptualise the body, first, as it morphologically inhabits space, and second, as it gauges time via the regulation of movement through space. First, the morphology.

It is self-evident to say that the most obvious boundary between self and world is the continuous, protective organ that surrounds our interior and keeps us intact: our skin. Gershon, however, disrupts this model of the body as a self-evidently enclosed object in space with a more complex image, elaborated through the aid of T.S. Eliot's poetic trope:

> We are indeed hollow men and ... women. The space enclosed within the wall of the bowel, its lumen, is part of the outside world. The open tube that begins at the mouth ends at the anus. Paradoxical as it may seem, the gut is a tunnel that permits the exterior to run right through us. Whatever is in the lumen of the gut is thus actually outside of our bodies, no matter how counterintuitive that seems. (Gershon 1998, 84)

Gershon's model of the body as a hollow tube through which the world passes is not a new one; any medical practitioner who focused on alimentary systems in the twentieth century would have proceeded on the assumption of such a model, among them Josiah Oldfield, whose article on constipation offers an exemplary version of this trope.

In one of several contributions to a special issue of the *Medical Press and Circular* devoted to 'Constipation: the Universal Malady' (1943), Oldfield applied himself quite methodically to the problem of how to remove obstacles to elimination in the human body. But to understand how constipation arose as a threat to the health and wellbeing of the human subject, he offered an elaborate account of the slow transformation, over evolutionary time, of an amorphous organism to that which, like Gershon's, was most notably characterised by its tube-like quality. We began as 'amoebas', whose 'selection of substances from the environment', 'absorption of them' and 'rejection of the remainder as being unwanted or unusable' was haphazard and indiscriminate (Oldfield 1943, 381). The world simply moved into and out of us with no particular directionality. But 'in common with those processes of evolution by which living organisms have become more complex, and their separate portions more specialised', we began to develop into beings that consisted of 'a tube running the length of the body. The food is introduced at one end. Selection, transformation and absorption of suitable elements from the mass takes place as the food passes long the tube, and then from the other end are cast out the waste, the unsuitable and the deleterious elements' (Oldfield 1943, 382). Now the world began to run through us with a particular directionality, entering at one end of the tube and exiting at the other. Moreover, to ensure that this movement occurred 'in rhythmic and uninterrupted flow', an 'elaborate system of nerves and muscles have been provided along the whole of this tube' (Oldfield 1943, 382).

Here we have the evolutionary story of man's 'grown-in tools', consisting most importantly of a tube, through which substances pass, and around which a network of mechanisms accretes, designed for the purpose of keeping the substances flowing through the tube. Oldfield pictured us as sites for 'processing' a world that was propelled through us as it in turn made us and sustained us. Moreover, to aid in illustrating peristaltic action, Oldfield borrowed the image of the 'ordinary garden worm' to give an inside-out demonstration of how we, as tubes, kept the world proceeding through us. Just as the worm moved through the earth thanks to the aid of a 'set of ripples running down the length of his body and pushing against the ground as they ripple' so, too, 'the ripples along the inner muscular coating of the intestines continue for awhile and then stop – and the intestinal contents stop. Each time the ripple runs along it carries the contents a little way forward' (Oldfield 1943, 382).

Having described the body as it inhabited and processed 'space', Oldfield then introduced the element of time, or rather, the means by which the concept of 'duration' became broken down into component parts, as the organism became more sophisticated. In our bodies as earthworm-like-tubes, the 'ripple does not go right down to the end, otherwise the human being would be constantly oozing out faeces' (Oldfield 1943, 382). The oozing, however, was prevented by the mechanism of a 'lock gate near the end, called the sigmoid flexure', resulting in a 'gradual heaping up of an increasing mass'. The contents of the body-tube waited in abeyance until a 'push button set of nerves' was triggered, forcing 'the whole collected mass clean out of the tube, and behold what is called "a motion" has been accomplished' (Oldfield 1943, 382).

That we were not 'constantly oozing out faeces' was apparently what set us apart from the lower species, according to this account of the human body. If in the 'lower rungs' of life, expulsion was almost continuous, in the higher creatures on the evolutionary ladder, more room was afforded for storage, allowing for emptying at less frequent intervals (Oldfield 1943, 382). Unlike caterpillars, mice, and cattle, all of which are characterised by constant defecation, humans made an important discovery that enabled them to introduce the concept of periodic accumulation into the flow that was animal life.

> When man discovered the value of time, and the manifold varieties of interests that it unfolded to him, he ... concentrated his feeding times into two or three hours or less, in the twenty-four. This freed his propulsory processes from continuous action and therefore eating, propulsion of foods along his alimentary canal, transformation, absorption, and expulsion, became alternated with long periods in which mental activities replaced the previous continual devotion to ... bodily nutrition. (Oldfield 1943, 382)

By this logic, an adult, according to Oldfield, had the impulse to eat only at intervals, and 'by the over-riding action of mentality upon the nervous system a regular sequence habit can be developed so as to ensure a complete freedom from an impulse urge, excepting at times that can be arranged for ahead – such, for example, as after breakfast or before going to bed!' (Oldfield 1943, 382). The exclamation point, rare in Oldfield's text, seemed to emphasise that we had arrived at nothing less than the juncture of the invention of history, born at the moment pauses were introduced into the natural flow of substances through the peristaltic tube that defined the organism as a body. Time now could be measured by the amount of substance that was stored up in the end of the peristaltic tube, kept in reserve for an evacuation that would happen only periodically, instead of continuously. Now time was characterised by periodicity, flows interrupted by stoppages, rather than an indistinguishable stream that allowed for no consciousness of one moment as opposed to another. As soon as this happened, a future could be imagined, and something planned for; the human subject now became capable of imposing will on the passage of time itself, by means of a holding in reservation, then a releasing, at a prescribed time. An 'impulse urge' might now be escaped insofar as it could be 'arranged for ahead' – making it no longer, after all, an impulse, since it could be counted among the known events that would occur according to the day's schedule ('after breakfast or before going to bed').

Laura Salisbury has called this notion of the human subject's evolutionally developed ability to impose will on the passage of time a 'sublimation theory', or 'the regulation of the body's appetite and inevitable consequences of ingestion that liberates time for thinking, for work, for culture' (Salisbury 2011, 68–9). In an article on Samuel Beckett's relation to his analyst, Wilfred Bion, Salisbury writes that for Bion,

> thinking ... not only makes tolerable the distension and dilation of time, it actually produces a sense of time, of experience that can be retained, by holding up the evacuation of the ... untransformed external world sufficiently for something to be taken into the self. Just as food can be metabolised and absorbed into the very matter of the body if it is allowed to linger in the lumen of the gut long enough to be digested, thinking produces a container for time, an archive for the experience of the world, within which the self might be nourished by its 'objects' rather than assaulted or contaminated by them. (Salisbury 2011, 68)

If Arendt's introspection 'has found within man – *not in his mind but in his bodily processes* – enough outside matter to connect him again with the outer world', it would seem that the turn-of-the-century theory of the enteric system is the corollary to this; metabolic peristalsis has evolved to make both bodily and mental archiving possible, for the simultaneous processing and thinking of the world (Arendt 1998, 312).

But what if the world is detained for too long in the lumen of the intestine? The real problem Oldfield had set out to address was not the 'constant oozing' that might be imagined if the peristaltic system worked without interruption, but rather the apparently widespread malady of constipation, when the contents of the bowel remained in their archive, and failed to make their way out the other end. While Oldfield mentioned, in passing, 'nervous irregularity in controlling muscular action' as a possible cause of intestinal stasis, the main culprit was our susceptibility to 'fashion, habit, and novel ideas' about what constituted good nutrition (Oldfield 1943, 383). We failed to consume the proper food in order to ensure that the contents of our bowels were of adequate 'quality' and 'mass'. Spicy foods, for instance, were 'irritants to the delicate nerve filaments along the colon, and thus injure their sensitiveness, so that in time they become inactive'; moreover, foods with too little 'mass' made for watery or meagre contents, giving the contracting and expanding intestinal walls nothing to grab onto, and thus 'the contents of the intestine provide no fulcrum for an onward push by the muscles. The contractile ring action in the intestine may, therefore, as easily push fluid content backward as forward' (Oldfield 1943, 383–4).

Oldfield's analysis touched on one of the key ways in which (as Marx put it) humans must mediate, regulate and control their metabolism with nature. It was up to us to provide the necessary fulcrum by making sure that we selected just exactly the correct part of the world to ingest, and thus to direct on its way through ourselves. Otherwise, the movement of the world through us might either reverse its direction, or come to a stop. This would happen if our intestinal contents were either too soft or too hard; in both cases, peristaltic motion would fail, and nothing would appear at the other end of the tube. Meaning, perhaps, that we would stop as well. The reversible worm image functioned doubly. To be sure, it gave us our model for understanding internal peristaltic action in the human body. But because of its reversibility, its susceptibility to being imagined inside out as well as backwards and forwards, it also carried with it the image of our own bodies as they moved through the peristaltic systems of our world of 'fashion, habit, and novel ideas'.

Even when diet is ideal, neither Oldfield nor Gershon seem prepared or willing to address the vexing question of what happens when the 'push button mechanism' that releases the contents of the bowel fails to function. What exactly is meant, for instance, by Oldfield's obscure passing reference to 'nervous irregularity in controlling muscular action'? What set of nerves is meant here? Who would be exerting the control? To approach this question, I return to Gershon's account of the division of nerves involved at each stage of the peristaltic journey, from mouth to anus. The reader is positioned as the traveller in this section, and invited to imagine herself journeying through a long passageway, coming, as she presses onward, now under the jurisdiction of a central sovereign authority (first brain), now under the control of local authorities (second brain), depending on which division of the nervous system is in play at a given point in time and space.

'In every body,' Gershon begins, 'the brain is king. Its writ is law. At the top of the bowel, the rule of the king is acknowledged, but as one descends deeper and deeper into the depths of the gut, the rule of the king weakens. A new order emerges: that of the second brain' (Gershon 1998, 113). From mouth to stomach, the sympathetic and parasympathetic systems are involved, taking their orders from the brain. But,

> to descend below the *pyloric sphincter* (the exit of the stomach) ... is to move almost beyond the reach of the king. This is the turf of the enteric nervous system where the brain can exert only quantitative effects and not make the basic decisions of what to do and when. It is an autonomous region that cares little for the brain and is happy to do without it altogether. (Gershon 1998, 113, emphasis in original)

It is as though one vanishes from all conscious and unconscious cognizance of the (first) brain while in the depths of the intestines; this is a curious territory, not 'in' the body proper, of course, because still separated from it by the walls of the intestine. This is a place where the world passes through us, and becomes in some sense 'unknown' to our central nervous system, while at the same time being under the control of our 'second brain', a brain which is inside us, transforming the world moving through us while we are unawares. It is also the very terrain of what Inglis calls our 'faecal habitus', where what seems to be our natural instinct to excrete has in fact been transformed through social metabolism into conventions of regularity at an unconscious level.

But where the world returns to 'itself', as it were, emerging from the end of the tube that is our body (or where, in Marx's terms, 'inorganic nature', having been worked on by the grown-in tools of 'organic nature', reaches the realm of the inorganic once more), the first brain takes over again, almost with a vengeance. As one passes from the colon to the rectum and the anus, the ambiguity about who or what is in control becomes particularly pronounced. For here, a quite complex set of conditions must come about before a 'motion' is accomplished. It is not as simple as Oldfield's 'push button mechanism' makes it sound, and even Gershon, whose real passion is the second, not the first brain, can give only a cursory account of the vicissitudes of the defecatory impulse.

So, what happens when the contents of the colon reach their endpoint, and the question of how they are to be expelled arises? For anyone who has noticed that only certain social, habitual, environmental or emotional conditions must be present before they can properly experience the urge to eliminate (and act upon the urge), this may be the most crucial part of the peristaltic system. 'As the rectum fills,' Gershon tells us, 'it delivers a "call to stool". This sensation is usually not painful, although it may become so as it rises to a crescendo; nevertheless, the "call to stool" is not a sensation that is easy to ignore' (Gershon 1998, 171). If the reader experiences some anxiety that we might spew the noxious contents of our intestines into the world, Gershon reassures us not to worry, that 'gravity is not a threat to our social well-being' since our rectum is 'well endowed anatomically to handle the heft and bulk of the stool it contains'. To maintain the 'veneer of civilization' the rectum is cunningly designed to store its contents for most socially necessary periods of time, and its exit is guarded not by one, but two tightly locked doors: the internal and external sphincters (Gershon 1998, 171).

Who is addressed, then, by the rectum's interpellation, its 'call to stool'? At first, it would seem to be these two sphincters that hold in the rectum's contents: they are summoned, and they open in response to this summoning. But no, Gershon says, 'these sphincters ... are not slaves that open as soon as the "call to stool" is issued. They can hold stool back and resist opening until the moment is right. In fact, a guiding principle upon which the smooth working of our society is based is that the anal sphincters of every individual who is not an infant will indeed hold stool back until the right moment' (Gershon 1998, 171). The 'smooth working' of society, it appears, depends on the temporary blockage of the 'smooth working' of peristalsis.

So now the question arises as to who or what determines when the 'right moment' is, thus permitting the sphincters, which have been putting up an oppositional resistance to the second brain's propulsive mechanisms, to open and allow expulsion of the rectum's contents. By the time we reach this last stage in the peristaltic process, the second brain has ceded most, though not all, responsibility once more to the first brain which, depending on information gathered as to the state of the social environment external to the body, authorises the sphincters to block or not to block. The perceptual and cognitive systems, passing information to the central nervous system, inform it that the 'right moment' has come, and the central nervous system in turn permits the sphincters to open, allowing for the final stage of peristalsis to be completed.

But, as might be suspected, it is not as simple as that. Consider, after all, that there is a question not of one, but two sphincters. Most of us are aware, of course, of the external anal sphincter, which is made up of skeletal muscle and is under our volitional control. We can decide whether to relax it or not. The internal sphincter is regulated, however, 'only by the enteric and autonomic nervous systems', and is thus 'on autopilot and out of our volitional control' (Gershon 1998, 171). Before the external sphincter even gets the chance to retain or release the contents of the bowel, based on the conscious signals we send it from the first brain, this internal sphincter has to have *already opened*, has to have already made a decision to respond to the 'call to stool' sent out by the full rectum. If this inner sphincter does not open for some reason, the outer one may relax all it wants, but nothing will pass through.

And here is where the question of constipation, or the inability to pass stool, becomes most perplexing. For, on what basis does this *internal* sphincter decide that the 'right moment' has arrived to respond to the 'call to stool'? It falls under the jurisdiction partly of the enteric nervous system, which Gershon would have us believe is oblivious to what's going on in the social world in which the body must conduct itself, and partly of the autonomic nervous system which, though connected to the first brain, operates independently of our conscious deliberation. Here, presumably, is where the question of the 'right moment', indeed, the very question of temporality, is taken over by unconscious mechanisms; where the conscious mind, detecting the 'call to stool', positions the outer sphincter over a perfectly acceptable toilet, gives the order to let go and, in some cases, nothing happens. 'Regularity' is far from being an uncomplicated autonomic function; nor is it strictly, I am arguing, a matter of individual dietary control, contrary to what Oldfield, Gershon and medicine in general would suggest. Constipation is the main obsession in the biomedical account of peristaltic workings, since it has to do with the vagaries of a valve over which we apparently have little conscious control as individuals, and which is thus the target of much disciplinary training. It is perhaps the biological location in the human body most sensitive to the predominant faecal habitus at any given time or place. In the next section I survey Western techniques of peristaltic discipline, in the form of routinised toilet training that was assumed to play an intrinsic role in one's health, happiness and even moral character.

## Toilet training, or the disciplining of the large intestine

I turn now to consideration of at least one early twentieth-century intervention into the governance of the 'brain in the gut': the emphasis on toilet training and other technologies for the control of childhood habits of elimination.[4] Since both metabolic transformation and our mediation of it unfold over time, the temporality of modernity moves to the foreground in our study, permitting us to ask not just what the body produces, but how it experiences, and deploys, time and duration in the process of production. The model of metabolism helps us to see how we govern the movement of substances through our own bodies, even as we ourselves move through larger networks of natural forces, human interrelations, commodities, money, information, pleasures, legislation and affect. It allows us, too, to interrogate an aspect of what Foucault, in *Discipline and Punish*, calls the accumulation and capitalisation of time in the body that has not yet been adequately theorised: in other words, on the visceral training of the body as a 'processor' of both nature and the world, not only in terms of physiological digestion and our cognitive participation in symbolic exchange, but also in terms of our unconscious implication in disciplinary structures (Foucault 1977, 157).

In the 'Docile Bodies' section of *Discipline and Punish*, Foucault turns to the school, the barracks and the manufactory to note the emergence of

> an important phenomenon: the development, in the classical period, of a new technique for taking charge of time of individual existences;

for regulating the relations of time, bodies and forces; for assuring an accumulation of duration; and for turning to ever-increased profit or use the movement of passing time. (Foucault 1977, 157)

'How can one capitalize the time of individuals,' Foucault asks, 'accumulate it in each of them, in their bodies, in their forces or in their abilities, in a way that is susceptible of use and control?' The disciplines, he argues, accomplish the individualising of humans through the training of the body to become a 'machinery for adding up and capitalizing time' (Foucault 1977, 157). Turning a Foucauldian eye to the modern peristaltic body reminds us that even before we enter the school, the barracks or the factory, we undergo the incremental disciplinary techniques of the nursery, the kitchen and the bathroom – domestic spaces presided over almost always by women, performing the meta-industrial labour that ensures accumulation of capital. We are subjected, thus, to the meticulous training not only of the voluntary skeletal nervous system, but also of the autonomic enteric nervous system, as the local version of our faecal habitus is developed.

In the late nineteenth and early twentieth century, the young subject, as a consumer of nutrients and producer of waste, was expected practically from birth, through a series of graduated exercises, to discipline the peristaltic system of his or her body – or rather, to *be* disciplined via the training of the lower intestine, bowel and sphincter muscles. This Q and A passage in one early childhood training manual sums it up succinctly:

*How may a child be trained to be regular in its bowels?*

By endeavouring to have them move at exactly the same time every day.

*At what age may an infant be trained to use the chamber or chair for its movements?*

Easily by the third month if training is begun early. (Holt, 1894, 50)

Toilet training involved nothing less than the mastery of the bodily regulation of time: the division of duration into evenly spaced evacuations of the large intestine, the measuring of progress by rhythmic contractions of smooth muscle, the guarantee of a distinction between the 'natural time' of the indiscriminately excreting animal and the 'cultural time' of the systematically excreting human being. The properly trained peristaltic system also served to confirm the uni-directionality of time, as evidenced by the efficient transformation of food into fuel and waste, and the distance maintained between point of ingress (the mouth) and point of egress (the anus). Moreover, as Inglis has put it, 'toilet training, a re-enactment of the civilization process in miniature', was and still is largely delegated to the female head of household, whose job consists of maintaining 'temporal routines and procedures . . . which operate implicitly in the service of the reproduction of the domestic sphere as one element in the overall patriarchal order' (Inglis and Holmes, 237).

Two temporalities were involved in this process: the cyclical time of ingestion and expulsion, and the developmental time of the disciplining of the viscera. While the world was detained and released, detained and released, an accumulation of a different kind occurred – not only that of faeces in the large bowel, but of a habitude that was stored in the musculature, nerves and viscera of the organism: what was stored was the ability to store in the first place, a capacity to hold in reserve before expelling, a talent for discerning the prescribed place and time. If time was thus 'capitalised' in the body, it was through the agency not only of the first, but of the second brain and its dealings with the world. It was this corporeal habituation to a learned regularity that formed the basis for what Inglis calls our faecal habitus.

Moreover, these dealings were as much about affective states of being as about physiological processes. Brian Massumi, for instance, classes the enteric nervous system as the 'deepest' among three systems of perception through which we take in, and act upon, sensory data. There are the 'exteroceptive senses' (sight, hearing, tactility, for instance) that make direct contact with objects in the world; this is followed by proprioception, which 'translates the exertions and ease of the body's encounters with objects into a muscular memory of relationality [that constitutes the] cumulative memory of skill, habit, posture' (Massumi 2002, 59). Finally, there is the 'interoceptive sense', which also occurs at the 'dimension of the flesh', where it

> intervenes between the subject and the object. It, too, involves a cellular memory and has a mode of perception proper to it: *viscerality* (interoception). Visceral sensibility immediately registers excitations

gathered by the five 'exteroceptive' senses even before they are fully processed by the brain. (Massumi 2002, 60, emphasis in original)

Massumi acknowledges Gershon's rediscovery of the 'second brain' as the basis of his speculations about the enteric nervous system, which, as he puts it, 'provides one of the physiological bases for the autonomy of affect' that drives the overall argument of his book (Massumi 2002, 266 n. 13). He spins out a mundane example of how the interoceptive perceptual apparatus of the gut registers an event in the external world: a scenario in which you are imagined crossing a busy street, and your stomach 'turns somersaults' even before you hear the sound of screeching brakes careening towards you. 'The immediacy of visceral perception,' he writes, 'is so radical that it can be said without exaggeration to precede the exteroceptive sense perception. It anticipates the translation of the sight or sound or touch perception into something recognizable associated with the identifiable object' (Massumi 2002, 60–1). The enteric nervous system is thus the means by which our body 'thinks with pure feeling before it acts thinkingly' (Massumi 2002, 266 n. 13). And although his example has to do with the 'functioning of "viscerality" in relation to shock', he argues that stress, 'which might be thought of as slow-motion shock' is also processed by and through the enteric nervous system.[5]

But in fact, we needn't even posit the events registered, and 'thought', by the visceral perceptual apparatus in terms of their function as disruptive pathogens (shock, stress) to imagine this condition in which our 'body thinks with pure feeling before it acts thinkingly', especially if we keep in mind the routine ways that we target the interoceptive senses, from the first changing of the diapers, through the disciplinary techniques of toilet training, to the designation of certain architectural spaces and their furnishings as proper locales for the relaxation of inner and outer sphincter, to the segregation of these spaces depending on the genitalia (or, as of 2016, birth certificate) of the one who is to defecate (the men's room versus the ladies' room), and to the availability of these spaces depending on whether one's skin is perceived by the exteroceptive senses of one's fellows as white or not, as untouchable or not. While the variations change, the fact of visceral training, and its implications for how we 'think with pure feeling' is in effect at any historical place or time.

A brief foray into the vast literature on the 'habits' of infancy and childhood in the early twentieth century demonstrates how the interoceptive senses were not only targeted, but also correlated with other affective and cognitive functions of the body. In the US and Britain, almost every publication on childcare from this period (ranging from self-help books marketed to parents, to inexpensive government manuals, to articles in medical journals) focused specifically on the habits of eating, sleeping and elimination. The extent to which the training of the bowels was understood to enhance the child's integration within the larger social sphere, indeed, within the nation, is perhaps best exemplified in one of three books published as the result of a 'White House Conference' on 'Child Health and Protection' in 1930. John E. Anderson's *Happy Childhood* opened with a quotation from President Herbert Hoover, who announced that the conference had gathered together all the best representatives of science to explore and understand the 'safeguards and services to childhood which can be provided by the community, the State, or the Nation – all of which are beyond the reach of the individual parent', but who hastened to reassure us that 'every scientific fact ... every public safeguard ... every edifice for education or training or hospitalization or play' were 'but a tithe of the physical, moral, and spiritual gifts which motherhood gives and home confers' (Anderson 1933, vii). Where parenthood left off, the state intervened; by the same token, the state, with its science, could never provide what the presumably magical maternal instinct would accomplish. But, as the prescription for proper potty training unfolds in the texts of this period, we find that the well-intentioned instincts of 'motherhood' functioned more often than not as impediments to the proper visceral training of the infant and child – hence the necessity to call on parents as agents of the 'home' insofar as this home was conceived as the primary locus in which the citizen was fashioned. What unfolds in these habit-training manuals is the process by which unremunerated meta-industrial labour is split off from, even as it works in the interest of, the accumulation of capital. The 'physical, moral, and spiritual gift' of motherhood may be ideologically located within nature's metabolic cycle of renewal and health, but it must also remain accessible to the intervention of the state.

As with most of the literature published throughout the 1920s, the chapter on bowel training in *Happy Childhood* presumed a progression from an inchoate state of the body to one that had learned to measure and portion time appropriately. If newborns excrete and urinate at irregular periods, they must, in order to 'take a place in society', learn to control those processes, i.e. 'must learn to withstand pressure in the bladder and intestine when necessary' insofar as those organs are 'muscular structures under nervous control and are subject to training' (Anderson 1933, 59). The ultimate objective was to reduce the habit of elimination to 'the mechanical level'; indeed, the book was entitled *Happy Childhood* precisely because one's very sense of happiness was presumed to be directly premised on the regularisation of otherwise unruly processes:

> Happy is the child who masters these basic responses in his early years and moves on from the orderly healthful regime established by his parents to face with confidence the new situations presented by his ever-changing environment. Unhappy is that child who finds that the building of basic habits has been done in such a way that he must build up control anew in a period that should be free for an attack on habits appropriate to a higher level of development. (Anderson 1933, 68)

In another publication, Anderson offered much more specific advice about the best timetable for the training of the bowels, as well as detailed instructions for how and when the infant's body should be positioned in relation to certain facilitative objects in the world, and the best way for parents to suppress or mitigate the transmission of their affect during the course of the training process. Training, he wrote, could begin as early as six weeks old, the mother being directed to hold the infant over a warmed receptacle on her lap, with a little hot water in it to induce a movement more quickly (Anderson and Faegre 1929, 136). He prescribed a clock-like regularity, advising the mother to choose the same place, hour and condition every day, making sure to remove distractions and to arrange a reward for success (Anderson and Faegre 1929, 137).

When the pressure of a vessel against the child's buttocks was not enough to stimulate peristaltic movement at regular intervals on a daily basis, then it could be helpful 'to use a suppository of soap or glycerine to alter the movement to a suitable time of day' (Anderson and Faegre 1929, 138). Indeed, the recommendation of the soap stick as a stimulant to the sphincter reflex was ubiquitous throughout the literature of toilet training, and was most vividly described in the following passage from another government publication that advocated 'training the bowels' as early as the 'end of the first month':

> Hold the baby in your lap or lay him on a table with his head toward your left, in the position for changing his diaper. Lift the feet with the left hand and with the right insert a soap stick into the rectum to act as a suppository. Still holding the feet up, press a small chamber gently against the buttocks with the right hand and hold it there until the stool is passed. The first time the soap stick is used the stool will come in 5 or 10 minutes. Later this time will be shortened. (Children's Bureau 1935, 59)

However, even the most assiduous adherence to a regular schedule would fail to systematise the baby's bowels if the mother or nurse did not also learn to properly calibrate the emotional atmosphere that accompanied the training process. More particularly, a regimen of repression was to be established, first with regard to the mother's affective states, and then with regard to the child's. 'The parent's attitude should show that she expects success by the child,' wrote one author, 'but under all circumstances irritation, scolding or punishment should be rigorously suppressed by the parent to avoid associating in the mind of the child this unpleasant accompaniment with his attempt' (Blatz and Bott 1928, 134).

While the irregularity of the bowel movements in infancy were to be replaced by clock-like punctuality, the infantile pleasure experienced by the defecating body should be retained and protected from the pernicious influences of negative parental sentiments:

> A child's reactions to eliminative functions will be largely conditioned by the attitudes of the adults in charge. Eliminative processes, involving as they do relief from bodily tensions, are normally pleasant and are almost always so regarded by the child. Yet many adults have themselves been conditioned to feel shame and disgust in connection with such functions; they must therefore re-condition themselves or else they will convey their own unfortunate attitudes to their children. (Blatz and Bott 1928, 137–8)

Anderson also emphasised the adoption of a 'casual, matter-of-fact attitude' to facilitate the 'development of control' over what he termed 'a perfectly normal process, quite as natural as eating or sleeping' (Anderson 1933, 60). Indeed, it would seem that a balancing act of freedom and restraint was called for, though always bound to fail, where proper bowel health was concerned. While it was important to 'preserve the child's normal sense of satisfaction', one must also build up 'inhibitions in regard to place and time of elimination' as well as prevent 'unnecessary discussion in relation to the act' (Blatz and Bott 1928, 138). Moreover, advice abounded on how best to coordinate the disciplinary practices being acquired with the proper discourse – a discourse of strategic silences as well as carefully modulated utterances. Vigilance must be practised about the linguistic surround that accompanied potty training; even before the child 'begins to speak', we are told, the mother should 'select the terms she wishes to use and employ them whenever she places the child on the toilet' so that the child will learn 'through conditioning' to 'employ them in anticipation of his needs' (Anderson 1933, 60).

Later, as the child became more deeply embedded in this discursive system, language was to be deployed even more insistently to make him aware of the inner processes of his own body:

> The young child should be given some elementary explanation of the relation between intake of food and the elimination of waste, of the part played by food in the building up of the body, of the variety of ways in which waste products are eliminated, and of the importance for health of the unimpeded exercise of these functions. He will then understand urination and defecation as necessary parts of the bodily economy and therefore free from any suggestion of uncleanness or shame. Undoubtedly chronic constipation in adults may have certain psychological aspects. By training the child not only in right habits but in right *attitudes* we may help to avoid such later difficulties. (Blatz, and Bott 1928, 138, emphasis in original).

As this passage shows, it was the role of the parent to facilitate the child's awareness not only of his own interiority, but especially of its economic nature, and of its place in the larger economy of production and consumption, or of what Marx would call social metabolism.

The establishment of 'habit clinics' in the late 1910s and early 1920s coincided with this proliferation of child-care literature. These clinics were perceived as institutional instances of, and safety nets for, the normal process of inculcating habit in the child (See Blatz and Bott 1928, 132). The home, as regarded from the point of view of the habit clinician, was 'considered the workshop in which the personality of the child is being developed' (Thom 1974, 28). But when parents failed to control their negative affect, if they failed to maintain the proper discursive balance between restraint and satisfaction, then the household ceased to be a productive facility for the fabrication of the future citizen/worker and resembled something more like a polluting miasma: 'too frequently the home becomes the reservoir into which are poured all the resentment, disappointment, grief, and frustration associated with the unhappy experiences of the day'. The children began to regard it as 'the dumping ground of all unhappy and unhealthy adult emotions – a place used by all its inmates in their efforts to air the grievances against a world that has cheated them of something vital to their well-being' (Thom 1974, 28–9). It resembled, in other words, an emotional cesspool rather than a 'workshop' where the child might develop the toilet habits that would ensure his or her own positive emotional and indeed moral development. That one's faecal habitus was a matter not of cleanliness but of a carefully calibrated regularity is made explicit by the meticulous detail with which every aspect of peristaltic training was mediated by the discourse of childcare manuals and habit clinics.

Just one paragraph from an article that outlined the history and role of the habit clinic in the United States demonstrates with a startling clarity how crucial regularity in early habit formation was considered to be:

> We begin to acquire habits at birth and continue to acquire them to a greater or less degree, depending upon our plasticity, until the end of life. The functions of eating, sleeping, and elimination become habitual. We develop habits of conduct toward those in authority. In some situations we acquiesce; in others we rebel. We have habits of conduct which include morals and manners. Our mental attitudes toward life are but habits of thought, and such traits as selfishness, shyness, cruelty, and fearfulness are merely emotional responses that have become habitual through repetition. Lying, stealing, and a disregard for the rights of others are likewise responses to certain situations, which through repetition become a part of the life pattern; in other words, they are habits. (Thom 1974, 26)

Every aspect of human experience, in other words, from mundane bodily functions to intellectual, emotional, and moral activity, to traits that make up a personality were considered matters of 'habit'; moreover, it is clear from the literature on the training of habits in very young life that the regulation of the bodily functions, right down to the alimentary tract, was deemed crucial to the regulation of the individual as a social actor in the world. Intense emphasis was placed on establishing good physiological habits, including those of elimination; to go astray in peristaltic regularity and efficiency was to risk delinquency of a more serious nature later on. 'Bad habits such as enuresis and temper tantrums may offer great difficulties when it comes to treatment,' one author wrote. But

> recent scientific researches in many fields have shown methods which are proving effective in solving these problems. These methods are being used by the Child Guidance Clinic to aid the child. They are especially effective with the normal child, helping him to develop free and unhampered by handicapping conflicts; to function at full efficiency in order that his debt to society may be adequately met by attainment of his maximum productivity. (Emery 1925, 663)

If he had trouble attaining an awareness of his own 'bodily economy', and thus modulating the flow and ebb of that economy, the child could be brought by the responsible parent to the habit clinic, where he would receive the physiological (indeed, neurological) training that would help him to coordinate his own bodily economy with that of the state. Only thus could he pay his 'debt to society', in regularly issued instalments, as it were. Reaching his 'maximum productivity', he could take his proper place in the social metabolism of the exchange and consumption of commodities.

If the enteric system is a 'second brain', this brain acquires if not exactly a language of its own, then an intelligible, rationalised functionality in relation to the world outside it, and the world it is called on to process. The stimuli it takes in, assesses, and then acts upon are not incoherent, meaningless sights, sounds, smells, sensations; rather, as is evident in even this short summary of toilet-training practices, the world with which the second brain comes into contact is itself regulated, deliberately structured to elicit correspondingly patterned responses, responses which are routed partly through the cognitive functions of the first brain, but largely also through the 'unconscious' (or rather, viscerally conscious) functions of the second brain.

Thinking back to Marx on metabolism, we begin to see how the regulatory discourse and routinised training of bowel habits are central to the 'mediation, regulation, and control' of man's relation to the metabolism of nature. In a direct and material sense, this mediation takes place as the manipulation of the human's internal organs – is, in fact, the 'organ-isation' of the human body, the honing of its visceral 'tools', as counterpart to nature's 'inorganic body'. These organs as 'grown-in-tools' are presumed to be essential to the coordination of bodily economy with the economy of the state, and to the fashioning of the citizen as a body capable of processing the world in a productive manner. Moreover, as must be evident by now, it is women in their role as mothers and childcare providers who are most intimately implicated in the mediation of the human peristaltic system, from birth through childhood.

This mediation, however, as evidenced by the persistent attempts of the state to administer it, is never complete, never comprehensive. The gut, amorphous and tractable though it may seem to be, has a 'mind' of its own. Hannah Arendt registers this ambiguous threat of metabolic agency in comments she made when discussing the introspective writing of Nathalie Sarraute. As Adam Kirsch put it, her 'love of the public and the political, and her fear of the private and the psychological, becomes almost neurotically intense' (Kirsch 2009, np). He quotes her as having written that our inner turmoil and *shapelessness* must be 'kept under strict quarantine [since] "It is no less indecent, unfit to appear, than our digestive apparatus, or else our inner organs, which also are hidden from visibility by the skin"' (quoted in Kirsch 2009, np). 'Quarantine' is Kirsch's term, not Arendt's, but it is apt, indicating as it does her desire to protect our public acting selves from catching the virus of shapelessness that characterises our inner organs and psyche alike. 'Our emotions are all the same,' she ventures, 'the difference is in what and how we make them appear' (Arendt 1995, 241). Or, to put it differently, she says, 'nature has hidden all that is merely functional and has left it shapeless . . . the inner organs of all living things are nothing to look at, as though they were haphazardly thrown together' (Arendt 1995, 241–2). If elsewhere she imagines Bergsonian introspection as discovering in one's 'bodily processes – enough outside matter to connect him again with the outer world', here she finds that the Cartesian '*cogito me cogitare, cogito me cogitare cogitare* [I think myself thinking, I think myself thinking the thinking]' has the effect that 'now the world is subject to the same endless kaleidoscopic change, infected as it were by the inner turmoil of the self, its *shapelessness*. In this inner turmoil, all identities dissolve, nothing any more to hold on to' (Arendt 1995, 242, Arendt's italics). As if to prevent our carefully crafted, fabricated 'world', that product of all our (masculine) 'work', from succumbing to the (feminine) shapeless obscenity of our inner organs and psyches, Arendt asserts the power of our purposive capacity for conscious communication: 'Speech, gestures, expressions of face – they all make manifest something hidden, and it is this manifestation that *changes* the shapeless, chaotic inside in such a way that it becomes fit for appearance, for being seen or heard' (Arendt 1995, 242). What is important for Arendt is that although every living organism 'seems to have an "urge" to appear', humans (unlike animals) make a 'deliberate choice' about that appearance. Our words, she says, 'survive and transcend the life-conditioned purposes' of the kind of functional communication of the 'language of bees or the sounds of birds', and in this way, our words 'become part of the world' (Arendt 1995, 243).

But as I am arguing, it is not only through the language of the first brain, our 'speech, gestures, expressions of face', that we 'make manifest' what is hidden. The gut would seem to exert its own communicative agency, and does it, in fact, in ways that 'transcend the life-conditioned purposes' of bees and birds (although we might put it differently now, as we come to acknowledge the cognitive competency or even superiority of non-human species). Her conviction that the 'shapelessness' of the internal will cause 'all identities [to] dissolve, nothing any more to hold on to' evinces an anxiety about getting lost in amorphousness, losing grasp of what allows an integrity of the self. But as I show in the following case studies, the psycho-biological ruminations, peregrinations and articulations at the level of the enteric system not only contribute to 'who we are' in our relation to our metabolic interlocutors, but also play a role in our world-making capacities.

I have all along been suggesting that neither the inner organs nor psychic life are, in fact, shapeless, though they may be considered as unfit or immodest for public view. The visceral detail with which I have investigated metabolism, particularly in terms of its peristaltic twists and turns, its propulsive advances and eruptive retreats, its cessations and redoublings, is precisely the kind of delving into the 'inner turmoil of the self' to which Arendt seemed most inimical. And yet, her own immersion in the vagaries of metabolic labour, nature, work and worldliness, and her recognition that biologically based introspection finds itself connecting back up to the world (that very world that has, all along, been passing through us) seems to argue for an understanding of the way the inner organs of the body, of the mind, of the psyche, are seemingly 'shapeless', but also susceptible to the shaping forces of the world with which they communicate. Arendt's anxiety that the 'shapelessness' of our inner organs, of our psyche, indeed of labour as autonomic functionalism will inhibit meaningful political action could just as well be expressed as the opposite: an anxiety that our inner workings have been all too thoroughly shaped by the regulatory routines and regimes of biopolitics. Perhaps in her unexpected recognition that 'introspection' leads through our biological processes right back out into the world, Arendt tacitly acknowledges that, however regulated these processes are, they are nevertheless capable of extending an enteric form of thought and deliberation into meaningful world-making.

Arendt's immersion in the metabolics of Marxian economic and political theory is in itself a kind of acknowledgement, however ambivalent, however blind to gender, of the potential for a 'subjective' dimension of action. This is especially true of her characterisation of interiority as 'shapeless', opening up, as it does, the simultaneous possibilities that what goes through us peristaltically is, after all, shaped by us, or that introspection benefits from going through the shapelessness of the internal before it finds the world once again, or that what labour and work share, at bottom, is the shape they exert onto otherwise formless material, or that (as I've already suggested) if our life processes are shapeless, this makes them all the more susceptible to being (externally) shaped.

As I shift from macro to micro peristaltic analysis, I move away from the discourse of Marxist economics, environment and sociological theory, to the discourse of the individual psyche. I will be drawing from and examining that other science of introspection, psychoanalysis, particularly as it emerged from and continues to intersect with biology and the physiology of the gendered body. This means that, to the sociological category of the conditioned bodily habitus we will add the concept of an unconscious, that is, of a motivating impulse that is not reducible to mere 'conditioning', even as it asserts itself within a context of the rituals and repetitions of social regulation. If there is an ideational unconscious in psychoanalytic parlance, we find also a kind of biological unconscious, a viscera whose communications are intermittent, variably accessible, socially consequential. And because psychoanalysis emerged at the turn of the century from the investigation of the narratives generated by a very particular sector of European society, I will shift my focus from the aggregated displaced farmers, factory workers, merchants, capitalists, bourgeois and proletarian excretors, as well as faecal recycling engineers that make up the theoretical terrain I've been surveying to the worlding activities of medical professionals and their 'hysterical' patients. The fact that psychoanalytic and physiological medicine unfolded in large part by way of case studies means I will be able to turn to the specificity of how faecal habitus, meta-industrial labour and gender play out on a minutely detailed scale, in the context of the European and English metropole in the early twentieth century.

## Notes

1 Michael Gershon dates the birth of 'neurogastroenterology', a subfield premised around the discovery that the 'gut contains nerve cells that can . . . operate the organ without instructions from the brain or spinal cord' to research conducted by Bayliss and Starling in the late 1890s, by Trendelenburg during the Great War, and by J.N. Langley, who published *The Autonomic Nervous System* in 1921 (Gershon 1998, 2–8).
2 For an account of the emergence throughout the eighteenth and nineteenth century of the concept of the vegetative nervous system, and Langley's renaming of it as the autonomic nervous system in the early twentieth century, see Ackerknecht 1974.
3 In his book, Gershon places emphasis on the gut's chemical processes rather than its potential for thinking and even learning; elsewhere, however, he seems to admit to the more speculative implications of a 'second brain'. Consider the anecdote he tells in a *New York Times* interview for instance:

> A big question remains. Can the gut's brain learn? Does it 'think' for itself ? Dr. Gershon tells a story about an old Army sergeant, a male nurse in charge of a group of paraplegics. With their lower spinal cords destroyed, the patients would get impacted. 'The sergeant was anal compulsive', Dr. Gershon said. 'At 10 A.M. everyday, the patients got enemas. Then the sergeant was rotated

off the ward. His replacement decided to give enemas only after compactions occurred. But at 10 the next morning, everyone on the ward had a bowel movement at the same time, without enemas', Dr. Gershon said. Had the sergeant trained those colons? (Blakeslee 1996)

For accounts of the 'brain in the gut' in a more popular vein, see Enders, 2015 and Roach, 2014.

4 For a recent overview of childcare advice manuals from the early twentieth century, with sections on toilet training, see V. Sue Atkinson (2017).
5 See also Elizabeth Wilson, who argues 'maybe ingestion and digestion aren't just metaphors for internalization; perhaps they are "actual" mechanisms for relating to others. That is, perhaps gut pathology doesn't stand in for ideational disruption, but is another form of perturbed relations to others – a form that is enacted enterologically' (Wilson 2004, 45).

# Part II: Micro-Peristalsis

5

# Unkinking, Streamlining and the Household Engineer

Feminists have written extensively about women's eating practices as they pertain to capitalist consumption and compulsory femininity; analyses abound of the cultural implications of anorexia, bulimia, dieting, fasting, or in other words, of women as *consuming* bodies. But little attention has been given to female bodies as sites of expulsion, or to the pervasive incidence of constipation or irritable bowel syndrome in women (to mention only the pathologised aspects of bowel habits), or to the way bowel 'regularity' becomes one of the means by which women exercise 'control' in their daily lives.[1] In Part II: Micro-Peristalsis, I consider three case studies regarding how women manage and attach significance to their bowel habits, or, more generally, to the movement of substances through their bodies, even as their bodies are moved through, or positioned within, social, political, domestic, erotic and ideological systems. Each chapter includes a glimpse of the larger systems of movement within which a particular bio-medical case emerges – beginning in this chapter with the simultaneous cultural emphasis on medical treatments for constipation and streamlining industrial and domestic production in the early twentieth century. In each case, I examine how the woman in question is partnered with a representative of the medical establishment, and how knowledge is produced about her peristaltic system through a disciplinary unfolding of observation, interpretation, experimentation, subjection, resistance and the general 'perpetual spirals of power and pleasure' Foucault writes about as the 'devices of sexual saturation' that characterise biopolitics. A 'sexuality of doctor and patient' might be said to be operating in these case studies, but our emphasis will be placed rather on what we might call the 'regularity of doctor and patient' as the prime mover of the regularisation of the modern metabolic subject (Foucault, *History of Sexuality, Part 1*, 1990, 45–7).

While both men and women have been interpellated as 'peristaltic subjects', I argue that the female body as a site of faecal production and management deserves particular attention, both because of its unique positioning in the history of modern health practices and domestic architectural design and its role in relation to 'meta-industrial labour' as the catalyst of metabolic transformations. As this chapter demonstrates, psychoanalysis as a discipline may have evolved around the 'hysterical' sexual aberrations of women, but psychoanalysis as an archive reveals material pointing to another facet of modern female subjectivity: that of a dissident gut, operating in the manner of a Deleuzian desiring machine, and offering lines of flight, however fragile, from an otherwise scripted trajectory of the housewifely duties of managing one's own and others' faecal output in the domestic space of heteronormativity.

As we have seen, peristalsis is at once an organic, autonomic process of the body and a psycho-social phenomenon, subject to the vicissitudes of emotion, cognition and disciplinary training – everything that goes into the development of a class or a culture's faecal habitus. Evacuation cannot be willed, but neither is it as automatic as breathing, the heartbeat, the pumping of blood through the veins, the growth of hair and nails. Some people experience more than others the necessity to engage in certain rituals, activities, postures in order to trigger the inner sphincter and bring on a movement. Peristalsis thus marks the indistinction between the organic and the psychological, between fuel and waste in the body-machine, between natural and technological operations, between the compulsive and the compulsory.

As our attention to the discourse of toilet training attests, the early decades of the twentieth century saw an intensification of the monitoring, measuring and enhancing of substances as they pursued a peristaltic progression through systemic structures. In his study of the history of 'inner hygiene', James C. Whorton has charted a persistent medical and cultural preoccupation with 'intestinal stasis' in the US, Britain and Europe. A widespread obsession with bowel regularity spurred an ever-increasing marketing and consumption of pharmaceutical, behavioural, dietary, surgical and mechanical cures for the costive that reached a climax in the 1920s. During this same period, as cultural historians Ellen Lupton and J. Abbott Miller have argued, American and European modernist architectural design was propelled by not only an aesthetics, but an economics of 'waste', consistent with Marx's elaboration of a 'law of movement' informing capitalist production and consumption. Situating their study of domestic kitchen and bathroom design in the context of a capitalist consumer ethos and of the adoption of time and motion studies to engineer the most efficient domestic workspaces, they lay the groundwork for a more thoroughly elaborated account of how the human digestive tract is caught up in larger systemic flows.

In the pages that follow, I will survey some of the historical details and arguments made, on the one hand, by Whorton in his account of constipation remedies in the early twentieth century and, on the other, by Lupton and Miller in their linking of domestic design with consumer capitalism. These twinned studies of a cultural preoccupation with the regularisation of movement will help us to understand how women were specifically targeted by a peristaltic imperative of regularity. Lupton and Miller's work will lead us to Christine Frederick's enormously popular book *Household Engineering: Scientific Management in the Home* (1915), in which the peristaltic health of the household is directly integrated with that of the female 'engineer' who maintains it.

### Inner hygiene

Josiah Oldfield's article on remedies for constipation is only one salient example characterising a wealth of popular and medical treatises on regularity in the early twentieth century. In the West, intestinal cleanliness variously had been linked not only to physical, but also to spiritual, moral and emotional wellbeing through the end of the nineteenth century. But with the advent of germ theory, bowel irregularity suddenly took centre stage as perhaps the single most significant root condition underlying most serious illnesses. Cultural historian James C. Whorton notes that although the existence of microorganisms had been known for some time, it was not until the 1860s and 1870s, when the work of Pasteur and German physician Robert Koch demonstrated the causal relation between microbes and disease, that germs entered the forefront of contagion theory. 'Over the ensuing two decades,' Whorton writes, 'the causative agents of most of the major infectious diseases were discovered, and medicine (and the public) came to think of virtually all illness as due to germs' (Whorton 2000, 23).

It was only a matter of time before such early theories of microbiology led to the discovery of a widely occurring condition in which the body harboured putrefying, bacteria-producing matter that slowly poisoned the rest of the organism if it was not frequently and adequately evacuated. Dubbed 'autointoxication', this condition served as the newly scientific account of why bowel regularity should be the first priority in the medical maintenance of the healthy body. Although other organs might be considered as harbouring harmful bacteria, the large intestine took centre stage as the place from which the body was most in danger of absorbing poisonous compounds (Whorton 2000, 22). Moreover, as Whorton writes, autointoxication served to provide

> an explanation and a diagnosis for all those exasperating patients who insist they are sick, but are unable to present the physician with any clear organic pathology to prove it. Autointoxication, in other words, became its era's catchall diagnosis, the category into which cases of headache, indigestion, impotence, nervousness, insomnia, or any number of other functional disorders of indeterminate origin could be dumped. (Whorton 2000, 24–5)

If the 'vapours' had played this role in the eighteenth century, and 'neuraesthenia' had come to play it in the late nineteenth and early twentieth, now autointoxication could be cited as the 'fundamental cause' of both these conditions (Whorton 2000, 25).

Whorton's book abounds with detailed accounts of the various remedies for autointoxication aggressively marketed throughout the first three decades of the twentieth century, ranging from purgatives and laxatives to contradictory dietary regimes (stressing, by turns, yogurt and sour milk, yeast, vegetarianism and the ever-popular bran cereal), from exercise regimes to mechanical devices for massaging the abdomen, from rectal dilators to electrotherapy, from the curative waters of European spas to 'internal lavage', or enemas, which could be administered in the privacy of one's own bathroom. Most striking perhaps was the rise in popularity of radical surgical intervention, as demonstrated by the success and prominence of British surgeon Sir Arbuthnot Lane, whose widely disseminated theories of intestinal stasis were typical of the popular understanding of inner hygiene in the modern subject of civilised society, and whose mostly female clientele attested to the links between bowel regularity and compulsory femininity.

A surgeon at Guy's Hospital in London, Lane had by the first decade of the century developed an elaborate theory of the causes and effects of intestinal stasis. The human digestive system had functioned perfectly in our distant ancestors who had not yet begun to walk erect, and it continued to function well in those precivilised races whose primitive modes of life, which presumably included much squatting and sleeping on level surfaces, offered periodic respite from the practices that endangered the civilised digestive system. But evolutionary forces took a toll on our evacuative capacities; when we developed into *Homo erectus* our colon was affected by gravitational pull, causing it to droop. The body in turn formed 'membranous bands or adhesions' to try to prop it back up until 'eventually the bands would come to grip the sagging organ so tightly as to contract it in places and form unnatural "kinks", as Lane termed them' (Whorton 2000, 58). This gravity-induced 'kinking' process was an inevitable result of the evolutionary movement away from the primitive crouching position, so that 'by early childhood, every civilised person was trapped in a vicious downward spiral of tightening of the intestine and retention of waste matter in the body' (Whorton 2000, 58).

During the first three decades of the twentieth century, Lane made it his mission to enlighten the public on the far-reaching consequences of intestinal stasis, comparing the 'kinked' human digestive tract to a blocked drainage system in the domestic space of the household: 'the stomach was the body's toilet bowl, the duodenum the toilet trap, the small intestine the drainpipe, "and the large bowel the cesspool"' (Whorton 2000, 60). The irregular patient should follow the example of the homeowner who sensibly has his clogged drains cleaned out, thus reducing the danger of releasing poisonous gasses into his domicile (Whorton 2000, 61). According to Whorton, Lane 'employed [this] analogy repeatedly, time and again describing the intestines as "the sewage system of the human body", demanding that people pay attention to "the paramount importance of effective intestinal drainage", [and] illustrating his books with diagrams of the alimentary tract laid out as a sanitary engineering network' (Whorton 2000, 61).

Even those who did not appear to suffer from constipation (i.e. infrequent and laboured bowel movements) were nevertheless likely victims of intestinal stasis if their daily evacuations were not entirely complete, thus leaving behind an ever-increasing residue. 'If only a fraction of each day's waste stayed trapped by the colon's kinks, feces would accumulate [. . .] and putrefy and poison the unsuspecting victims no matter how unconstipated they were' (Whorton 2000, 60). Consequently, it was not only patients who came to Lane (and other physicians of the era) with explicit complaints of constipation that were ultimately diagnosed with intestinal stasis; since the condition was not easily detected by the layman, yet was considered to be the cause of almost all other physical and mental ailments, from nervousness to cancer, almost anyone coming for a consultation would be found to be suffering from autointoxication.

Lane began by treating his patients with paraffin oil, enemas and application of the Curtis belt, an abdominal truss meant to support the sagging bowel (Whorton 2000, 63–4). If these remedies did not clear up the patient's symptoms, then Lane resorted to the radical surgery that he became famous for: 'what he called the "short circuit operation", the bypassing of the large intestine from the point where it's joined by the small intestine (a common site of kinking, he believed) all the way to the sigmoid flexure, the s-shaped stretch of colon just above the rectum' (Whorton 2000, 64). His surgical procedures became more invasive over time, until eventually he was simply performing complete colectomies on his patients, removing the colon from the body altogether.

It is troubling enough that Lane carried out these surgeries with astonishing frequency over a period of twenty years. What is even more disturbing is that most of the patients who went under his knife were women. Three reports published by Lane and his assistant Harold Chapple document 106 cases of surgical treatment of autointoxication, of which 89 were women. Why the predominantly female clientele? While there was some speculation that women were more prone to autointoxication due to their reluctance to retire for a bowel movement when in the company of others, or to their relative lack of physical activity, the most significant root cause, according to Lane, was that the female intestine was just entirely more susceptible to being kinked (Whorton 2000, 66). This could be chalked up to a combination of factors, starting with their 'untoned abdominal musculature', which offered 'no resistance to the sagging of the digestive tract', and the use of the English corset, which constricted the abdomen and thus exaggerated a downward displacement that prevented the passage of faeces through the large intestine (Whorton 2000, 66). Once afflicted with intestinal stasis, a woman began to lose weight, thus depriving her abdomen of the fat that would otherwise support her internal organs, and making them likely to kink more severely than in men (Whorton 2000, 67).

But the above explanation merely accounts for why Lane believed women to be more prone to intestinal stasis; a more difficult question arises when we consider the ambiguity of the status of this 'medical' condition: in what sense did it exist? Was it (like the unconscious in psychoanalysis) merely hypothesised by the physician through a semiotic reading of evident symptoms? In other words, regardless of whether women 'really' suffered from constipation or not, they were hailed, by doctors such as Lane and more broadly by a popular cultural preoccupation with bowel regularity, as subjects whose identity was 'rooted' in their abdominal health. And though it is debatable as to whether women were squeamish about answering the call of nature, it seems evident that they responded enthusiastically to the call of medicine and 'found' themselves in its characterisation of them as in need of intestinal adjustment.

Predictably, when women were diagnosed with intestinal stasis, their bowel regularity was routinely linked to their gynaecological health and by extension to the way in which their femininity succeeded or failed. Chapple went so far as to assert that many gynaecological conditions could not even be considered as separate diseases, but had to be classed with the many other abdominal maladies whose primary cause was intestinal stasis (Whorton 2000, 67). One of Lane's theories was that pregnancy, because it restored the fat lost by sufferers from backed-up colons and thus straightened out some of the kinks, could serve as a cure for intestinal stasis, with the result that 'a toxic, thin, miserable girl may be converted into a plump, clean, happy one' (Whorton 2000, 67). However, since the majority of his patients were unmarried (forty-four out of fifty-seven, as reported in two of his articles), it might be problematic to prescribe pregnancy instead of surgical intervention. Besides, Lane and his colleagues promulgated the notion that women suffering from autointoxication were in any case unmarriageable, insofar as their physical and mental condition made them undesirable as objects of sexual exchange. In promoting his surgical treatment, Lane made the following kinds of claims:

> The poor, wretched, stupid, feeble woman, who is rendered ugly and unattractive by her [...] general appearance of irritable old age, with her cold, clammy hands, with the aches and pains in her legs, loins, and arms, becomes in a few days a bright eyed woman, sweet smelling, active mentally and physically. Each week and each month shows a steady improvement and she gradually recovers her youth. (Whorton 2000, 69)

His surgery could eliminate all disagreeability and unruliness; indeed, he argued that a man was better off living 'with a drunken woman rather than a toxic one, [since] a drunken person is occasionally merry, but a toxic one never!' (Whorton 2000, 69). Moreover, the autointoxicated woman, according to the medical practitioners of the period, was not only irritable and unpleasant, but also physically repugnant as a result of disfiguring toxins.[2] Once intestinal stasis was diagnosed and treated, however, a woman's health, youth, good spirits and beauty would be restored, thus increasing her matrimonial prospects. Lane reported that many cases of unmarriagable autointoxicated women were able to find matrimony after his surgery (Whorton 2000, 69).

It is still unclear as to the extent to which women were complicit in the medical establishment's invasion of their abdominal cavities as a mode of domestic 'taming'. Whorton reports that autointoxication had made these women's lives so 'unmanageable [...] that they demanded surgical help even when Lane advised against it' (Whorton 2000, 68) and elsewhere that 'Lane's patients worshiped him' (Whorton 2000, 70). Even when post-operative results were far from felicitous, Lane's female patients still expressed a mixture of 'misgivings and faith' in his treatment. One of his colectomy patients wrote to him a few years after her surgery to describe her ongoing troubles:

> 'I am still having mucus colitis [likely a mistaken self-diagnosis, since she no longer had a colon], and it keeps me very thin'. She was plagued by 'bleeding piles' as well, 'but I could not have another operation. [...] I feel afraid to see you. I have got such a coward lately'. Nevertheless, she requested his advice on nonsurgical remedies, and hoped 'you will not mind my writing. I have such faith in you'. (Whorton 2000, 72)

As a result of the discourse of the colon throughout the late nineteenth and early twentieth centuries, we might, following

Foucault's lead, say that a new 'species' of individual was born: the 'abdominal woman'.[3] Indeed, this species had achieved enough of a public profile to be lampooned by dismissive commentators of the period, who described her as a 'veritable vampire, sucking the vitality of all who come near her: [...] half an hour with her reduces her doctor to the consistence of a "piece of chewed string"' (Whorton 2000, 76).[4] As we often find in such satirical representations of female types, the real conditions of production are reversed here: it is not the medical professional who subjects hundreds of women to unnecessary surgeries, but rather the ludicrous abdominal woman who vampirically sucks all the vitality out of her doctor. Is it precisely an anxiety about being sucked into the alimentary system of the all-devouring female patient that symptomatically produces this image of a 'piece of chewed string'?

By the early 1920s, Lane's surgical solutions to intestinal stasis had fallen into disrepute within the medical establishment, and he returned to less invasive means of treatment. But the condition of autointoxication continued to be propounded as the root cause of physical, psychological and social ailments well throughout the next decade, with women as the special targets of campaigns to promote internal cleansing and regularity.

## Architectural modernism, hygiene and domestic space

During roughly the same period that the medical, pharmaceutical and popular media were emphasising the importance of intestinal regularity in the modern woman's body, architectural designers began to replace ornate Victorian interiors with streamlined domestic spaces, giving new importance to the kitchen and the bathroom as paradigms of a seamless modernist aesthetic. As design historians Lupton and Miller point out, this new emphasis on streamlining coincided with capitalist strategies of planned obsolescence in which 'products were mass produced and mass distributed, designed to be purchased and rapidly replaced by a vast buying public' (Lupton and Miller 1992a, 1). Our consideration of Marx's metabolic model of capitalist circulation and transformation, with its emphasis on sustained velocity, has already prepared us to understand the specifically peristaltic nature of streamlining. Lupton and Miller's compelling study of the rise of the modern(ist) bathroom and kitchen is an extended elaboration of the phrase 'process of elimination', which, they explain, concerns the 'overlapping patterns of biological digestion, economic consumption, and aesthetic simplification' (Lupton and Miller 1992a, 1). They make explicit the continuity between Marx's human metabolism with nature and the social metabolism of economics in industrialised capitalism, the process of consuming, digesting and excreting fully implicated in the process of buying, using and disposing.

Streamlining in modernist architectural design arose from an American obsession with waste – a fascination, on one hand, with strategies for 'managing the intimate processes of biological consumption' through a full cycle from food preparation to the elimination of faeces, and on the other hand, an economy premised on planned obsolescence with its constant discarding and replenishing of commodities. As a process of elimination, streamlining performed 'a surreal conflation of the organic and the mechanical: its seamless skins ... fluidly curved yet rigidly impervious to dirt and moisture'. Its moulded forms amounted to what they call 'an excretory aesthetic', in celebration of 'natural and cultural digestive cycles' (Lupton and Miller 1992a, 2).

By streamlining, Lupton and Miller mean both the smooth, curvilinear forms given to kitchen and bathroom fixtures in the early decades of the twentieth century and the increasingly seamless, unornamented design of household objects (telephones, irons, small appliances, etc.). But it also includes the ascendance in the same period of standardised packaging for food products: boxes and cans that enclosed products 'in a smooth, continuous skin, giving the organic, shapeless substance inside a clear geometric shape' (Lupton and Miller 1992a, 4). As an incitement to amp up consumer buying velocity, streamlining 'invoked a body gliding through fluid' and thus 'served to accelerate a product through the cycle of purchase and disposal, stimulating sales and hastening the replacement of objects not yet worn out' (Lupton and Miller 1992a, 5). The policy of planned obsolescence 'pictured the economy itself as a "body", whose health depends on a continual cycle of production and waste, ingestion and excretion' (Lupton and Miller 1992a, 5). Advertising was, of course, the 'crucial lubricant for keeping this cycle regular' and 'a laxative for hastening the flow of goods through the economy' (Lupton and Miller 1992a, 5).

In accordance with this emphasis on a regular flow of productive waste as necessary to the health of consumer economy,

Lupton and Miller point to a transformation of how domestic architectural space is configured in the middle-class home: the activities of 'cooking, bathing, and defecating' were shifted from 'positions of invisibility to dominance in the home. Formerly relegated to the cellar, exiled to the outhouse, or merged with the bedroom, these functions came to command the most expensive and technologically advanced features of the modern dwelling' (Lupton and Miller 1992a, 7–8). The bathroom and kitchen thus came to be articulated as the 'erotogenic zones of the domestic body' (Lupton and Miller 1992a, 8). As such, they required 'continual maternal maintenance' and were the 'locale of oral [and I would add anal] pleasure and personal care of the whole family' (Lupton and Miller 1992b, 504). While Lupton and Miller do not use the term, it is clear that what they are talking about is the female head of household as 'meta-industrial labourer', duly carrying out her role as she 'mediates, regulates, and controls' her family's metabolism with nature.

Women, as the meta-industrial providers of such 'maternal maintenance', were of course situated very prominently within the domestic/consumer circuits described by Lupton and Miller. In the public sphere, men earned the wages that women then spent on merchandise, the care and maintenance of which became their responsibility. 'For the male employee, the home became a sanctuary from the pressures of production, while for women it became an isolated site for the economically devalued yet demanding labors of consumption' (Lupton and Miller 1992a, 11). As women thus came to influence the shape of domestic space, modern technologies of consumption addressed them more insistently, at once empowering and manipulating them (Lupton and Miller 1992a, 8).

Lupton and Miller's study of what they call the 'aesthetics of waste' is especially extraordinary insofar as it never makes mention of the cultural anxiety around 'autointoxication' and 'intestinal stasis' promulgated by the health industry that I outlined in the previous section; and yet, they nevertheless discover this same anxiety, this same cultural obsession with peristaltic motion and cleanliness, in the discourses of design and domestic engineering.[5] While James Whorton was documenting Arbuthnot Lane's characterisation of the modern body as a house with backed-up sewage, Lupton and Miller were documenting the modern house as a body that must regularly produce and circulate waste in order to fulfil its proper role in the consumer economy. I would like to turn now to a text that occupies a peculiar juncture where these peristaltic scenes come together: Christine Frederick's enormously influential manifesto for domestic efficiency, her 1915 book *Household Engineering: Scientific Management in the Home*.

### Household peristalsis

Lupton and Miller quote Frederick as giving voice to 'the ethos of disposal' in the early twentieth century. In *Selling Mrs. Consumer*, Frederick writes, 'we have learned that the way to break the vicious deadlock of a low standard of living is to spend freely, and even waste creatively' (qtd. in Lupton and Miller 1992a, 7). This notion of 'creative waste', according to Lupton and Miller, promoted the garbage of consumer culture as an important element of 'positive production' – not because it could be recycled and reused, but in order to valorise 'destruction and replacement of objects as a pleasurable and socially instrumental act'. Waste, in this respect, was not just an incidental by-product of the consumption cycle, but a 'generative, necessary force. In the consumer economy, "production" finds a place inside the process of consumption, a cycle that reiterates the body's own form of "creative waste", excrement' (Lupton and Miller 1992a, 7).

Frederick was part of a trend in the 1910s and 1920s to adapt corporate models of Taylorism in the factory to develop 'scientific' strategies for household management. Through photographic techniques, workers' movements were monitored, timed and analysed in order to reveal and eliminate unnecessary gestures or inefficient postures, thus increasing the rapidity with which products passed through the assembly line. Frederick and fellow domestic theorists Frank and Lillian Gilbreth borrowed these same time and motion studies to chart the passage of the 'household engineer' through the kitchen as she prepared, served and washed up after meals, or as she cleaned the rest of the house, publishing the results as bases both for improving domestic architectural design and for advocating for more efficient movement of the homemaker through the domestic interior. Their publications inevitably included comparative floor plans of kitchens, juxtaposing an old-fashioned kitchen design, congested and clogged by a criss-cross of dotted lines representing the woman's inefficient movement through the space while she prepared a meal (and reminiscent of Arbuthnot Lane's diagram of the kinked colon), with a modern, streamlined design, through which only one or two dotted lines passed, to represent the smooth and continuous motion of the woman's body through space.

A detailed reading of Frederick's *Household Engineering*, so popular that it was reissued in 1919, will allow us to consider some of the implications of Taylorism in the domestic sphere, particularly as it pertains to the peristaltic imperative for the female homemaker. To begin with, let's consider Frederick's account of the function of nutrients as they travel through the body in relation to her advice about financial budgeting. In her chapter on food planning, Frederick remarks that 'cooking is all too frequently done to feed the family, without planning to nourish it' (Frederick 1919, 80). It is thus paramount for the home economist to familiarise herself with Frederick's list of the main nutrients found in food and how each functions in the body: protein 'is the only nutrient which can furnish the material to replace old or grow new tissue'; carbohydrates 'furnish "fuel" for heat and muscular energy to the body' (Frederick 1919, 180); fats 'furnish over twice the "fuel" for heat and energy as same weight of carbohydrate or protein. Excess of food supply is stored in the body as fat'; mineral salts 'form the greater part of the body structure and are a very small, though necessary, part of every tissue in the body; they are necessary for the digestive secretions and for the blood' (Frederick 1919, 181). These four nutrients are followed by two additional substances: bulk or waste products, which creatively 'serve to give "bulk" to the meal and act as "brooms" to the system, stimulating the intestinal and muscular walls', and water, which is 'necessary in dissolving the food, carrying away waste products, and in regulating the temperature of the body through the blood' (Frederick 1919, 181).

A similar tabulation of divisions and distributions is found in her chapter on 'Family Financing and Record Keeping'. According to Frederick, household income is to be divided among the following categories of expense: shelter (rent or mortgage, taxes, repair and upkeep of house); food; clothing (including mending supplies, dressmaker and pressing,); operating (light, heat, ice, telephone, wages of maid, as well as house furnishings and labour-saving devices); savings (life insurance, bonds and savings account); luxuries (cigars, barber and hairdresser, candy and other indulgences); and a final category called 'advancement' that comprises 'Education, music, books and periodicals; club dues, church, charity, gifts, amusements, vacations, health (physician, dentist, medicine), postage, toilet articles, telegrams, etc.'. What makes this ultimate category interesting is that 'toilet articles' (which include grooming items such as brushes, razors, soaps and lotions, but also undoubtedly an array of products designed for inner hygiene) are classified along with 'education' and various expenses associated with one's civic duties as part of the family's 'advancement' (Frederick 1919, 273). Frederick explains that many fail to see the connection between health and advancement. But:

> [t]he care bestowed upon the family's teeth, eyes and health, all items for sanitary use, mark the difference between the family with a low standard and one with a higher view. All spiritual needs, all educational expense, or the means of increasing knowledge, training, development or the making of the members more efficient to themselves and to society, must be classed here. (Frederick 1919, 283)

In other words, products not just for the healthy, but more pointedly, for the 'sanitary' functioning of the body are to be classed under advancement because they help to mark the family as having a 'higher view' of how to make their bodies more 'efficient to themselves and to society'. This no doubt includes all products for the maintenance of intestinal regularity, over and above what might be classed in the 'food' category (in terms of what nutrients are taken in) and what might be classed in the 'operating' category (plumbing and waste removal costs).

Moreover, there is a continuity here between how the body and the household (as semi-organic architectural structure) are imagined as one extended metabolic system: while proteins are 'furnish(ing) the material to replace old or grow new tissue', thus physically augmenting the body in which one is housed, so income classed under 'shelter' is directed toward providing the household dwelling place; while carbohydrates 'furnish "fuel" for heat and muscular energy to the body', so income designated for 'operating costs' supplies energy to the internal workings of the household; while 'excess of food supply is stored in the body as fat', so some income must be stored in the bank as 'savings'; and finally, just as bulk and water 'act as "brooms" to the system' and 'dissolv[e] the food, carrying away waste products', so the hygienic items classed under 'advancement' help to keep the individual household bodies efficiently regular. Production and management of waste,

## Unkinking, Streamlining and the Household Engineer 123

whether through the proper valuation of nutritional categories or through the recognition of the importance of the bathroom as site of hygiene and elimination, is stressed throughout Frederick's book as key to a household's avoidance of 'stasis' in the realm of social betterment. Indeed, Frederick's book is first and foremost a compendium of strategies for keeping substances moving efficiently and regularly through space, with the understanding that this is the only way to facilitate spiritual, social, national 'advancement': food must be purchased and prepared with an eye to its most useful progression through the household members' bodies; monetary income must be apportioned, saved, spent, invested (and even creatively 'wasted' on luxuries) for the most efficient buying power; kitchen fixtures, furniture, appliances and supplies must be arranged for the most efficient trajectory through the kitchen and dining space of the body that is preparing and cleaning up after meals. This is where the modern housekeeper is urged to follow the example of Taylorism in the factories:

> Emphasize the importance of 'beating your own record' and making time-studies of each particular task. The housekeeper in the servantless home has widest opportunity to make original kitchen and housework time-studies. Where does your time go? How long does it take you to make the beds? How long to clean the downstairs rooms? Do you wash dishes three times a day, or only once? (Frederick 1919, 388)

Frederick advocates washing the dishes only once a day, for instance, rather than after every meal, since it takes less time overall to wash the dishes of three meals in one batch (Frederick 1919, 389).

In Frederick's book, of course, no body is more rigorously subjected to the logic of time-and-motion studies than that of the female 'household engineer'. It is no surprise, then, that *Household Engineering* culminates with a chapter titled 'Health and Personal Efficiency', in which the author stresses the importance of keeping the body of the female head of household in proper working repair:

> We may put a worker into the most efficient kitchen, we may hand her the most useful labor-savers, we may show her the easiest way to wash clothes, but all our teaching will be in vain if the worker is ill, if she 'fags' easily, or if she is subject to headaches. (Frederick 1919, 481)

In addition to tips on the benefits of 'fresh air during work hours' (Frederick 1919, 483), good eating habits (Frederick 1919, 485), the 'importance of right posture' (Frederick 1919, 489), 'relaxation through reclining postures' (Frederick 1919, 491), proper clothing (Frederick 1919, 496) and daily physical exercise (Frederick 1919, 498), Frederick devotes an entire subsection to the 'Evils of Constipation' and 'poor elimination of the colon and alimentary tract' (Frederick 1919, 486).

'Headaches, dizziness, fatigue and similar symptoms' are 'directly traceable to an overstuffed and inadequately emptied colon, or lower bowel' (Frederick 1919, 487). Frederick's familiarity with the popularised intestinal theories of Arbuthnot Lane comes through in the following passage:

> Physicians call such conditions 'auto-intoxication', meaning that the contents and poisons of the intestines which are not removed quickly enough, 'back up' (just like an overful waste pipe or sewer) and thus poison the blood supply. It is this poisoning of the blood with waste and decaying food residues, that makes the 'head-aches', the 'tired feeling' of which so many women constantly complain. (Frederick 1919, 487)

Once again, the analogy between body and house comes to the forefront, much along the same lines that Lane and other medical specialists deployed it in their descriptions of intestinal stasis in the two decades prior to Frederick's book. But in the case of Frederick's book, the domestic space of the household is imagined in much more detail, and the 'internal' process of the household engineer's individual system of elimination is articulated as an organic element in the larger peristaltic composition of the house itself. The movement of products through the house, the movement of the woman's body through the kitchen, the movement of nutrients and roughage through the woman's body – all are hooked up to each other in an economic-hygienic assemblage, or, more to the point, in an over-arching metabolic system that the household engineer 'mediates, regulates, and controls' (Marx 1976, 283). When the functioning of this assemblage experiences a breakdown, a blockage, a lag, a rupture, or when the metabolic circuit experiences a rift, it can be traced directly back to disturbances in the 'homemaker' segment of the household peristaltic system.

Indeed, overworked women who attribute their fatigue, for instance, to endless routines of cooking, cleaning and childcare learn in this chapter that their exhaustion is in fact due to another cause altogether. 'Many women think they are "tired" from work, whereas the truth is that they are suffering from a slow poisoning of their systems due solely to inactive sluggish elimination of food waste' (Frederick 1919, 487). While the household engineer may safely stack and save the after-meal dishes for one washing-up per day, the movement of 'food waste' through her intestines must progress at a more lively rate: 'Three times a day is the natural, normal evacuation of the bowels, or a movement after each meal to keep the system in the most healthful condition' (Frederick 1919, 487).

Frederick warns against dangerous medicines and cathartics, advocating instead for a healthy diet, and stressing that 'the home-maker, as a specialist in food values, should be the very woman to make intelligent use of such diets to improve her own health and thus retain and increase her personal efficiency' (Frederick 1919, 487). The 'anti-constipation' foods are listed, with an emphasis on the bulk, roughage and water categories that had appeared in the nutrients chapter. That bowel regularity is understood to be the largest underlying factor in maintaining a healthy and therefore efficient homemaker's body is evident in Frederick's remark that 'Emphasis is here laid on this point of right feeding and adequate elimination, because no one other single health point is so vital to women's efficiency and so generally neglected, with the result of "nerves", irritability, and greatly impaired work power' (Frederick 1919, 488).

Indeed, when Frederick later reiterates her belief that it is not excessive, monotonous labour that leads to fatigue, but rather improper health measures, most of the problems she lists are directly or indirectly linked to impaired peristaltic movement in the working body:

Thousands of women think that as homemakers they are 'overworked'. Some, indeed, are working beyond their strength. But the plain facts are that most of these thousands of women who think they are being overworked are instead victims of bad air, wrong diet, poor elimination, body poisons, lack of exercise and worry and mental disquiet [. . .]. There are some women, perhaps, working beyond their capacity, but on the other hand their working capacity is only a fraction of what it would be if they took exercise, if they were not constipated, if they did not eat wrong foods, if they did not worry. (Frederick 1919, 499)

Since constipation is to be found at the source of most psychological distress, it appears that even worry and 'mental disquiet' belong to the category of peristaltic disturbances. Moreover, as we find elsewhere in the 'Health and Personal Efficiency' chapter, another category of psychological distress, 'emotional fatigue', is directly attributable not just to faulty peristalsis in the body, but to the sluggish elimination of objects in the larger peristaltic system of the household in general. Frederick warns against 'disorderly, upset kitchens and overcrowded sinks, and rooms which have been allowed to "look like a sight"'. This kind of domestic overcrowding not only leads to bodily fatigue (through the necessity to clean) but, more importantly, to severe mental fatigue as well, since 'clutter' will cause discouragement, and lower a woman's efficiency.

> Therefore, those methods which prevent confusion, such as [a] definite place for grouped equipment, the cleaning up of mixing bowls in cooking, the 'pick-up-as-you-go' habit, are to be followed not only because they save time, but because they save emotional fatigue. (Frederick 1919, 495)

It is not the motion of labour that causes fatigue, it turns out, but rather the stasis of constipation: the overburdening of the intestines with faecal matter and the cluttering of household channels with things. Streamlining for smooth movement is the solution not only to physical debilitation but also to psychological distress. Moreover, to facilitate the unimpaired functioning of the homemaker component in the household peristaltic system, Frederick suggests that she be removed from the system at least once a year and placed temporarily in an institutional space designed for the inventory, repair, fine-tuning and maintenance of her psychophysical workings. Here, in the sanitarium, the household engineer should have an annual survey and diagnosis conducted of 'all body conditions and organs' even though she may feel in perfect health.

> Such a 'survey' of heart, blood pressure, sex organs, eyes, teeth, etc., may reveal slight indications of wrong which, taken in time, will never

become the aggravated symptoms and illness they might develop into if unobserved at the start. One week spent in a sanitarium under the constant observation of trained health specialists will more than repay the cost, especially if the woman later follows the course of diet, or exercise, or hygiene planned for her special problems. (Frederick 1919, 500)

It is not simply that the woman ought to consult her physician once a year for a check-up, but rather that she check in to a sanitarium for a week, so that the functioning of her body may be observed over a period of time; so that her own 'time and motion studies' may, as it were, be supplemented by those studies that can only be carried out in the clinical space of the institution.

## Notes

1  The work of Elizabeth Wilson is a notable exception to this lacuna. And Myra Hird (2012), following on Hannah Landecker's work, offers a provocative meditation on how metabolism might function as a 'foil' to the concept of sexual difference. See also some of the essays in Forth and Carden-Coyne, eds. *Culture of the Abdomen: Diet, Digestion, and Fat in the Modern World* (2005), and Mathias and Moore, eds. *Gut Feeling and Digestive Health in Nineteenth-Century Literature, History and Culture* (2018).
2  As one London doctor explained, 'Toxins [...] springing from the intestinal cesspool [...] prowl about the tissues seeking what they may convert from the beautiful and useful into the ugly, the painful, and degenerate' (Whorton 2000, 70).
3  'Four figures emerged from this preoccupation with sex, which mounted throughout the nineteenth century – four privileged objects of knowledge, which were also targets and anchorage points for the ventures of knowledge: the hysterical woman, the masturbating child, the Malthusian couple, and the perverse adult' (Foucault, *History of Sexuality* Part 1, 105).
4  'The age now belonged, in a London physician's phrase, to the "abdominal woman", a female conditioned to let "abdominal troubles colour her life and personality", women generally "neurotic" or with "unstable nervous systems, who are much more given to thinking about their insides than about getting into the kingdom of heaven". Her mind in "perpetual revolution round her umbilicus", she traveled a long road to "chronic abdominalism" that was "paved

with operations", while her estimate of the skill of her surgeon rose and fell "with the number of kinks which he can discover in them [her intestines]". A self-absorbed hypochondriac, the abdominal woman was "always discovering fresh symptoms", never admitting "any improvement in her condition", carting about "a box full of roentgen-ray plates" to dramatise the congested state of her intestines. She was "a veritable vampire, sucking the vitality of all who come near her: [. . .] half an hour with her reduces her doctor to the consistence of a "piece of chewed string".' (Whorton 2000, 76)

5  It should be noted, however, that Christina Cogdell (2010) brilliantly extends Lupton and Miller's work on streamlining into the study of eugenics in American culture, thus drawing out the connections among the national obsession with intestinal stasis, the imperative to keep the contents of the white, civilized body on the move, and even the promotion of a national highway system 'as the cure for America's "communications constipation"' (Cogdell 2010, 142). She points to the 1932 book by doctor Ettie Hornibrook, which suggested that constipation hindered 'civilized' women's sexual desire, thus reducing the eugenic birthrate (Cogdell 2010, 134), and argues that the 'causes, consequences, and cures of constipation became a site where the broader goals of smooth flow and national efficiency were telescoped downward and turned inward' (Cogdell 2010, 135).

6

# The Peristaltic Desiring-Machine of Miss Louise

Lupton and Miller report that Frederick's *Household Engineering* was translated into German in 1922 and point out its influence on progressive German architectural designers as they sought to implement streamlined kitchen designs 'featuring built-in, continuous-height cabinets and work surfaces organized in a coherent L-shape' (Lupton and Miller 1992a, 48). Undoubtedly, her book also spoke to a broader inter-war audience of European women who, like their British and American counterparts, were already being interpellated as peristaltic subjects and urged to find their proper positioning as domestic consumers and producers of waste. Not long after the appearance of the German translation of Frederick's book, Viennese psychoanalyst Wilhelm Stekel published his *Frigidity in Woman*, which included among its hundreds of case studies the story of one patient whose sexual aetiology is clearly implicated in the larger systems of consumption and excretion referenced by the discourses of hygiene and domestic engineering that pervaded the popular consciousness of the era. If what I have outlined in the previous chapter concerns how women were addressed and positioned through certain cultural apparatuses and disciplinary structures (as though they were passive, docile bodies), Stekel's case study offers a glimpse of how at least one woman responded to this cultural interpellation, speaking back in the very mode in which she was addressed, that is, through a kind of intestinal grammar of desire.

In his chapter titled 'The Psychology of the Frigid Woman', Stekel hypothesises that an underlying bisexuality, or a repressed homosexuality, is often the cause of frigidity in normal (read hetero) sexual life. By repressed homosexuality, Stekel refers not to unconscious homoerotic impulses, but rather to explicitly felt homoerotic desire that has been deliberately repressed by women who refuse to face up to the 'truth' of their desire. Aware at one time or another of their attraction to other women, they consciously reject it and 'turn their yearnings the more eagerly to the male' (Stekel 1967, 105).

The first case study presented by Stekel in this chapter concerns one of these 'unwilling' women who display a flight from homosexuality 'which may assume the strangest forms': the thirty-year-old, unmarried Miss Louise K who has consulted the analyst for 'a very perplexing trouble' (Stekel 1967, 105). The trouble, as Stekel presents it, concerns Louise's daily bowel habits and thus appears at first to have little to do with frigidity. Indeed, it is not until halfway through the case study that Stekel attempts to integrate the striking account he has given of Louise's uncommon intestinal routines into his standard Oedipal hypotheses about female sexual pleasure. In this chapter, I turn to an account of the complex bowel practices devised by this woman, as well as the attempt Stekel makes to subordinate her peristaltic assemblages to the familiar tale of arrested heterosexual development. In the process, I will supplement Stekel's perspective on this case with one that asks a different set of questions, thereby allowing me to explore Louise's story not simply as an instance of pathological neurosis, but rather as a site of desiring-production embedded in a modern metabolic system.

Louise K apparently comes to consult Stekel after having lived for some time in a boardinghouse, where she has just terminated a two-year, unsatisfactory love affair with a married physician. As Stekel describes it, the problem she brings to him is not that her sexual relationship with the physician has gone wrong, but rather that she has developed a peculiar set of circumstances regarding her bowels. It would appear that her erotic life is entirely hooked up with her peristaltic processes, in particular, with the rituals and practices associated with her daily regularity. In Stekel's account, everything circulates around a troubling paradox that dominates her life. 'As soon as she comes near anybody', we are told, 'she feels the most unpleasant intestinal sensations. Intestinal gas begins vehemently to stir and the noise is often audible' (Stekel 1967, 105). She fears the escape of wind, which 'renders her appearance in company impossible'. Yet – and here is the paradox – 'she is driven almost to worse despair' by the fact that she needs these rumblings caused by her 'appearance in company' in order to move her bowels (Stekel 1967, 105). Even if she decided to content herself with a solitary life, remaining secluded from others so as not to experience the fear that she might offend them with her gas, her body would not allow it, because she would thus be condemned to intestinal stasis.

It appears that, faced with the prospect of permanent constipation, Louise has devised a complex strategy for moving her bowels: a carefully calibrated series of experimental activities that include preparatory fantasies, washing rituals, the positioning of her body at the correct distance from other bodies, engagement in social interactions, a meticulous attention to timing, a delicate and finely attenuated understanding of the relation between affect and organic processes. For some, nothing more than a cup of coffee, a cigarette, a little reading is required to trigger the autonomic release of the inner-sphincter muscle that allows the contents of the lower bowel to signal a readiness to be expelled. For Louise, the requisite conditions have become more elaborate, more consciously articulated, and therefore more instructive for us in terms of understanding how bowel habits can become a form of discourse, a means, whether consciously or unconsciously, of exercising control over one's cultural positioning.

Stekel describes her daily routine as follows:

> In the morning, on awakening, she begins to day-dream about the various men of her acquaintance. This she calls her 'warming up'. She pictures herself enjoying the company of these men undisturbed by her bowel symptoms. These day-dreams she carries to the utmost extreme, picturing to herself marriage and sexual intercourse, childbirths and various other strange adventures. (Stekel 1967, 106)

Thus, the first stage of the process involves a preparatory series of romantic or sexual fantasies, which Louise consciously terms 'warming up' and 'baking'. It is as though the fantasy activity works like an internal combustion mechanism to fuel the heating of her body like an oven. Stekel comments that she says she 'never indulges' in this 'baking' with a woman, that 'such a thought never enters her mind'; but given what follows, it would seem that these vigorous protestations imply that her preparatory fantasies are, indeed, just as likely to be homo- as hetero-erotic (Stekel 1967, 106).

The baking process is succeeded by a two-hour 'washing ceremonial' that Stekel links to her preoccupation with bowel regularity: 'if she has a thorough bowel movement she feels properly cleansed,' he remarks. The next page details the means by which such a thorough movement will be attained, but first we are given some insight into at least one of the social apparatuses that has doubtless mediated her understanding of her peristaltic processes:

> For a time she was taking large amounts of purgatives, especially if she expected to go in society. Afraid of being found 'smelly' she would scour her bowels so thoroughly with purgatives that before venturing out of doors she had to take large doses of opium to check diarrhea. These foolish habits – the taking of drastic purgatives and checking their over-effect with opium – she learned in a sanitarium. (Stekel 1967, 106)

Louise's residence in the boardinghouse has, it appears, been preceded by at least one episode in a sanitarium, though it is not clear whether she was being treated there for physical or nervous ailments. Whether she was one of the thousands of European women of the period who came to sanitaria seeking a cure for 'neuraesthenia', looking for a rest from the pressures of civilised daily life, or, as recommended by Christine Frederick, to have a '"survey" or diagnosis made [...] of all body conditions and organs', it is not surprising, given Whorton's account of the prominence of autointoxication as the root of all psycho-physiological disturbances, that purgatives and opium would be administered to her regardless of her symptomatology. Whatever 'toilet training' Louise brought with her to the sanitarium was modified by the institution's pharmaceutical interventions, with the result, no doubt, that she came to be much more vigilant about her faecal habitus than she might have been before her stay there. By the time she leaves the sanitarium, she has gotten into the habit, as Stekel puts it, of 'taking drastic purgatives and checking their over effect with opium to check diarrhea' with the result that she is unable to move her bowels 'without the aid of purgatives and the accompaniment of anxiety' (Stekel 1967, 106).

Interestingly, however, it would appear that Louise has found a way to wean herself off the pharmaceutical manipulation of her bowels and to replace it with a psycho-physiological self-treatment, that is, with 'anxiety centered either on a man or on a

## The Peristaltic Desiring-Machine of Miss Louise   133

woman' (Stekel 1967, 106). When the description of her morning routine is resumed in the subsequent passage, we understand that the necessary 'purgative' is now no longer a drug, but rather another person whose nearby body will, under the right conditions, produce the proper metabolic reactions in her own:

> In the morning, her first thought was: 'Whom shall I use as a "purgative" today?' It had to be a person towards whom she was not indifferent. Full of tension she would go to the breakfast table, if she lived in a boardinghouse, a sanitarium, or a hotel, to sit down near the person she had chosen as her anxiety objective. But she could not be too close to the person or she suffered such tortures that she had to leave the table in the midst of her breakfast. (Stekel 1967, 106)

While the loaves are baking in the warmed-up oven, Louise sets in motion the couplings and gears that will move them through their internal chambers. The question of proper proximity is crucial at this point: she must be close enough to someone to whom she is 'not indifferent' that the requisite enteric reaction will be produced within her intestines and yet not so close as to short circuit the operation before its satisfactory conclusion. Moreover, only certain bodies are serviceable as 'purgatives'. As Stekel explains it,

> our patient became accustomed to attain her bowel movements through a form of sexual excitation. It is noteworthy that already at this stage she was able to obtain the desired excitation through persons of either sex. If the housekeeper or a woman acquaintance sat near her at the breakfast table she achieved the same excitation as when Mr. X or Mr. Y was in the room. Always the fear of exhaling a bad odor played a great role in this connection. Unfortunately Mr. X suffered from a nasal catarrh and he had the sniffles; consequently she could not get her excitation in his presence because he could not smell. Miss N uses strong pomades. At the sanitarium it was said that she does this to cover an unpleasant body odor which she exhaled. Our patient promptly loses her anxiety in the presence of Miss N and the latter can no longer serve her effectively as a 'purgative'. (Stekel 1967, 107)

The circuit now appears in more detail: a person can only function as an 'anxiety objective' if he or she possesses the proper olfactory proficiency. Mr X's blocked sinuses mean that he will be of no use in the deblocking of Louise's bowels because he is incapable of smelling odours and therefore of being offended by intestinal gas; Miss N is reputed to 'exhale' her own unpleasant odour and hence is also unlikely to be a properly impressionable receptor of Louise's bodily emissions. But given an individual whose nasal passages are alert and sensitive, the actions and reactions progress smoothly: Louise arrives at the breakfast table and situates her own body the proper distance from another body which sexually excites her. She imagines that her breakfast companion inhales the air that has been imbued by her odour, and expects at any moment to be the object of disgust or repugnance. Stekel continues:

> While eating breakfast her bowels would begin to stir most vigorously (without gas rumbling) the intestinal agitation becoming truly unbearable. She began to fidget, her face turned red and she ceased taking part in the table conversation. She controlled herself until she could endure the torture no longer. Then she was sure of results. She would suddenly leave the table to rush to the toilet, where she attended to the ceremony of bowel 'cleaning' with more or less success, depending on the degree of her agitation. (Stekel 1967, 106)

Louise comes to the breakfast table to get plugged in to at least three complex social transactions engaging all the senses. She and her companions eat, taking in the substances that begin a peristaltic journey through the oesophagus, the stomach, the intestines. As they eat, they also converse with each other, listening, speaking, taking in and emitting discourse – in general, delineating the social space they inhabit together. Meanwhile, Louise is conscious of another silent network of flows and ingestions, potential repulsions and intensifications, a circuit that runs on an olfactory-intestinal principle: the proximity of her companion, the one she has chosen as her 'anxiety objective', the one whose interiority might at any moment be invaded by Louise's bodily odour, now makes Louise's bowels begin to 'stir'. This internal agitation in turn precipitates a series of other reactions in Louise's body: she 'fidgets', her face 'turns red' and she ceases to 'participate in the conversation'. But this apparent foundering of the social machinery is in fact just one of the necessary breaks in the systemic flow that allows for the next threshold to be attained. The fidgeting, the coursing of blood to the face, the subtraction of her voice from the conversational exchange, all of these are calculated elements in the desiring-production process. Such 'torture' must be endured for a specific duration of time, and then, finally, 'she could be sure of the results'. The more agitation that is produced by the breakfast companion, the more torture that is endured, the more successful is her subsequent bowel cleansing.

Stekel treats this bowel cleansing ritual as a metaphorical rendering of a deeper sexual condition, subject to an interpretation that will reveal its true significance. The 'cleaning,' he asserts, is 'a symbolic act meant to render her pure again. If she sinned at the breakfast table she could cleanse herself at once by the adequate punishment involved in the mental anguish of dwelling on the sinful thoughts' (Stekel 1967, 106). But to treat this preoccupation with internal cleansing simply as the legible symptom of an individual pathology is to ignore how it is absolutely in keeping with the broader cultural emphasis on 'inner hygiene': as I have shown, medical experts and popular health magazines alike routinely warned about the dangers of autointoxication, reiterating in detail the short- and long-term effects on women of putrefying waste allowed to build up in their intestines. The medical definition of intestinal stasis was not just the condition of constipation, but rather the backing up of faecal matter that has not been 'systematically completely removed' from the colon every day, up to three times a day (Whorton 2000, 60). With this in mind, one might think of intestinal cleansing as a compulsory rather than a compulsive activity – the result of a broad social mandate to keep one's intestinal contents moving rather than of an individual sexual development that has strayed from the norm.

This is not to say that there is no sexual aspect to Louise's bowel habits. Indeed, Stekel is correct in recognising that she attains her movements through 'a form of sexual excitation', and that it is her sexual attraction to the women and men at the breakfast table that makes them viable as purgatives. But while Stekel, as psychoanalyst, would claim that this is a case study about a certain sexual type (a sub-category of the frigid woman), it is more to the point to consider Louise as a variation of a certain kind of peristaltic subject. It is not that the excretory function works in the service of a certain sexual identity for Louise, but rather that the sexual function works in the service of keeping the peristaltic desiring-machine going, at once affording a pleasure not assimilable to the codifications of Oedipus, and ensuring for Louise an unpredictable position in the usual cycles of social production and consumption.

I will follow this through in more detail by looking at Stekel's conclusions about Louise's condition.

After having detailed Louise's morning routine, Stekel sums up its sexual significance in the following manner:

> We have already pointed out that her intestinal irritation was erotic in character. It constitutes her form of sexual gratification. No person thinks all day long about the excreta unless he finds in the 'anal function' his secret gratification. The rank bodily odors constitute a compromise representing not only self-punishment and a pleasure premium; they represent also a protective defence reaction. (Stekel 1967, 107)

The implication here is that having arranged a means of propelling her intestinal contents via social interactions, producing internal sensations and intensifications, Louise can simultaneously experience a bodily enjoyment (the 'pleasure premium') and punish herself for such indulgences. But what does it mean, exactly, to find in the 'anal function' one's 'secret gratification'? Is this complex morning ritual merely a substitute for anal intercourse? Or is it producing precisely the sensations that it is designed to produce, that is, the intestinal rumblings as experienced in relation to other peristaltic bodies within a larger metabolic system of physical, emotional and social flows and blockages? How does the psychoanalytic fixation on 'genital sexuality' involving penis, clitoris and vagina prevent Stekel from exploring the intensification of internal organs in this scenario, an intensification produced in part by their public circulation as targets of medical and social intervention?

Stekel accounts for Louise's intestinal drama by reconstructing her erotic development as a series of repressions and substitutions, as a surface heterosexuality beneath which lies a consciously repressed homosexual libido. If she is frigid when having sexual intercourse with the doctor in the boardinghouse, it is because, as analysis reveals, her lesbian fixation on her mother has never been successfully overcome, due to circumstances surrounding her first heterosexual seduction. The full story goes like this: as a child, she was reprimanded by her female principal at boarding school, who threatened to expel her for pranks she had committed. Anxious to please the principal, she promised to change her ways, and became 'docile, zealous, obedient and very punctilious in her conduct' (Stekel 1967, 108). This suppression of her otherwise lively personality, however, exacted a price; the conflict between outward obedience and inward yearning for freedom led to a 'flight into illness', or an attempt 'to postpone deciding the momentous conflict which obsessed her' (Stekel 1967, 109).

When graduating from the school, she is rewarded by her female principal for being a model pupil for so many years: 'The teacher gave her a present and a single kiss. During this kiss she felt such rapture as she had never experienced before nor since. At the same time the thought crossed her mind: "For Heaven's sake! Am I homosexual?"' (Stekel 1967, 109). This Stekel takes as confirmation that Louise has all along been in love with her principal and therefore especially susceptible to a desire to please her with the docile behaviour that results in her inner conflicts. As soon as she becomes conscious of her intense libidinal attraction to the principal, however, Louise puts herself on guard against further homoerotic temptations, taking pains to avoid further intimate contact with women:

> In Paris, where she lived for a time, a friend of hers, a Frenchwoman, invited her to share the same bed. Coolly but firmly she declined. She also developed a marked coolness towards her mother, toward whom she was formerly demonstrative, having indulged in slight tendernesses involving fondling. (Stekel 1967, 110)

It is worth noting that a discourse of suppression and release characterises Stekel's account throughout; in familiar psychoanalytic fashion, he imagines the structure of desire to function almost like a peristaltic system, in which libido is by turns blocked or backed up, only to be either released later or to find an outlet in some other channel (the 'flight into illness' that has its counterpart in the poisoning of the bloodstream by backed-up faecal matter). Of the rapturous first kiss, for example, Stekel says 'the long-brewing homosexuality suddenly released this pent-up libido' (Stekel 1967, 110). If Louise subsequently persists in suppressing this newly released libido, by showing 'coolness' towards her mother and the would-be French seductress, she must discharge the blocked-up energy through another outlet: 'She sought and found her release through masturbation, achieving highest orgasm during the act' (Stekel 1967, 110). But the solution of self-pleasuring is short-lived: she hears that 'such indulgence renders women frigid' and thus forces herself to give it up (Stekel 1967, 110–11).

In her relations with the doctor at the boardinghouse she finds herself 'wholly anaesthetic' and is unable to achieve a climax even when she resorts once more to masturbation. This is because, according to Stekel, a fear of harming herself 'suppresses' the orgasm. Suspecting that it is the doctor's fault that she fails to 'achieve gratification', she tries experimenting with other men and

> would have been willing to try all of them. At least she would have liked to kiss each one. Occasional 'trials' yielded varying results. Usually the libido she achieved was weak and very indefinite. At any rate various disturbing influences always interfered with success. During the initial stage of kissing her conscience already began to trouble her and this was enough to prevent her from achieving a satisfactory orgasm. (Stekel 1967, 111)

By the time Louise comes to consult Stekel, she has already established an extensive knowledge of her own erotic aspirations and conditions for gratification, not hesitating to pursue alternative practices when the results are not to her liking. Stekel elicits from her the history of this experimental trajectory and reproduces it for us as a series of suppressions, releases, interferences and preventions. As he reaches the conclusion of this account, he attempts to reintegrate it with the peristaltic symptoms:

> Even more remarkable was the fact that after indulging in masturbation her intestinal rumblings ceased and for a day she had peace. This plainly proves that sexual gratification rendered superfluous the erotic muscular excitation of the intestines. In the same way the intestinal rumbling ceased whenever the doctor or some other man kissed her. More than that! After a kiss she sometimes enjoyed precious freedom from her trouble and for several days could move her bowels without the aid of her customary symbolic 'purgatives'. (Stekel 1967, 112)

It is evident that, according to the closed system of stasis and motion, repression and release, Stekel understands the 'erotic muscular excitation of the intestines' to be nothing more than a 'superfluous' substitute for a 'sexual gratification' more conventionally attained through masturbation or heterosexual kisses. If only her libido could flow through normal channels, by way of the proper sexual organs and in relation to the appropriate heterosexual partners, it would cease to be diverted through its compensatory intestinal routes. That the cure Stekel envisions for Louise (but despairs that she will ever achieve) is that she become properly Oedipally heterosexualised is confirmed in his summary conclusions about her case.

Coming back to sexual anaesthesia during heterosexual intercourse as the condition in need of treatment, Stekel remarks that the 'orgasm with the woman teacher', as well as 'orgasms during masturbation, probably attained with the aid of homosexual fantasies', prove that there is no organic impediment to Louise's sexual gratification: she is not 'natura frigida' (Stekel 1967, 113). These homoerotically produced orgasms are thus accorded a double meaning by Stekel: on the one hand, they unfortunately indicate a lesbian fixation that must be overcome if Louise is to enter into culturally permissible adult heterosexual relations. On the other hand, they at least attest to the fact that her biophysical libidinal system is functioning and is only in need of proper channelling.

A classic psychoanalytic understanding of how this channelling would have to be accomplished is revealed in Stekel's final remarks. 'The woman teacher was an Imago of her mother,' he begins. 'The kiss enkindled an infantile libido in her' (Stekel 1967, 113). It would seem that there is no present moment of sexual excitation, therefore, that is not the 'enkindling' of what the doctor presumes to be the earliest experiences of erotic pleasure. If a woman is aroused by another woman, it must be because she unconsciously recalls her mother's arousal of her as an infant. Arrested in a pre-Oedipal stage of her sexual development, according to Stekel, Louise has never moved beyond the infantile sexual attachment to the mother, has failed to exchange the mother for the father as object of her libido, and thus failed to complete her proper Oedipal orientation. To be thus pre-Oedipally oriented is necessarily to be homosexually oriented.

This is not necessarily a problem in itself, according to the psychoanalytic account of sexual development. Given the proper conditions, one may move out of this infantile stage of sexuality into a more mature stage, the stage of genital heterosexuality. But Louise is prevented from making her transition. As Stekel points out,

> a heterosexual leaning on her part could have arisen only after successfully overcoming her moral inhibitions. She would have surely been responsive in the embrace of a man she loved if she had been married to him. She had no chance to submit herself to this test. Having been

> deprived of her virginity she lost, according to her own estimate, the chance of marrying and was reduced, she thought, to 'unlawful relations'. (Stekel 1967, 113)

By 'heterosexual leaning', Stekel means that the formation of a heteroerotic orientation could have 'leaned' on or been supported by the already established capacity for sexual pleasure evident in her infantile desire for the mother. This is, presumably, what happens to most 'heterosexual' women: a basis for sexual pleasure is formed through the intimate infantile relations with the mother, and heterosexualisation 'leans' on this basis, eventually leaving behind the maternal training ground, so to speak. 'Moral inhibitions' prevent Louise from making this transition, however: in her own mind, to have sex outside of marriage is to sink into sin, to become a prostitute. This fear inhibits her from experiencing sexual pleasure with a man, a pleasure she would, according to Stekel, surely have been capable of had marriage removed the moral inhibitions.

Yet, neither is Louise able to gain satisfaction from lesbian arrangements with women; so strong is the taboo on lesbianism, she quite consciously avoids all intimate contact with other women, her mother in particular. Instead, she pursues heterosexual liaisons with men, while at the same time defending against such 'unlawful' relations through the mechanism of her 'neurosis': 'Therefore her defense reactions [a reference to her bowel practices] fortified themselves. Her neurosis grew; a cure was almost out of the question' (Stekel 1967, 113). The olfactory-intestinal peristaltic desiring-machine is to be understood thus as primarily a 'defense reaction' to heterosexual enjoyment, rather than as a pleasure-producing mechanism in its own right.

It is worth noting that the peristaltic practices that were elaborated in such fascinating detail at the beginning of this analysis become less and less prominently referenced as Stekel continues. As soon as the psychoanalytic account of a heterosexualisation-gone-wrong takes hold, Stekel seems increasingly reluctant, or unable, to explore Louise's complex bowel habits with the same kind of thoroughness that characterised his initial description of them. Finally, in the concluding point-by-point summary of the case, an Oedipal schema takes over completely, and the intestinal aspect of the study drops out altogether. Stekel leaves us with the terse observation that 'the woman's anaesthesia had a fourfold root: 1. Homosexuality. 2. Moral inhibitions. 3. Hatred against the father. 4. Infantile fixation on the mother' (Stekel 1967, 113). Deleuze and Guattari's exasperated criticism of the tendency in psychoanalysis to 'make Oedipus the sole measure of desiring-production' seems apropos here, such that 'the entire process of desiring-production is trampled underfoot and reduced to (*rabattu sur*) parental images, laid out step by step in accordance with supposed pre-Oedipal stages, totalized in Oedipus' (Deleuze and Guattari 1983, 45–6).

While I would not want to trivialise the real mental pain Louise no doubt experienced as a result of her compulsive rituals, I also want to keep open the possibility of exploring the intricacies of her particular olfactory-intestinal desiring-machine. This would entail a new set of questions about a European woman's desire within a modernity understood as a metabolic system of flows and breaks, consuming and producing, hoarding and purging. Rather than treating her bowel rituals as symbolic symptoms of an underlying sexual pathology; rather than assuming that the question posed by desire is, as Stekel asks, 'What does it mean?', one might instead ask:

> 'How does it work?' How do these machines, these desiring machines, work – yours and mine? With what sort of breakdowns as a part of their functioning? How do they pass from one body to another? How are they attached to the body without organs? What occurs when their mode of operation confronts the social machines? (Deleuze and Guattari 1983, 109)

To ask how Louise's desiring-machine 'works' within the context of the kinds of 'social machines' I outlined in the first sections of this discussion is not to diagnose her, but rather to approach some understanding of what her intestinal routines produce for her, how they situate her within, alongside or in confrontation with the larger peristaltic systems of consumer capitalism. If to be properly heterosexualised, for instance, is to finally take up one's sexually destined position in the Oedipal scheme of things, it would appear that Louise's desiring-machine produces her precisely as the anoedipal subject, as never yet wife to a man, mother to a child – never yet inserting herself into the reproductive chain.[1]

Stekel characterises her as dominated by two 'tendencies' struggling for 'supremacy in her inner self: the longing for purity and a glowing yearning for sinful pleasure'; in other words, she can easily be classified with other 'frigid' women who are 'usually a combination of "prostitute" and "nun"' (Stekel 1967, 107). But surely Louise's relation to these well-worn stereotypical categories is an oblique one. She is also, as colonic subject, by turns costive and cleansed, the orchestrator of precise social arrangements for the production of regularity in her body, a metabolic system of schizzes and flows. Her identificatory impulses extend beyond 'human' models for existence. As Stekel reports, she 'read in a textbook that the muskrat protects himself against his ferocious enemies by emitting an obnoxious odor' (Stekel 1967, 107–8). Thus, 'in self protection and as a protection against others (from the dangers of intimacy) she developed her distressing bowel activity. It seemed to her impossible to trust herself alone with a man without endangering her virginity. As soon as she was alone with a man a few minutes, the muskrat function asserted itself' (Stekel 1967, 108). If Louise experiences a becoming-homosexual ('For Heaven's sake! Am I homosexual?'), a becoming-nun, a becoming-prostitute, she also experiences a becoming-oven (the 'warming up' and 'baking' before breakfast), a becoming-purged, a becoming-muskrat; all the while, her breakfast companions are, in relation to her, becoming-purgatives. While Stekel remains convinced that Louise's muskrat-function is primarily designed to protect her chastity, I would suggest that it is also, perhaps more importantly, the means by which she ensures the absence of her body from a very specifically defined architectural space.

What spaces, after all, has Louise occupied in her thirty years? She has moved from the domestic familial space of her family (where already her siblings and parents were experienced more in terms of their purgative value than as Oedipal nodes), to the institutional space of the boarding school, to the hotel, the sanitarium, the boardinghouse, the Frenchwoman's apartment. Her intestinal desiring-machine has ensured, in other words, that she never take up residence in the domestic space of the suburban family dwelling, that she never assume her role as 'household engineer'. Her attraction to women and men alike, as well as the capacity of these 'anxiety objects' to smell the gas she emits, keeps not only intestinal but also domestic stasis at bay. To come to rest in the familial ménage would be to bring Louise's own metabolism to a complete stop, both internally and externally – while at the same time, it would be the means by which the metabolism of consumer capitalism is kept going. If the bathroom and kitchen have become the erogenous zones of the familial household, it is not Louise who will provide their maternal maintenance; if goods must be kept flowing regularly through cycles of consumption and waste, it is not Louise who will be facilitating their peristaltic movement through the domestic dwelling; if the peristaltic health of a capitalist economy relies on Oedipally placed female consumers whose sexual pleasure has been channelled through the proper sexual 'organs', Louise will remain somewhere on the periphery of this channelling, with intensifications happening along her internal organs, those not conducive to an efficient Oedipalisation.

If Marx had defined metabolic rift in terms of a broad-based breach in the metabolism between human and nature, it would seem that another kind of metabolic rift emerges as a deviation in the faecal habitus at the level of the individual. This rift entails not only a swerve away from a conventionally defined sexual development, but also away from a tacit trajectory meant to be taken by the middle-class European woman in the larger scheme of capitalist production and consumption. That this swerve is facilitated by the unconscious 'thinking' of the second brain, by an inner sphincter that has a mind, and almost a social life, of its own, points to a biological aspect of affective life that psychoanalysis, at least in Stekel's version of it, seemed unable to accommodate.

Unlike the 'abdominal women' I described in Chapter 5, Louise brought her peristaltic symptoms not to someone like Arbuthnot Lane but to a psychoanalytic doctor whose specialty was to cure 'frigidity' – or, in other words, to lead the way to sexual satisfaction for the patient. But what Stekel's work with this patient produces is insight into how sexual excitement can be deployed for peristaltic regularity.

My emphasis in this book is on the peristaltic vicissitudes of white women in a given historical moment. But I want to remark, by way of a corollary to this case, a differently inflected case in Alice Walker's fable about racialised pornography in *You Can't Keep a Good Woman Down*. The fable follows the relationship between a middle-aged man and his wife, both African American. In the opening episode, the husband comes home from a long day at work, greets his wife who has made dinner for him, but retires to the bathroom first, for the purpose of masturbating to a porn magazine he's brought home. 'He studies the young women – blonde ... with elastic waists and inviting eyes – and strokes his penis. At the same time, his bowels stir with the desire to defecate'. Ten minutes later he emerges, 'spent, relaxed – hungry for dinner' (42–3). When his wife comments that she feels erased by the white women in his porn, he brings home a Black-themed mag the next day, but it is no less unsettling to the wife. On the cover is a 'well-dressed black man, carrying a brief case'. But she can't quite make out what is at his feet: she has to turn around the magazine cover to make out that it is 'a brownskin woman like herself, twisted and contorted in such a way that her head is not even visible. Only her glistening body – her back and derriere – so that she looks like a human turd at the man's feet' (43). By the end of the fable, the husband comes to realise that while white women are at least depicted as human bodies, 'black women are depicted as shit', and moreover, that 'the black man is portrayed as being capable of fucking anything ... even a piece of shit' (52–3). The fable is a compelling account of how the porn industry, but also popular culture in general, is bred of a long history of sexualised racism in the United States, a history with which the husband needs to come to grips in order to experience sexual pleasure with his wife that is not dependent on an internalised racist self-image. But the fable doesn't address the other side of the masturbatory fantasy on the toilet: the fact that it seems to be the husband's route to peristalsis, to relaxing his inner sphincter muscle, and defecating. If he gives up the racialised masturbatory fantasies, how is he supposed to stay regular? His faecal habitus is as deeply imbricated in violent racist history as his sexual pleasure.

In the next chapter, a woman consults an internist to address her intestinal problems. But as we shall see, there is an unacknowledged erotic side to the repeated experiments they engage in together as they seek to establish the truth of her bowels. Their partnership in medical knowledge production leads to publications not only on the workings of peristalsis, but on the tertiary sexual characteristics in hysterical women.

## Notes

1   'In reality the problem has nothing to do with pre-oedipal stages that would still revolve around an Oedipal axis, but rather with the existence and the nature of an anoedipal sexuality ... the break-flows of desiring-production do not let themselves be projected onto a mythical locale; the signs of desire do not let themselves be extrapolated from a

signifier. . . But rather than ensuring, or tending to ensure, the reversion of the entire unconscious according to the anoedipal form and within the anoedipal content of desiring-production, analytic theory and practice never cease to promote the conversion of the unconscious to Oedipus, form and content' (Deleuze and Guattari, 74).

7

# The Creative Devolution of Reverse Peristalsis

### A London physician finds his patient

While Arbuthnot Lane was operating on women to remove the kinks that caused their intestinal stasis, and Wilhelm Stekel psychoanalysed his client's eroticised bowel habits to cure her Oedipalisation gone wrong, a London physician sought to reduce unnecessary surgeries in a patient whose peristaltic symptoms seemed hysterical rather than organic in nature. This chapter continues our focus on doctor/patient pairings in the domain of female peristalsis, as we turn to Dr Frederick Parkes Weber, who worked in a public hospital that catered to patients of German (and Jewish) origin living in London and treated a woman whose metabolic peculiarities raised the question of whether the human peristaltic system could function entirely in reverse. Parkes Weber's fascination with his patient Rosa Strosmann extended over several decades, resulting in a plethora of material that allows us to delve more insistently into the question of the ambiguity between what is experienced as the lived body, on the one hand, and its biological substrate, its 'grown-in tools', on the other. I put Parkes Weber's case studies of Rosa in conversation with the work of Elizabeth Wilson on the gut, particularly as she draws from Sándor Ferenczi on the dynamicism of the biology of the enteric system. If psychoanalysis posits an unconscious aspect to the 'first brain', then might we ask if the gut, as a 'second brain', is subject to the vagaries of its own 'unconscious'. This Ferenczian model of a biological unconscious enriches our understanding of a local metabolic rift in the faecal habitus of at least one Jewish woman in the British working class, a rift developed through her repeated consultation of a member of the medical establishment. Parkes Weber's sustained consideration of his patient's peristaltic feats leads him to speculate on a Darwinian theory of 'tertiary sex characteristics', traits that emerge over evolutionary time as a solution to combative tensions between the male and female of the species. Peristaltic hysteria or neurosis is at once the object of this doctor's study, but also the medium through which he himself plays out the early twentieth-century dynamics of tertiary sex characteristics, in his long-term relation to his patient.

Dr Frederick Parkes Weber had attended the Salpêtrière lectures near the end of Jean-Martin Charcot's life, and was keenly interested in cases whose symptoms could not be traced back to organic causes or lesions, and which therefore had to be categorised as hysterical. As a medical doctor practising in London, however, he did not seem to have shown an interest in acquiring training in Freud's talking cure, even in the years when other English doctors travelled abroad for analytic training with Freud's colleagues. It should be noted, however, that as a speaker and reader of German, Parkes Weber kept abreast of Freud's and others' publications on hysteria and neurosis throughout the 1910s, 1920s and 1930s.

Before delving into this physician's preoccupation with his patient, and their long-term association, I'd like to introduce Parkes Weber by way of a dream he recorded in the early 1930s, during a period when he published several articles emphasising what he (and most of his physician colleagues) considered to be the extravagances of Freudian explanations. In 'The Storming of the New Jerusalem: A Dream', Parkes Weber takes on the mock heroic persona of a Dante who, 'well on in the fourth quarter' of his earthly life (and after having read some of the *Divina Commedia*) is visited by a guide who shows him how those who seek the power of true knowledge attempt to find it by gaining admission to the 'City of God'. Parkes Weber is delighted and terrified to be conducted 'through the ether', to be shown the 'storming of the New Jerusalem', where he witnesses thousands of men falling back as they endeavour to scale the walls via ladders. After having visited the 'real gates of entry' through which only a few are permitted, he is taken by his host to a back door – which turns out to be the true focus of the article. Here it is worth quoting at length:

> He took me to a relatively dark portion of the walls, where was the city-cloaca. There stood a large notice, EXIT ONLY, but nevertheless

a small army of the besiegers was trying to gain entry that way. They constituted, indeed, a gallant body of men, though drenched in the mud, and defiled with faeces. The more difficult and extraordinary the path the greater praise does the endeavor deserve, they said, and to rally and refresh each other, they carried banners with all manner of strange symbols and slogans on them, many of which my guide told me hardly anyone could understand. I recognised most of the symbols, even if I could not always understand their special meaning. Some of the rallying words and expressions, such as 'Oedipus complex', seemed familiar to my ears, but others seemed to me altogether suggestive of insanity, for instance, 'anal sadistic patricide', or 'patricidal anal sadism', if I remember rightly. My guide, however, informed me that, strange as it at first sight seemed, some of this grimy band not only had gained entrance to the golden city, but had revolutionised and regenerated the whole study of psychology. He convinced me even that some of their names had become immortal in the minds and on the lips of grateful and admiring men, and so he left me. It was a dream. (Parkes Weber 1932, 217)

I need hardly emphasise that Parkes Weber's primary objective in the analysis of this dream is to cast it as an allegory for the perplexing success of psychoanalysis. Why, despite its 'grimy' preoccupations, has it earned the praise of so many admiring men?

The article was a hit among his fellow British physicians, attracting jovial and punning follow-up letters, one advising him against letting his 'clean mind' dwell too much on the prurient. But this image of a city under siege, being penetrated via its cloacal orifice (whose proper use is EXIT ONLY), tells us as much about Parkes Weber's own personal and professional anxieties as it does about the extravagances of the talking cure that had come to flourish in the first half of the twentieth century. 'I do not know whether anyone will think it worth while making a psychoanalytical study of my dream!' he writes, before offering up his own pithy interpretation. The exclamation point, meant to serve as a challenge to anyone who dares to assail his psyche via his dream images, functions also as a sort of apotropaic barrier to such an attack. 'Just try it!' this mode of punctuation seems to say. You, too, will end up looking like one of those besiegers, so 'defiled with faeces'. But as we will see, Rosa Strosmann, a patient whom he first met in the 1890s, treated on and off until 1913, and about whom he was still thinking even after the Second World War, would have made it difficult for Parkes Weber to completely distance himself from those dabblers in anal sadism.[1]

## The metabolism of scientific research

It should be noted that Parkes Weber had an extraordinarily wide range of medical research interests and published over a thousand articles on diverse topics. Although known as a generalist, he was highly respected for his contributions to the medical understanding of diseases of the chest, to pathology and to dermatological conditions, among other domains of medicine. That he made it a practice to 'collect' rare and unusual diseases, of which 'his "profound knowledge and phenomenal memory" was internationally renowned', accounts no doubt for the plethora of materials he amassed on conditions, like Strosmann's, that had no observable organic origin (Hall 2001, 524). Rosa's symptoms were not the only ones he researched, documented and ruminated on with an insatiable appetite for accumulation, but they were, because of their peristaltic aspects, perhaps the closest allied with his own professional hoarder's sensibility.

Anyone who consults the Parkes Weber collection at the Wellcome Archives in London is first and foremost struck by the disordered voluminousness of his papers. As curator Lesley Hall has put it:

> The accretional method by which the collections and bundles were built up can be clearly seen ... where an initial description has been added to, further information inserted over time, and in fact Parkes Weber appears to some extent to be conducting a dialogue with his own earlier conclusions. This accumulative procedure can also be seen in his case-notes, in particular in the volumes of his longhand reports on consultation with and observations of his private cases. Parkes Weber added for reference cuttings as well as related correspondence, and this close relationship between his own clinical observations and his perusal of contemporary literature was similarly manifested in his collections – on very diverse medical subjects. (Hall 2001, 528)

Considered from a peristaltic perspective, we can say that a pattern of intellectual ingestion, accumulation, absorption and production characterises the life of anyone devoted to research and publication. But in Parkes Weber's case, this process was so enthusiastically pursued, and with so little concern for the kind of regulated digestion and 'waste disposal' that might bring a more patent scientific orderliness to his papers, that the messy bundles he deposited at the Wellcome, near the end of his life, attest to the intimacy between scientific pursuit and the vicissitudes of the body's somatic processing of the world. Parkes Weber himself confessed that 'the bundles had become "gradually very extensive, and many of them have become dislocated and unmanageable", so that "sometimes there is a good deal of disorder"'. If in earlier years his 'accumulations' had 'been bound up in volume format, most of them were [now] in envelopes which had become increasingly tattered and strained over the years, some of which had completely disintegrated, scattering loose papers' (Hall 2001, 528–9). Put another way, it is as though the ratio of input to output, of data-gathering to publishing, is overwhelmingly on the side of intake, despite Parkes Weber's extraordinarily distinguished professional publishing record; the storing up, the accumulation, the hoarding of precedents, data, related conditions, far outweighs the capacity to impose order on what came in, so that even the 'enveloping' attempts to keep similar papers together failed, as the casings through which the evidence flowed burst and expelled their contents.

The 'Rosa' bundles are no exception to this rule: in 1904, for example, Parkes Weber published a comprehensive study of Strosmann's condition in the London neurological journal *Brain*. (This was one of at least seven published papers by Parkes Weber based on Rosa Strosmann – in addition to at least two more by other doctors whom she consulted.) He kept a bound offprint of this article, and over the next several decades, packed its margins with additional handwritten, precisely dated notes about subsequent encounters with his patient, or reports from other doctors who had seen her; he pasted in clippings on related topics, published before and after 1904, and also appended additional dated notes jotted onto envelopes or scraps of paper, or correspondence from colleagues that might have bearing on the case. The pages of the original offprint thus swelled and thickened, far exceeding the width of its binding, the paste and paper contents crinkling like so much *papier mâché*. To proceed through the article from start to finish is to encounter a palimpsest of notations, and to enter a bewildering temporal realm, dates referring backward and forward in time with no perceivable logic. It wasn't that Parkes Weber suffered from intellectual constipation or diarrhoea; it was rather that what had become, by the early twentieth century, an ideal of peristaltic regularity, underwent, in the form of this doctor's practices, a kind of libidinal capaciousness and temporal disorder.

Parkes Weber's files insist that we consider, for a moment, what might be called the 'metabolism' of scientific research, or of any research, for that matter. In the collecting of measurements, of observations, of experimentation with the human body in a clinical context, let's say; in the arranging of data to correlate with or to challenge other data; in the publication of findings, as raw material is prepared for a public sphere, we can say that some researchers have a more efficient metabolic system than others, with little waste, and much transformation of ingested material into processed, usable knowledge. By the same token, a less efficient metabolism involves the obsessive collection of voluminous materials, with very little transformation of what is ingested into published documents. And yet, who is to say what the ratio of accumulation to metabolised data should be, and whether the undigested material to be found in archives such as the Wellcome is to be thought of as useless waste or precious evidence, whose time has not yet come?

## The working woman in the urban metropolis

In 1896, twenty-two-year-old Rosa Strosmann (née Abraham) received a devastating shock on her wedding night. We don't know whether or not this resident of London's East End, where the city's working-class Jewish population was concentrated, consummated her nuptials with Mr Strosmann. But what we do know is that on that night, her new husband coughed up a quantity of blood, and died soon afterwards, likely from tuberculosis, which had reached epidemic proportions by the late nineteenth century (Parkes Weber 1904, 171). From this night, Rosa, who had been 'quite healthy up until the time of her marriage', suffered the first set of symptoms that brought her to Parkes Weber, an attending physician at the German Hospital in Dalston; together, doctor and patient, professional and working class, engaged in a series of what we might call visceral communications that persisted, on and off, for the next fifteen years, and about which Parkes Weber continued to publish until his 1950 paper reflecting back on the case, long after losing contact with his patient.

Rosa Strosmann, in her collaboration with Parkes Weber, offers what I want to suggest is an instructive model of the modern peristaltic subject as she is situated within, and defines herself through, an overarching urban metabolism. That the human body might be understood as functioning like a component in a vast, complex metropolitan organic system was nowhere more succinctly suggested than in Georg Simmel's well-known 1902 essay 'The Metropolis and Mental Life': 'Man does not end with the limits of his body or the area comprising his immediate activity,' he writes. 'Rather is the range of the person constituted by the sum of effects emanating from him temporally and spatially' (Simmel 1950, 419). The temporal aspect of this implication in a larger series of flows and stoppages was understood by Simmel and others to have intensified by the turn of the century:

> the technique of metropolitan life is unimaginable without the most punctual integration of all activities and mutual relations into a stable and impersonal time schedule.... Punctuality, calculability, exactness are forced upon life by the complexity and extension of metropolitan existence. (Simmel 1950, 413)

If, as Simmel puts it, the 'individual has become a mere cog in an enormous organisation of things and powers which tear from his hands all progress, spirituality, and value in order to transform them from their subjective form into the form of a purely objective life', then one feels all the more acutely the need to summon the 'utmost in uniqueness and particularization, in order to preserve his most personal core. He has to exaggerate this personal element in order to remain audible even to himself' (Simmel 1959, 422). Before sharing the details of Rosa Strosmann's remarkable attempts at 'particularization', I want to sketch out a relevant aspect of the 'enormous organization of things and powers' that marked city life in turn-of-the-century London: the ongoing debates about whether and where public lavatories should be provided for the use of women as they circulated about the city.

By the late nineteenth century, public conveniences had been built, mostly for men, but some for women, too, in many commercial districts of the city. In order to be financially viable, most of these facilities charged for the use of toilets in private, locked stalls, though in the case of the men's lavatories, free urinals were always available. This meant, of course, that though men could relieve themselves at no cost, women always had to 'drop a penny', except in rare cases where a 'free' stall was included for use of the poor. Even at a penny a go, the cost was prohibitive for the masses of working-class women going to and from factories and other places of employ (Penner 2001, 42). Architectural historian Barbara Penner offers a detailed account of a dispute over a proposal to construct a women's public lavatory in the Camden Town district of London in 1900 – a dispute that typifies the discursive tensions around the metabolic infrastructure of the city. The district vestrymen had received a visit from local residents and omnibus proprietors, opposing the location of a women's lavatory at Park Street and Camden High Street, ostensibly because it would lower property values and impede traffic. One opponent claimed that the presence of a Park Street lavatory would offend ladies passing through the area, though he 'seemed to find it unremarkable that for years they had endured the sight of a gentleman's convenience at the very same intersection, without suffering any obvious ill effects' (Penner 2001, 41). A representative of the omnibus trade argued against the convenience on the grounds that 90 per cent of the women passing through actually lived in Camden Town, and thus could avail themselves of their own facilities at home (Penner 2001, 41). This comment was countered by the sole vestrywoman to be represented in the debate, who asserted that 'a women's convenience near Park Street was desperately needed for the "thousands of women and girls on their way to and from the factories of the district"' (Penner 2001, 41), and indeed, none of the other vestry members attempted to 'deny the sheer volume of women in the streets' (Penner 2001, 41). They, in fact, pointed to 'congestion' in the streets as a reason *not* to go through with the proposal, since a public lavatory might impede the free circulation of traffic. This argument raised the prospect of competing streams: women passing through the area would not be permitted to relieve the 'congestion' of their own internal flows, due to the external congestion of vehicular circulation.

Penner points out that it was disingenuous to imply that women who lived nearby had access to toilet facilities at home. 'Only middle- and upper-class residences of this period were regularly equipped with water-closets and baths: . . . working-class housing would not regularly enjoy such facilities until the 1920s, relying instead on chamber pots, outdoor privies and common urinals' (Penner 2001, 41). The bourgeois faecal habitus had not, as yet, been fully extended to the proletarian class, and given the dearth of public facilities for women, even less to women engaged in meta-industrial labour.

Underlying the explicit objections to the Camden Town toilets (property values, traffic obstruction) was most likely an unexpressed ambivalence about the public nature of such amenities – the intimate association of the lavatory, as Penner puts it, 'with the female body, as the container of its natural functions: urinating, defecating and menstruating. Owing to its provocative corporeal associations, a female lavatory [as opposed to a male] evoked the spectre of sexuality which ... encompassed a nebulous constellation of issues above and beyond sexual conduct itself' (Penner 2001, 45). Indeed, when vestrymen decided to postpone the building of the Park Street facility in favour of seeking out a nearby house where women could relieve themselves, the solution was put in the following jocular manner: that they would find 'a suitable house for the use of ladies' – provoking laughter at the sexual double entendre. 'The easy slip from lavatory to brothel,' Penner remarks, 'betrays the most extreme prejudice of the concerned citizens, the Vestry, and of women themselves: that, in using a public convenience, women would be little better than "public" women, prostitutes, who exposed their bodies in the streets' (Penner 2001, 45).

What I want to emphasise about this debate, though, is not so much the discursive shape it took in published accounts of the vestry's proceedings, but its embodiment in a form of aggressive street theatre. To test the safety and viability of the lavatory, a wooden model was erected on site, to be observed throughout the day. In that period of time, it was struck 'an incredible forty-five times, causing several accidents and very nearly a serious casualty,' as reported by the representative for the bus company. But George Bernard Shaw, himself a vestryman in the district, offered a different account of events:

> In one day every omnibus on the Camden Town route, every tradesman's cart owned within a radius of two miles, and most of the rest of the passing vehicles, including private carriages driven to the spot on purpose, crashed into that obstruction with just violence enough to produce an accident without damage. The drivers who began the game were either tipped or under direct orders; but the joke soon caught on, and was kept up for fun by all and sundry. (Penner 2001, 35–6)

The men Shaw accused were not 'mere pranksters involved in a spontaneous joke', but respectable citizens whose indirect opposition delayed the resolution of the debate, so that public lavatories would not be installed for another five years (Penner 2001, 36). The question of where women, in particular, could be permitted to void their bowels was thus debated not only in popular print venues, but in a performative vehicular argument carried out in the streets. A threatening spectacle was conjured: should a woman enter the proposed public convenience, raise her petticoats and make a contribution to the city's sewer system, she risked injury or death from the omnibuses and carriages that would likely, at any moment, plough into the structure that inadequately sheltered her. Implied is a distinct disciplinary lesson: if the 'technique of metropolitan life,' as Simmel puts it, requires 'punctuality, calculability, exactness' of every modern subject, it would seem to be all the more intensely required of London's working-class woman, whose calculations about when and where her waste might be eliminated were bound up with the very traffic patterns of the city. Simmel's idea that 'from each point on the surface of existence ... one may drop a sounding into the depth of the psyche so that all the most banal externalities of life finally are connected with the ultimate decisions concerning the meaning and style of life', this image of 'sounding' an interiority resonates with the biosciences of the era, and their concern to plumb the depths of the organic interiority of the body – its major organs, its viscera and, above all, its nervous system – a system so subtly modelled that it continually gets caught up into the liminal space between the physiological, the social and the psychological (Simmel 1950, 413). What could be a better example of Simmel's 'banal externalities of life' than the daily necessity of ridding oneself of the body's waste products? This 'banal externality' of defecation is linked also to one's most intimate depths, the depths of the nervous system that regulates the viscera, and that determines the velocity – and, it turns out, the direction – of the world as it literally moves through one's gut, as well as the periodicity at which one lets go of it, and the appropriateness of the 'spatial and temporal' locality where the world will be reunited with itself.

### Reverse peristalsis

Now that we have considered this glimpse of London at the turn of the century, its working-class women moving in masses through the streets, travelling from home to work to shops, an official uncertainty hanging in the air about where their waste should be eliminated, we may return to Rosa Strosmann, who made her way to more than one hospital after her traumatic wedding night. In 1896, she at first comes to the German Hospital, where Parkes Weber is a resident physician, and presents her symptoms to him, as well as to other attending physicians. After two laparotomies show nothing amiss, she is discharged, but immediately presents herself at the London Hospital. After some tests, and yet another laparotomy, she is discharged again, and she winds up back at the German Hospital soon after, where she is treated on and off by Parkes Weber until 1904. The symptoms, as reported by Parkes Weber, are as follows: 'Vomiting (sometimes with a little blood), distension of the abdomen, and great constipation... The vomiting persisted on and off. At one time there was undoubtedly faecal vomiting. Actual scybala or formed faeces from the large intestine were certainly vomited on more than one occasion' (Parkes Weber 1904, 171).

What made Rosa Strosmann an extraordinary, rather than ordinary case for study was this presence of 'formed faeces' in her vomited matter. This vomited faecal matter immediately interested Parkes Weber as medical researcher, suggesting, as it did, that it might be possible to reverse the direction of one's peristaltic system, not just from the stomach upwards (as with normal vomiting), but along its entire length. But several investigations had to be carried out before this vomited scybala could be submitted as the evidence of a medical discovery. Parkes Weber had to prove that what emerged from Strosmann's mouth during her vomiting episodes was fully formed faeces that had truly travelled, in reverse, almost the entire length of her peristaltic system – that is, from her large intestine to her mouth. This involved ruling out two alternative explanations for the symptoms she presented, one of them organic in nature, the other, a case of fraudulence. Her doctors, both at the London Hospital and at the German, first try to determine whether there has been a 'fistulous communication between the colon and stomach or duodenum' – that is, a lesion or opening through which the contents of her large bowel could have moved directly into the stomach, thus by-passing the peristaltic motions of the small and large intestines – or in other words, taking a short cut. Laparotomies showed 'no abnormal condition whatever' (Parkes Weber 1904, 172). The symptoms, in other words, had no organic origin in the gut itself that the doctors could detect.

But it was also necessary to rule out another alternate path by which the faeces could have found their way into Strosmann's vomited material, and indeed, in his reading of prior cases, Parkes Weber found many an instance where, for example, an apparent faecal vomiter was found to have 'some hard faeces wrapped in paper' under her pillow (Parkes Weber 1904,182). It had to be proven, in other words, that Rosa Strosmann was not consciously and deliberately simulating her condition. To this end,

> In order to guard against imposture and to obtain an accurate diagnosis, an enema coloured with methylene blue was administered by the nurse. Some of the methylene blue appeared in the vomited matter within ten minutes after the administration of the enema. Any deception on the patient's part was altogether impossible. (Parkes Weber 1904, 171)

What this proves, in the emerging language of non-organic pathologies, is that Strosmann was not merely 'malingering' – that is, consciously simulating illness for some form of gain (or at least not yet) – but was truly engaged in what Parkes Weber termed '(neurotic) actual faecal vomiting' or 'hysterical faecal vomiting' (Parkes Weber 1904, 183). The terms neurotic and hysterical signified that the vomiting was not due to an organic ailment, and the designation 'actual' meant that the vomiting was not feigned.

By 1904, news of Freud's psychoanalytic method of treating hysterical somatic symptoms had barely begun to circulate within the English medical establishment. Though it is probable that Parkes Weber, as a German speaker, had access to the earliest of Freud's publications in German (his and Breuer's co-authored *Studies in Hysteria*, for instance), it would not have been likely, once he had diagnosed his patient as a hysteric, that he would begin treating her with the talking cure. And yet, it would seem that he saw the trauma of her husband's death after a violent expulsion of vital matter from his mouth as akin to what Freud might have called the 'ideational content' of the somatic reaction in Rosa Strosmann's own body – otherwise he would not have mentioned it. I will come back to this acknowledgement of a psychological shock, followed by indifference to its significance, but first let's consider what Parkes Weber set out to accomplish in this case study.

Drawing from no fewer than fifteen similar cases of faecal vomiting that appeared in the medical literature of the 1880s and 1890s, Parkes Weber offers a composite 'typical history' of this rare 'symptom complex':

> The patient, generally a young woman, but sometimes a man or a child (of either sex), may seemingly be in blooming health before the attack. Some distressing mental emotion or other physical or psychical shock is followed by a period of great constipation, and this constipation is accompanied or followed by meteorism (hysterical tympanites [i.e. a swelling of the abdomen]) and abdominal pains. There may be severe attacks of vomiting and even some haematemesis [vomiting of blood]. The constipation becomes absolute and the other symptoms get worse, and finally the condition of 'hysterical ileus' [i.e. hysterical intestinal obstruction] is reached. Then everything taken by mouth is returned. The vomit becomes faecal in character and even pieces of formed faeces may be ejected by the mouth. Enemata and suppositories may likewise be vomited. (Parkes Weber 1904, 183–4)

It is instructive to recast this account in terms of its documentation of how a 'natural' directionality of the flow of things becomes completely reversed. We begin with the individual 'in blooming health', which is to say, occupying an unremarkable position with regard to the intake of food, its flow through the peristaltic system, and its ejection at regular intervals through the proper channel. A shock occurs – mental or physical – resulting in an internal blockage of this movement: 'a period of great constipation'. The patient may still be taking in nutrients through the mouth, in other words, but these substances only travel so far through the peristaltic system until they reach a point of stasis, and nothing emerges from the other end. Now, all that has been ingested begins to collect inside the body, as evidenced by the swelling of the abdomen. In time, the motion from mouth to obstruction is reversed, and vomiting commences: anything 'taken by mouth' is returned at this point, while stasis still characterises the peristaltic system below the obstruction. Eventually, the contents of the vomited matter become more faeculent, until fully formed faeces appear, indicating that now, even below the point at which obstruction has occurred, motion has been restored, although in the wrong direction. Section by section, from the oesophagus to the stomach, to the small intestine, to the large intestine, the musculature of the peristaltic tube reverses its autonomic contractions so as to move the contents upward toward the mouth, rather than downward towards the anus. Finally, attempts to introduce nutrients into the mouth are abandoned, replaced by the insertion of substances into the anus (i.e. 'enemata and suppositories' administered, presumably, by medical personnel). A complete reversal has thus been achieved, and motion along the full length of the peristaltic system restored; now, however, it begins at the anus and ends at the mouth.

Reading through the many cases quoted by Parkes Weber to build his composite model (they take up a full third of the article), one is struck by the ingenuity of the nurses, doctors and researchers in their efforts to prove or disprove the authenticity of the reversal of the peristaltic flow: 'an enema of coffee was partially returned by the mouth fifteen minutes after its introduction per rectum'; 'a coloured substance was injected into the rectum to settle all doubts on the question, and twelve minutes afterwards some of it appeared in the vomit'; 'intestinal movements were increased when an enema was administered, and ceased after it was vomited'; 'the faecal masses which were vomited on one occasion were coloured blue by some henna, which had been administered in the form of an enema'; 'Indigo administered with an enema was ejected, together with faeces, from the mouth in less than fifteen minutes'; 'The patient was carefully watched, so that deception could be excluded, and yet nine minutes after the enema was administered she vomited a feculent mixture of milk coagula with indigo'; 'Bregman, who was often present during the attacks, was able to exclude trickery'; 'Nothnagel showed that coloured salt solution injected per rectum could be carried by antiperistalsis through the ileo-caecal valve into the small intestine, and Grutzner thought that small particles of charcoal, when injected as an enema suspended in salt solution, could under favourable circumstances reach the stomach within a few hours'; 'in two girls who were being fed by nutrient enemata ... some of the material used for the enemata must have found its way by antiperistalsis to the stomach'; 'a large nutrient enema of hot milk and brandy was given.... The patient afterwards began to throw up uncurdled milk, evidently derived from the enema' (Parkes Weber 1904, 176, 177, 181, 182, 187, 188). By the time he came to write his 1950 follow-up article, Parkes Weber had added a few more, the most striking perhaps coming from the earliest published account, dating back to the fifteenth century: a twelve-year-old girl who vomited 'suppositories introduced into the rectum ... "in the time it takes to say a paternoster and an ave maria"... When an attempt was made to keep a suppository in place by a string, the string broke and it was speedily vomited. Another one was attached by four strings, but these strings also broke'. Not even the girl's mother, who is enlisted (but fails) to 'hold a suppository in the rectum and keep it there', is able to prevent the vigorous display of reverse peristaltic action (Parkes Weber 1950, 122).

Taken together, these accounts build up a picture of a striking cooperative arrangement between patients and hospital personnel; if at first the patient appears to have reversed the normal course of things on her own, very soon doctors, nurses, researchers, even family members join in the enterprise, volunteering to facilitate the transit of substances from anus to mouth, all the while verifying and documenting the process. On the one hand, this collaboration seemed to have been essential to guarantee the authenticity of the phenomenon. On the other hand, as Parkes Weber well realised, it was this very libidinally charged professional excitement around the patient that could produce the phenomenon in the first place – as with the hysterical patients that Parkes Weber had witnessed during Charcot's lectures at the Salpêtrière.

Parkes Weber tries to limit himself to one carefully chosen aim in his 1904 article on Strosmann's condition: to solve the physiological riddle of whether the peristaltic system can really operate in reverse. If doubt about the matter has dominated the literature to the end of the nineteenth century, his patient's symptoms, along with a careful review of other cases, finally allows him to conclude with a resounding affirmation: anti- or reverse peristalsis is most definitely possible. But then he must answer the question as to what is the source of such reversed peristalsis; it is unlikely, he says, when there is some weakening or an organic disturbance somewhere along the peristaltic tube itself, and all its components. Much depends on the 'ileo-caecal valve', i.e. the valve that permits substances to exit the small intestine into the large intestine in normal peristaltic action. Is this a one-way valve, marked 'EXIT ONLY', or will it permit, under some circumstances, the entry of

## The Creative Devolution of Reverse Peristalsis 161

substances in the opposite direction? Parkes Weber surveys the options: 'It is possible that in cases of faecal vomiting the backward passage of the intestinal contents through the ileo-caecal valve may be due (1) to acquired incompetency resulting from forcible distension of the colon [i.e. too much faecal matter backs up in the colon, pushing so hard against the exit door that it makes its way back into the small intestine] or (2) it may be due to congenital incompetency, the valve having retained its infantile type (like the muscular sphincter of lower animals), or (3) it may be due to opening of the valve by muscular action connected with antiperistaltic movements in the colon' (Parkes Weber 1904, 185). Previous cases offer conflicting evidence, but Parkes Weber finally opts for number three, and concludes that 'in spite of what surgical text-books say ... the most typical cases of faecal vomiting are due, not to organic obstruction in the large intestine, but to intestinal contraction and antiperistalsis of nervous origin' (Parkes Weber 1904, 186). One doesn't find true formed faeces in the small intestine in the case of 'organic obstruction', for instance, only faeculent matter. 'Violent antiperistaltic movements are probably required before pieces of formed faeces can be passed up from the colon through the ileo-caecal valve, and violent movements are more likely to occur in a gut with normal muscular walls than in a gut weakened by disease and over-distension; in fact, violent antiperistalsis sufficient to produce the passage of formed faeces through the ileo-caecal valve is more likely to be due to nervous derangement than to organic disease or obstruction of the gut' (Parkes Weber 1904, 187).

Organic disease and obstruction of the gut having been ruled out, Parkes Weber must now answer the question heading his next section: 'What portion of the Nervous System is chiefly at fault in cases of Faecal Vomiting of Functional Nervous Origin?' (Parkes Weber 1904, 194). Support for the hypothesis that the location of the 'fault' is in the brain itself can be found in the fact that when there is an organic disease or injury of the brain (tumours, concussion), vomiting will occur; likewise, when there is no 'gross change' in the brain (as with sea-sickness), not to mention when there are 'purely psychical causes (such as ideas connected with disagreeable smells and sights)' (Parkes Weber 1904, 194). Add to this the fact that 'patients with functional nervous vomiting mostly exhibit characteristic signs of hysteria [hemianaesthesia and the like]' and his belief that such symptoms are also 'of cerebral cortical origin', and one arrives at the idea that faecal vomiting, like any nervous vomiting, must also have a cortical origin. Parkes Weber here reminds us of Pavlov's experiments showing that 'mental conditions can have a great affect on appetite', and that 'anger, fear, and other emotions have been proved to influence peristaltic movements in the alimentary canal of cats and dogs' (Parkes Weber 1904, 195). If the 'almost physiological cerebral disturbances corresponding to ordinary fear or anger can thus influence the movements of the alimentary canal, how much more, I would ask, may the very pathological cerebral disturbances corresponding to the psychical states of hysteria be expected to do so?' (Parkes Weber 1904, 196).

As to 'why the vomiting in functional brain disease should be sometimes actually more violent and severe (faecal vomiting) than it is in organic cerebral disease. . . I cannot understand, unless it be that disturbance of function can show itself in a more pronounced form in a brain without any gross organic disease than it can in a brain the finer mechanism of which has already been impaired by severe organic disease, such as cerebral tumour' (Parkes Weber 1904, 196). The corollary of this may be found if the vomiter is compared to the paralytic: 'a delusion is apt to be less stable and not so well "organised" in a general paralytic, whose brain is the site of grave organic disease, than in a monomaniac, whose brain, could it be examined, would probably show no obvious organic changes' (Parkes Weber 1904, 196). Anti-peristaltic action so powerful as to bring faeces up to be vomited can only occur, in other words, when both brain and gut are organically healthy. Only the most robust, indeed one may say dynamic, biological substrate is capable of the violent peristaltic action it takes to get fully formed faeces to travel in reverse along the entire length of the alimentary system.

### Dynamic biology

Parkes Weber's insistence on the 'health' of the gut and the cerebral cortex (both conceived as part of the body's biology) as the essential foundation for faecal vomiting brings me to the question of how the condition was to be cured. What are the implications of the fact that Parkes Weber does not go down the path of psychoanalysis, that is, to devise a treatment around the presumed ideational link between mental trauma and its somatisation in the body? Even as late as 1950, he recommends more or less the same treatment regime he had followed in 1904, that is, bromides, strict isolation and 'mental antihysterical treatment' (which in 1904 included 'fresh air, ordinary personal hygienic measures and the persistent avoidance of alcohol, tea and stimulating drinks'), though in retrospect, he adds that 'nowadays, [i.e. in 1950] psychotherapy would be much more employed' (Parkes Weber 1950, 122). Parkes Weber does not elaborate on which psychotherapeutic method he is thinking of here, but it might be worthwhile to consider that Rosa (and the other examples Parkes Weber adduces) was the kind of patient whose symptoms, because of their location in the enteric system, would have been the perfect candidate for the experimental, more biologically inflected analytic treatment practised by Freud's colleague Sándor Ferenczi. As Elizabeth Wilson points out,

> As Freud was elaborating complex psychological (ideational) explanations for conversion, Ferenczi was becoming fascinated with the biological material itself: Can we explain the mechanism of hysterical conversion in biological terms? What does a hysterical conversion tell us, not only about the psyche but about the character of biological substrate? (Wilson 2004a, 71)

Ferenczi was particularly interested in afflictions of the digestive tract, such as 'globus hystericus' [the hysterical presentation of a lump in the oesophagus], swallowing air, conjuring a child in the intestines, and in fact hysterical vomiting. He seems less concerned about the ideational content of a symptom like a 'lump in the throat' (unconscious fellatio, etc.) and more curious about how the lump literally 'materialises':

> The patients themselves speak of a lump that stuck in their throats, and we have every reason to believe that the corresponding contractions of the circular and longitudinal musculature of the oesophagus produce not only the paraesthesia of a foreign body, but that a kind of foreign body, a lump, really is brought about. (Ferenczi 1926/1952, 92)

As confirmed by Parkes Weber's careful observations, his research into like cases, and even his participation in facilitating the backwards movement of substances through her body, Rosa

Strosmann's reversed peristaltic system was not just an imagined, or hallucinated, but an actual phenomenon; its origins might have been obscure, but its reality could be proven.

In a classical Freudian interpretation, the source of such a phenomenon would have been traced back to ideational content in the mind; through the analytic process, the ideational material might have been worked through in an effort to mitigate the incursion of unconscious or conscious affect into the proper domain of the flesh. Or as Wilson puts it, the focus of traditional psychoanalytic models of hysteria 'fell . . . on the ideational contortions that hijack bodily function' (Wilson 2004a, 76) and 'the goal of psychosomatic practitioners . . . was to rid the affected organ (e.g., liver, kidney, stomach) of its entanglement with the psyche' (Wilson 2004a, 77). She quotes Felix Deutsch, Freud's personal physician: 'What is really essential is to loosen psychosomatic ties, to purify the organs from their psychic cathexis, so to speak, and to assure their organic function unaffected by too strong libidinal forces' (quoted in Wilson 2004a, 77). In Rosa's case, then, a psychoanalytic aim would have been to purify her alimentary system of its psychic cathexis to whatever ideational content emerged (through the talking cure) as a precipitating cause.

But in Ferenczi's model, there can be no 'purifying' of an affected organ. The physiological transformation of the flesh suggests

> that an aptitude for condensation, displacement, connotation, repetition, or identification cannot be contained to the ideational realm (dreams, parapraxes, and so forth); these capacities are also part of the nature of the body's organs, vessels, and nerve fibres. The aid given by the musculature of the intestines is not that of passive substrate awaiting the animating influence of the unconscious but, rather, that of an interested broker of psychosomatic events. (Wilson 2004a, 73)

Moreover, materialisations in and through the flesh are not 'the effect of a leap from the mental to the somatic; rather, they are the product of a regression to a protopsychic state. That is, hysteria materializes the protopsychic (ontogenetic and phylogenetic) inclinations native to the body's substrata' (Wilson 2004a, 74). Here Wilson is explaining Ferenczi's 'reformulation of the metapsychology of hysterical conversion', which proposes an evolutionary model of human biology in which a desire to 'return to the womb' repeats a desire also to 'return to the water' from which, as a species, we were traumatically forced to emerge as a result of the 'recession of the oceans' after an 'aboriginal piscine period' (Wilson 2004a, 74). If our biology (as 'organic matter') is normally so 'solidly organized that it is not affected even by strong disruptive stimuli', it is nevertheless capable of being 'exploded' (in the sense that atoms explode) by overwhelming traumatic forces. Our very 'substance' in such circumstances 'recovers its psychic quality, not utilized since primordial times. In other words, the capacity to be impelled by motives, that is, the psyche, continues to exist potentially in substances as well' (quoted in Wilson 2004a, 74–5).

> In moments of great need [i.e. when suffering a trauma], when the psychic system proves to be incapable of an adequate response, or when these specific organs or functions (nervous and psychic) have been violently destroyed, then the primordial psychic powers are aroused, and it will be these forces that will seek to overcome disruption. In such moments, when the psychic system fails, the organism begins to think. (Ferenczi 1995, 6)

According to Ferenczi's logic, the classic division of the psyche into conscious/unconscious (where our 'conscious' motivation behaves according to logic, rationality and voluntary choice, and 'unconscious' motivation, according to desire, irrationality, involuntary impulse) finds a corollary in the substrate of our very biology. That is, the organism, too, can be divided into two registers, with the 'conscious' level thought in terms of 'utility for the preservation of life', and the 'unconscious' level, in terms that are not reducible to the functionality of survival. 'If biological substrate was studied dynamically, the excessive concern with the utility (rationality) of organs that characterizes traditional biological knowledges could be supplanted with a more intricate account of their capacity for pleasure, for the expression of wishes, and for complicated thought' (Wilson 2004a, 76). Or as Ferenczi puts it, the 'semisubstances' of our body 'would ... have the extraordinarily or wonderfully pleasing quality of being both body and mind simultaneously, that is of expressing wishes, sensations of pleasure-unpleasure, or even complicated thoughts, through changes in their structure or function (the language of organs)' (Ferenczi 1995, 7).

For Wilson, Ferenczi's model is of particular value for dealing with a symptomatology very much like the one we find in Parkes Weber's patient Rosa, though the 'antiperistalsis' Wilson focuses on is that of chronic bulimia, not of faecal vomiting. She quotes from Ferenczi's *Thalassa* (the book in which he elaborates his theory of a primordial phylogenetic longing for the piscine era) to open this section of her essay: 'behind the symptom of vomiting,' Ferenczi writes, one perceives 'not only its manifest immediate etiology but also tendencies towards regression to an embryonic and phylogenetic primevality in which peristalsis and antiperistalsis were mediated by the same digestive tube' (Ferenczi 1938, 86). Even the *normal* functioning of internal organs depends on what Ferenczi calls the operation of 'amphimixis' or intermingling of their functions, which can also be figured as a conversation or communication among organs. In this respect, for instance, 'the bladder acquires a degree of retentiveness from the rectum, the rectum a degree of liberality from the bladder – or scientifically stated, by means of an amphimixis [mingling] of the two eroticisms in which the urethral eroticism receives anal admixtures and the anal eroticism urethral' (Ferenczi 1938, 12). 'Without such interorgan exchange,' Wilson adds, 'the bowel would become hopelessly constipated and the urinary tract incontinent' (Wilson 2004a, 81). This admixture is a sign of the dynamicism (rather than flatness) of the organs themselves, especially as it spills over into genital eroticism, which 'conjures eroticisms from all the organs of the body' (Wilson 2004a, 81).[2] At the other end of the digestive tract, the 'gagging capacities of the fauces have borrowed from the pharynx and become more like swallowing; and ingestion has become a technique for expulsion rather than digestion' (Wilson 2004a, 81). More importantly, 'in chronic bulimia, episodes of binging and vomiting are often no longer directly tied to meaningful, analyzable events in the patient's internal or external world' (Wilson 2004a, 81). If bulimia is so difficult to treat, it is because, in Ferenczi's words, 'the organism begins to think' and the analyst has not yet learned the language in which it thinks (though pharmaceutical treatment seems to have an effect on it). And here, Wilson makes her intervention into what she sees as a failure of feminist theory, that is, a failure to understand biology itself as dynamic.

> Distress, anger, need, depression, comfort, and attachment have become primarily organic, and their capacity to respond to cognitively or ideationally oriented treatments is greatly reduced. My argument is that the bulimic capacities of the throat should draw our attention

not just to behavioral intent or cultural transformation or disorder in higher cortical centers or mechanisms of unconscious representation but also to the Ferenczian language of the digestive organs. The vicissitudes of ingestion and vomiting are complex thinking enacted organically: binging and purging are the substrata themselves attempting to question, solve, control, calculate, protect, and destroy. (Wilson 2004a, 82)

We may or may not want to go along with the postulation of a 'Thalassal' origin of the capacity of organs to communicate, think, desire, express, 'question, solve, control, calculate, protect, and destroy'. I am not entirely persuaded of the need to turn to a phylogenetic past to account for why the organism, far from a flat substrate, might act as an 'interested broker of psychosomatic events'. If organs 'think', or even more to the point, if they express affect in ways that exceed their strictly utilitarian purpose, why is it necessary to presume that they acquired this ability in a primeval past, but that it lay dormant until awakened by a trauma in this life that was remindful of the original trauma of a prehistoric life?

I agree with Wilson that we have much to gain by thinking of the organism as more dynamic than psychoanalysis may have given it credit for. But if we wish to think of hysterical somatisations as 'regressions' to an earlier state rather than as 'leaps' between psyche and soma, we needn't go beyond the experience of a single lifetime – or if we do, we might want to consider the vicissitudes of a much more recent historical past before we take recourse to an evolutionary primeval era. Where peristalsis alone is concerned, we have only to consider what happens in the course of the routines of toilet training, variable according to culture and era, but nevertheless always leaving its social traces, in the form of 'faecal habitus', on an autonomic system that, as it turns out, is not so autonomous after all.

Wilson sort of gets at this in her discussion of bulimia: having given us a glimpse of the effect chronic bulimia has had on the capacity of patients to swallow a 'nasogastric or an orogastric tube' (bulimics had no problem since their gag reflex could no longer be stimulated), she objects to the explanation that the reflex has simply been 'reconditioned'.

> Is the gag reflex a simple mechanical action distinct from psychic or deliberative impetus? Does its disconnection from higher cortical

centers (and so from conscious cognitive processing) render it a nonpsychological event? What is conditioning anyway? (Wilson 2004a, 80)

Let's consider these three questions as they might pertain to the complex peristaltic operation necessary for bowel movements: Is the moving of one's bowels *a simple mechanical action distinct from psychic or deliberative impetus*? If this is the case in the very earliest stages of infancy (when the baby excretes indiscriminately, according to the autonomic whims of the large intestine) it quickly becomes something else, even before efforts to 'potty train' the toddler take over. The rhythm of infant care, feeding, changing of diapers, bathing, cuddling, playing – all components of an external environment – most assuredly has the effect of attuning autonomic flows and ebbs to a social world. If a predictability, a regularity of intervals between bowel movements becomes evident, it may not (at the earliest stages) be a result of 'psychic or deliberative impetus', but it is certainly not a 'simple mechanical action' independent of external environment either. Arguably, communication has been going on at a pre-linguistic level, as the responsive autonomic system of the large bowel replies and relates to both the world that passes through it (ingested milk and later food) and the world that interacts with it.

Does excreting's *disconnection from higher cortical centres (and so from conscious cognitive processing) render it a nonpsychological event*? As we will recall from Michael Gershon's neurogastroenterological account of the brain/gut relation, the peristaltic system does, at some points in the alimentary tube, make decisions all on its own – that is, receives information, processes it and functions according to its own evaluation of the situation. Gershon calls this reflex action the 'thinking' of a second brain. But at other points, and particularly near the end of the tube, where the contents seem ready to make their way out, the autonomy of the system is not so clear cut: the 'higher cortical center' may have decided (given the availability of an appropriate place to excrete, and a felt internal pressure) that it is time for a bowel movement to occur. But if the inner sphincter, governed as it is by the gut's brain, not the 'first brain', refuses to relax, no movement will occur. I'm not talking about the kind of constipation due to lack of roughage in the diet, but the more mysterious kind, that seems to have to do with the second brain's whims about when to open the inner sphincter and propel the contents through.

The chapter on Stekel's patient, whose inner sphincter only deigned to open when she became sexually excited by a neighbour at the breakfast table, is just one example of how complicated is the brain/gut relation, especially when we consider that there is more than one 'brain' involved. And even if the movement is not governed by 'psychic or deliberative' activity by the first brain, it is plausible to imagine that such psychic and deliberative activity is going on in the second brain. Does this render the bowel movement a psychological event after all, even if some of the 'psyche' we are talking about resides not in the first, but in the second brain? If we ask now whether this is simply about the 'conditioning' of a reflex action, we might ask, as Wilson does, *what is conditioning anyway*?

In the case of the bowels, we might respond that there is no unconditioned bowel reflex in the first place – all excretion occurs in the context of 'conditioning', with the understanding that some of the conditioning is accomplished through linguistic means (once a child has learned language) but that most of this conditioning is pre-linguistic, and para-linguistic, accomplished through a plethora of rituals, rhythms, regimes and affectively imbued interactions between the infant and the other humans, animals, edibles, objects and architectural features in its immediate environment. If an aspect of the gut is disconnected 'from higher cortical centers', it is not, after all, disconnected from the immediate tactile, aural, visual, gustatory environment – an environment immediate to the process of its becoming.

Ferenczi had put emphasis on the relational or intersubjective implications of hysteria, that is, that the body's 'materialization' of somatic symptoms appeared in response to and as a communication with the social environment, including the doctor. Thus, as Wilson puts it,

> maybe ingestion and digestion aren't just metaphors for internalization; perhaps they are 'actual' mechanisms for relating to others. That is, perhaps gut pathology doesn't stand in for ideational disruption, but is another form of perturbed relations to others – a form that is enacted enterologically. (Wilson 2004b, 45)

I prefaced the details of Rosa Strosmann's symptoms with two related environmental contexts: the immediate spectacle of her newlywed husband who vomits blood and dies, right at the juncture where Rosa is prepared to enter the domestic routine of married life; and the more diffuse discourse, involving print media and crashing omnibuses, around the question of where or even whether women like her could respond to nature's call when circulating outside the domestic space. If the properly functioning peristaltic system was to serve as an assurance of the distinction between the 'natural time' of the indiscriminately excreting animal/infant and the 'cultural time' of the systematically excreting adult human being, it was also expected to confirm the uni-directionality of time, as evidenced by the productive transformation of food into fuel and waste, and the proper distancing of the point of ingress (the mouth) and the point of egress (the anus).

But Strosmann's peristaltic system, trained and mediated in the context of the London metropolis, responds to these imperatives by refusing to guarantee the forward 'progression' of bodily time. Moreover, once she brings this visceral response to the German Hospital, a staff of participants joins in to confirm and perpetuate her body's contradiction of time's peristaltic arrow. One could say that both patient and medical practitioners participate in a fantasy of 'turning back' through the reversal of the peristaltic flow – a return to a 'before', or an undoing of what time has accomplished, or the acting out of a principle of retreat or backtracking.

Parkes Weber establishes that her vigorous antiperistaltic performances meet the criteria of true hysterical vomiting: she has not feigned the condition by hiding faeces under her pillow, and laparotomies have revealed nothing organically amiss in her abdomen. As a medical doctor (not a psychologist) he mentions, but then leaves aside, the news that Strosmann's symptoms began only after the trauma of her wedding night. He does not consider that the source of the disturbance in her gut might be an 'organism' that 'begins to think', or that she is speaking to him in 'the language of organs', or that he is encountering a 'biological unconscious'. Through a sort of 'upward displacement' of the trouble, he proposes that the source is to be found in her 'cerebral cortical center', though no organic lesion would be found there any more than it would be found in her gut.

### Hysteria, malingery, athletic feats

If it is impossible to 'purify' organs of psychic influences, in the case of Rosa (and others like her), Parkes Weber finds that it may be just as difficult to discover a patient who is 'purely' hysterical. For almost as soon as the authenticity of Strosmann's condition is verified, she begins to slip out of the category of the *bona fide* hysterical patient, whose symptoms are produced unconsciously, and morph into the malingerer, who deliberately simulates disease for gain. Parkes Weber thus is unable to remain rigorously focused on the strictly psycho-physiological nature of his scientific paper (to prove the existence of anti-peristalsis) and finds himself wandering down a number of side pathways: that Strosmann shams a fever by tampering with a thermometer, for instance, throws doubt onto the whole credibility of her status as ill person, deserving of hospital care. Rosa Strosmann thus leads Parkes Weber to focus more than he would have liked on the finer distinctions among the categories of the organic, the functional, the hysterical and the voluntary condition of malingering, all entailing differing degrees of conscious, unconscious or organic 'will'. Each time he attempted to keep his patient in the realm of the strictly neurological (as a physician who sought to follow all somatic symptoms back to a 'functional' if not an 'organic' disturbance), she thwarted him at every turn.

In his search for other cases of faecal vomiting, Parkes Weber has run across more than one instance of fakery.

> In endeavouring to settle the functional nervous origin in a case of faecal vomiting it may be very hard to exclude simulation, which, however unnatural it may seem, especially in the absence of any intelligible motive, has sometimes certainly been practiced. Hysterical patients, like insane persons, are known to have swallowed faecal masses before vomiting them, or to have placed faeces and enema material in their mouths and then pretended to vomit them. (Parkes Weber 1904, 190).

In this case, the patients belong to 'the class of hysterical or neurotic simulation' (Parkes Weber 1904, 191). They seem to have no 'intelligible motive for their deception, unless to become objects of interest or sympathy, and they seem rather to invite than fear the big surgical operations that are likely to result from mistakes in diagnosis' (Parkes Weber 1904, 191). A solid diagnosis is further complicated by the fact that 'persons with functional nervous symptoms [a true hysterical faecal vomiter] sometimes afterwards simulate their old symptoms' (Parkes Weber 1904, 191).

It seems indeed as if the wish to simulate all kinds of frightful diseases and court dangerous surgical operations depended on an abnormal condition of the nervous system similar to those neurotic states which lead to genuine hysterical vomiting, &c. It seems also as if the interest excited by their illness amongst those around them sometimes acts as an inducement to neurotic patients to simulate symptoms which originally were genuine, especially those symptoms on which the medical interest obviously centres. The incessant cross-questioning and suspicion to which such patients are often subjected may sometimes, by making them think of the whole matter, indirectly furnish them with the suggestion to simulate. (Parkes Weber 1904, 192)

This certainly seems to have been the case with Rosa, he adds, who demonstrated true faecal vomiting, but then tampered with a thermometer and wilfully produced the distended abdomen of 'hysterical tympanites'. There is an interesting progression in these pages, from the establishment of a solid, proven hysterical vomiter of faeces to the faecal vomiter who is at first hysterical, but then whose 'simulation' of hysteria must cause her to be reclassified as a 'malingerer'. But the distinction between the true hysteric and the malingerer who is merely shamming her hysteria is a slippery one. Eventually Parkes Weber has to admit that there are cases where 'ordinary hysterical vomiting ought really to be regarded as on the borderland between hysteria and malingering' (Parkes Weber 1904, 193). This is because there are young women who seem to have a 'marvelous facility for vomiting' and can bring it on just by looking at food for which they have an aversion. They may cultivate this facility, to be able to vomit on cue, or they possess the 'power of voluntarily vomiting' in response to a psychical condition that they can induce at will. The physician can thus expect difficulty dealing with hysterical patients who are both 'gifted' with this power of vomiting and are 'at the same time desirous, as hysterical patients often are, of attracting attention to themselves by malingering if they cannot do so by other means' (Parkes Weber 1904, 193).[3]

It almost becomes impossible, in other words, to make a hard and fast distinction between the hysteric and the malingerer, when one is dealing with an autonomic function that has come under the influence of the first brain. This 'marvelous facility', troublesome though it may be for the physician attempting to categorise pathologies, nevertheless becomes a trait to be admired when encountered in Britain's colonial outposts. Pasted into this section of the 1904 article is a note that Parkes Weber made to himself dated 1925, in which he recalls an apparently well-known fact, that some Indians are capable of cleaning the large bowel by sucking water in through the anus and then discharging it again as often as they like, though he can't recall the special term for such 'gymnastic' operations. And here he copies out a passage from Edward Carpenter's *From Adam's Peak to Elephanta: Sketches in Ceylon and India*:

> We pride ourselves on our athletic feats, but some of the performances of the Indian fakirs in the way of mastery over the internal processes of the body – processes which in ordinary cases have long ago lapsed into the region of the involuntary and unconscious – such as holding in the breath over enormous periods, or reversing the peristaltic action of the alimentary canal throughout its entire length – are so astonishing that for the most part the report of them only excites incredulity among us, and we can hardly believe – what I take it is a fact – that these physiological powers have been practiced till they are almost reduced to a science. (Carpenter 1921, 169).

Parkes Weber does not comment on this, but it raises the question of whether the same facility for reverse peristalsis in his own patient could potentially confer on her, as it does (according to Carpenter) on the Indian fakir, the status of scientist – or at least, the status of one who has mastered an internal process so completely as to 'reduce' it to a science. Since this reference (via Carpenter) to the Indian fakir is pasted in among a plethora of articles about malingerers, it is difficult to say whether the fakir is to be pathologised alongside the malingerer, or the malingerer is to be revalorised via our astonishment over the fakir.

## Phylogenetic aspect of hysteria redux

It seems pertinent to mention that his work with Rosa, as well as at least one other patient exhibiting symptoms on the borderline between hysteria and malingering, led Parkes Weber to publish two overlapping articles in which he speculates about the evolutionary development of male versus female gender traits. In 'On the Association of Hysteria with Malingering, and on the Phylogenetic Aspect of hysteria on Pathological Exaggeration (or Disorder) of Tertiary (Nervous) Sex Characters', Parkes Weber carefully demonstrates where the Malingering Hysteric (or the Hysterical Malingerer) may be placed within a developmental schema that accounts for female versus male 'sex characters'. First, he lays out the difference between primary, secondary and what he calls 'tertiary' sexual traits, where primary refers to the sexual organs and secondary to 'breasts, facial hair, the features, the voice, the form of the skeleton', etc. The tertiary sex characters are where hysteria comes in, since they are 'dependent on the nervous system, including both characters of instinct and ... mind (reasoning)' (Parkes Weber 1911, 26). It is really this less obvious area of the 'tertiary' characteristics that he is concerned with in this and the article he published a year later ('Two Strange Cases of Functional Disorder, with Remarks on the Association of Hysteria and Malingering').

After first offering the caveat that, unlike primary sex characters, the tertiary are 'not the exclusive property of either sex' but may 'predominate' in one or the other, he presents his thesis that 'much of what is now grouped together as hysteria, may be regarded as a pathological exaggeration (or disorder) of certain tertiary (nervous) female sex characters' (Parkes Weber 1911, 26). Present-day hysterical simulations of organic conditions or diseases can be understood as 'exaggerations' of the tertiary sex traits that, in prehistoric times, were 'useful in regard to selection by the other sex'. Thus, functional muscular paralysis, spasms and hysterical convulsions as well as hysterical pains and paraesthesiae are exaggerations of 'the slight ailments to which the "weaker sex" are supposed to be naturally more liable than the "stronger sex" and which call for the sympathetic interest of the protecting males' (Parkes Weber 1911, 28). Or hysterical palpitation, pulse irregularity and vaso-motor disorders are understood to be exaggerations of things like the 'facile blushing' that is attractive to the opposite sex. And the 'well known suggestibility' of hysterics is 'an exaggeration of the tendency of the female mind to bend to the opinion of (male) authority, a tendency which when recognised as present is (or, has been) often gratifying (flattering) to the male' (Parkes Weber 1911, 28).

I will hold off commenting on the logic of Parkes Weber's argument here until we have occasion to examine another dream of his, in which it seems doubtful that 'ailments' in the weaker sex are likely to elicit 'protection' from the stronger. But I want to point out that the presentation of hysterical symptoms as exaggerations of normal tertiary sex characteristics is merely a preamble to the real preoccupation of this, and the subsequent article he wrote about gender. For he must admit that 'some functional nervous symptoms usually classed as hysterical are not readily explained by my conception of hysteria', like 'so-called "hysterical vomiting"', which seems to be 'a pathologically exaggerated action of the reflex defensive mechanism by which poisonous or irritating ingesta are normally rejected' [and not related to the sexual traits so crucial for selection] (Parkes Weber 1911, 31). Prior to this admission, he has put forward what seems to be a fifth category of tertiary sex characteristics, one which seems to embrace all of the former categories: that is, a tendency toward 'simulation or deception of various kinds' that was necessary in 'past ages (from early prehistoric times onwards)' and which 'must often have been serviceable to the weaker female in protecting herself from the stronger (and sometimes cruel) male, as well as in enabling her sometimes to get her own way by "getting round" her male partner' (Parkes Weber 1911, 29). Deception and mimicry, thus, would have to be understood as essential for 'survival of the fittest' in a 'barbarous age', and would gradually increase in females until it had 'become a tertiary sex character' (Parkes Weber 1911, 28–9). This observation then allows him to emphasise not the differences between, but the commonality of hysteria and malingering: both could be said to involve 'mythomania', or the simulation of 'disease, accident, or injury' (Parkes Weber 1912, 135). And here, malingering becomes subsumed under the category of hysteria, insofar as

> hysteria is frequently characterized by two kinds of simulation of disease, or 'pathomimia', ... (1) the unconscious mimicry of disease, so well referred to in the writings of Charcot, Sir James Paget, etc., to which the term 'neuromimesis' has been usually applied; and (2) the conscious, more or less voluntary, imitation of disease that may be termed 'hysterical malingering'. (Parkes Weber 1912, 135–6)

The vomiting of faeces, then, whether it be hysterical and real, or malingered and feigned, can be seen in this light as the exaggeration of 'an instinct which is normally greater in women than in men, the greater prominence in woman of the tendency or instinct to deceive constituting a normal psychical sex character' (Parkes Weber 1912, 138). This kind of deception is not 'acquired by means of memory and reason' but is an 'inborn or developmental' instinct which can only be eliminated through 'sexual selection and eugenics' (Parkes Weber 1912, 138).[4]

But the 'greater frequency of simulated diseases … in women than in men' was not only attributable to evolutionary instincts; Parkes Weber seemed to recognise that it was also a result of differing social conditions for men and women in the present moment, for he urged the reader to remember:

> that when a woman is depressed and altogether discontented with the life she has to lead she is more likely than a man would be to try to attract attention or pity by simulating disease or injury. A man usually has much more open to him; he can seek a new country or (if he does not endeavor to obtain relief by drink or gambling) he can take part in dangerous ventures of various kinds which bring excitement and temporary relief. (Parkes Weber 1911, 32)

Embedded in this image of the man, free to seek travel and adventure as a solution to his 'discontent', is the implied vista of faraway geopolitical lands, a whole world of colonial outposts, beckoning with transformative promise. A woman like Rosa, perhaps, if things were 'much more open' to her, and indeed, if she belonged to a different social class, might find relief in travel and dangerous ventures rather than the attention or pity she seeks in the many hospitals to which she brought her disturbed peristaltic system.

Parkes Weber was ambivalently suspended between these two explanatory models of Rosa's symptomatology, casting back to an evolutionary past to account for her exaggerated 'tertiary sex characters', even as he recognised that there were elements of present-day society that might reverse a woman's peristaltic system. I want to share one more dream of his, of which he included an unpublished, handwritten account in a file labelled 'Psychoneuroses, malingering etc. 1910–1949'. Though the dream is undated, it likely occurred in November 1912, since Parkes Weber remarks that he had just seen Max Reinhardt's *Sumurun*, which had returned to London for a reprise in the winter of 1912–13 (Styan 1982, 26–7). A classic orientalist pantomime, complete with scantily silk-draped dancers, a hunchback, bustling bazaars, harems in a palace, doors guarded by eunuchs, scimitars and minarets in the background, Reinhardt's fantasia of the 'East' was so evocative that 'the Times correspondent … found himself writing his notice like a pastiche of *The Arabian Nights* itself' (Styan 1982, 29–30). Under the title 'A dream of neurotics in past ages', Parkes Weber describes falling asleep under the influence of the Reinhardt play, and fancying that he is part of a group of London surgeons and physicians who are whisked away one winter on a magic carpet that transports them not only to a warmer climate, but to a pleasant world of eleven centuries ago, where they mingle with the pulsating life that resembles the Arabian Nights evoked by Reinhardt's play. He and his fellow professionals are shown the utmost courtesy, as though they are magicians or philosophers with superhuman knowledge. They even gain access to the harems of wealthy dwellers of this magical world, and although he refrains from describing the oriental filth and splendour he has witnessed, he does recall that they are able to cure many sick and ailing people they meet.

There is one class of illness that stymies them, however, to be found in the harems of both rich and poor. Here they encounter women afflicted with all sorts of nervous ailments, and who are nuisances to themselves and to everyone around them. What is striking about this scenario is that, far from eliciting protective or sympathetic reactions from their husbands, these women are treated by turns with kindness or with harshness, and are whipped as often as they are fondled. Parkes Weber and his colleagues can find no organic causes for the women's symptoms, though occasionally (remindful of Rosa) they would spit blood, which apparently came from their mouths or throats, and force clinical thermometers to rise as high as 110 degrees Fahrenheit. The physicians (like Parkes Weber) attribute the symptoms to hysteria, while the surgeons (like Arbuthnot Lane) attempt operations to correct moveable kidneys, but everyone is forced to return on the magic carpet before a proper diagnosis can be ascertained clearly.

Although Parkes Weber offers no interpretation of this dream, he has pasted onto the bottom of the page a 1911 letter to the editor in *T.P.'s Weekly*, in which an Esther Mullens remarks on an earlier letter in which the author has inexplicably defamed her own sex. Mullens decides that the previous writer must have 'dark blood in her veins unknown even to herself', a conclusion based on the many 'women of Eastern, Negro, and Indian descent' she has met who seem to hold the same opinion; moreover, a 'descendant of the Princess Pocahontas' whom she knows has 'no respect for her music master, because she knew it wasn't in him to strike her'. She concludes that in women who 'think they would like to be ruled', it has 'always been a case of atavism' (Mullens 1911, 538).

Both the dream and the letter to the editor participate in a model of the feminine rooted in the same fantasy of an evolutionary past that Parkes Weber wants to bring to bear on his classifications of hysterical symptoms – though with an added overlay of racialised difference thrown into the mix. The mention of 'atavism' to account for present-day women's desire to be ruled finds its parallel in Parkes Weber's estimation that an exaggerated tertiary sex trait in women would have been the 'well known suggestibility of hysterics' that finds its origin in 'an exaggeration of the tendency of the female mind to bend to the opinion of (male) authority, a tendency which when recognised as present is (or, has been) often gratifying (flattering) to the male'. At the same time, as though to reinforce the idea of a primitive past surviving into a contemporary present, Mullens asks us to imagine a panoply of racial and colonial others, all of whom exhibit this 'atavism', though it would appear that even someone who seems white on the surface might harbour 'dark blood' of the past in her veins.

But if Parkes Weber has conjured a feminised Orientalist past in which to set his fantasy of the modern wonders of (masculine) medical science, as though to carry out a dream investigation of his theories about the phylogenetic origins of hysteria, he comes away just as frustrated by what he finds there as he is by what Rosa brings to her encounters with him at the German Hospital. For he is no more enlightened as to the pathology of the harem women than he is when repeatedly confronted by Rosa's hysterical malingery in present-day Dalston. Moreover, it would seem that his dreamlife contradicts at least one of his assumptions about the evolutionary origin of those 'slight ailments to which the "weaker sex" are supposed to be naturally more liable than the "stronger sex" and which call for the sympathetic interest of the protecting males'. The husbands of the distant 'Arabian' past are just as likely to beat their hysterical wives as to be inspired by a protective impulse. Even Parkes Weber and his fellow men of science, split as they are between the scalpel-wielding surgeons and the physicians with their non-organic evaluations, are unable to extend a 'protective' hand to these suffering women, much less a cure.

## Occupational treatment

After her initial treatment at the German and other hospitals in London, and after Parkes Weber's comprehensive 1904 paper on her case, Rosa Strosmann was not heard from for a few years. She returned, however, in 1909 after having worked as a cook at a south coast boardinghouse, and seemed to be suffering from some of the same symptoms, though she was no longer bringing up faeces in her vomit. Parkes Weber kept detailed notes on her during her in-patient stay, and over the next few years, when she came for out-patient treatment until 1913. It was during this period that Parkes Weber wrote his 1911 and 1912 papers on hysteria and malingering as 'tertiary sex characters'. As one might guess, he was unable to carry out his suggestion that hysterical malingering of this sort might best be eliminated (if not actually treated) through a eugenics program that would somehow, thanks to calculated breeding practices, result in subsequent generations of women who no longer needed to exaggerate their otherwise healthy tertiary sex traits, so useful for finding suitable male counterparts. Or rather, he was not in a position to replace with scientific modes of reproductive coupling the outmoded breeding practices guided by women's Darwinian deceptive qualities. But on a more immediate level, Parkes Weber did devise an ingenious treatment for Rosa's condition, and although it succeeded only for a limited period, it is worth considering how it served as a 'reply' to the vociferous organ-speech of Rosa's reversed peristaltic system.

I want to mention, first, one more metabolic cycle that informed the doctor–patient relationship I have been considering here – i.e. the economy of the English hospital system, premised as it was through the nineteenth and early twentieth century on a combination of philanthropic systems and investment returns. The German Hospital was one among a very few in London that fed its Jewish patients through a Kosher kitchen, which in turn relied on regular contributions from organisations like the Jewish Board of Guardians. As one woman observed at a landmark 1902 conference of Jewish women philanthropists:

> I have already mentioned how gladly I would have given money for the adding of a Jewish wing to some existing hospital, but as I failed to obtain any sufficient assurance that our patients would be supplied

with strictly orthodox Kosher food, or would be allowed the free practice of their religion in these institutions, nothing remains but to create the supply for ourselves. It is our duty to lighten the burdens of the afflicted in sickness, and not to add fresh ones by asking of them sacrifices [i.e. being made to eat non-Kosher meals] which affect them deeply. ('Report' 1902, 26)

It would appear that such philanthropic organisations provided not only the flow of capital and perhaps foodstuffs to supply the Kosher kitchen, but also a sponsorship system that allowed the kitchen to be staffed by qualified cooks. As an interesting exchange of letters shows, to become an employee in the Kosher kitchen, one would be 'elected' or sponsored by the Board of Guardians; the labour force of the hospital was facilitated, in other words, by a flow of letters attesting to and guaranteeing satisfaction. The Kosher kitchen at the German Hospital was thus the nexus of a philanthropic flow of both financial capital and the less calculable currency of individual sponsorship.

I was struck, in reading the patient notes for Rosa on her return to the German Hospital after her hiatus at Bournemouth, that she supplied Parkes Weber with letters attesting to her gainful employment while gone. It did not seem customary for patients to bring such recommendations to their doctors, as though applying for a job; but Parkes Weber, it appears, had inquired as to her occupation while away, and a letter of reply is pasted into his patient notes affirming that 'Rosa Jackson [she had by this time remarried] was in my employ, as cook, during the time you state. I always found her very hard working. Yours, faithfully, N Goetz' (in Parkes Weber 1904–1951). Parkes Weber further observes that the

Patient has likewise (10 Jan 1910) shown me a certificate from Mrs. Goetz, 'Pinewood', St Peters Rd, Bournemouth, where she seems indeed to have given every satisfaction. It is dated June 2nd 1908 – 'This is to certify that Rosa Jackson has been in my employ here 18 months as cook, and previously at "Dr Butler's Head", Mason's Avenue, London, E.C. for 5 years as "vegetable cook" and for 12 months as "pastry cook", and after that she was for 4 years in my private house at Highbury. I have always found her honest, sober, hard working, very economical, and can thoroughly recommend her, in fact I am sorry to part with her' (signed N. Goetz).

But some light was shed on the presence of these letters of reference when, among the same patient notes, I found the following observation: that in Rosa's case, 'hypnotic suggestion might be tried, but I am rather against hypnotism from the practical point of view'. Instead, Parkes Weber decides, 'I think it will be better to try to interest her in the kitchen and praise her work'. And indeed, it seems that Rosa was soon after employed in the German Hospital's Kosher kitchen.

While it had become fairly common by this time to offer some sort of manual employment as a treatment for neurosis, I think the particular version of work therapy offered here is significant. For in order to intervene in Rosa's disordered internal enteric nervous system, Parkes Weber has come up with the solution of inserting her into the hospital's larger metabolic system, where she will prepare the alimentary sustenance that travels from the kitchen through the respective bodies that make up the hospital's Jewish clientele. If the problem is that Rosa has reversed her own peristaltic system, in a bid to occupy the hospital in the capacity of a patient, Parkes Weber attempts to reorient the flow in the correct direction by shifting her status to that of employee (facilitated by the letters from her previous employers). This solution worked only temporarily, however, and did not prevent Rosa from insisting that her body continue to enjoy the medical gaze of the professional practitioners. It would seem that the troubles moved from the inside to the outside of her abdomen during this period, as she complained that the scars from the most recent exploratory surgery that had been performed on her (several months prior) were refusing to heal. When it was discovered that she had been irritating her own scars by applying cantharides powder to them, Rosa was questioned as to where she had acquired the irritating substance. Her letter in reply (as well as another letter from a fellow cook in the Kosher kitchen) is the last document to be found in the Rosa bundles. Among Parkes Weber's extensive conglomeration of articles, hand-written comments, letters to the editor, communications from other physicians and scrupulously dated patient notes, all accreting around the mysteries of a reversed peristaltic system, this letter is a poignant one indeed, serving as the only direct expression of Rosa's take on the matter of her appearances over the years at the German Hospital. In the letter, she mentions having been refused medical attention by another doctor at the hospital because she has not divulged the source of the powder. She now points to a Mrs Rosen, a fellow cook in the Jewish kitchen, and apologises for not having earlier come out with the truth. 'Since I want the German Hospital very badly,' she adds, she has thus made up her mind to confess, adding that she meant no harm to the hospital, but only wanted to relieve her pain. She now awaits an answer, in hopes that the hospital will attend to her again.

The other cook responds with an outraged letter of her own, laying out her own history; as a widow for eleven years, struggling to bring up her children, she was given assistance from the board of governors, who eventually sponsored her so that she could be hired to cook for the Jewish kitchen. She denies ever having given the powder to Rosa, and if her veracity is doubted, she offers to show the references that were given to the Jewish Committee when she was elected to her present position at the hospital. The outcome of this dispute remains shadowy; but since Parkes Weber's patient notes end soon after this contretemps, it is safe to assume that Rosa was forced to take her symptoms, and her cooking expertise, elsewhere.

In the context of a reluctance to provide public conveniences for women to relieve themselves, Rosa Strosmann elected to bring her peristaltic system to the city's hospitals, on a regular basis, over decades; while most of the doctors she encountered were reluctant to welcome her, Parkes Weber not only oriented his discursive production of the normal and the pathological around her complex of symptoms, but found a logic for making her own habitation of the institutional space more like his own: though she continued in the status of a 'patient' receiving 'care' – she was also inserted into the hospital's labour routines, as a cook – and so became, like Parkes Weber himself, an employee in the institution. While her peristaltic system offered an object of scientific study, at the same time, she became a producer in the hospital's larger alimentary system, assuring the flow of appropriate food from the kitchen, through bodies, to the hospital's waste system. Meanwhile, if the hospital was, for her, a locus for the reversed deposits of her peristaltic system, then his cathexis to her body in the hospital context was the generative source of the research process that led to the messy bundles that Parkes Weber eventually, at the end of his life, left to the archives.

## Postscript

I had opened this chapter with an account of a dream Parkes Weber presented as an allegory of psychoanalysts besmirching themselves as they try to force entrance through the cloacal 'EXIT ONLY' into the New Jerusalem. But by now we have had occasion to consider the role Parkes Weber played during decades of preoccupation with the peristaltic gymnastics of one of his most inspiring patients. I want to come back, for a moment, to his thesis that the sort of hysterical symptoms Rosa presents are an exaggeration of a tertiary sex trait developed in a phylogenetic past, a 'pathomimia' whose original aim was to attract the attentions of the male of the species, and thus help in the evolutionary survival of the fittest. If you bring the logic of this thesis to bear on the immediate context of Rosa and her male physicians, it raises the question: what is it about Parkes Weber and his colleagues, at the turn of the twentieth century, that makes the faecal vomiter so attractive, even the object, one might say, of a libidinal charge? That such a question would have been outrageous, completely unacceptable to a doctor like Parkes Weber, is suggested by his dismissive, or one might even say, defensive remarks in an essay that resonates with his dream analysis of the New Jerusalem. In 'Extravagance in Freudian Teaching and Freudian Explanations', Parkes Weber informs us that he has just consulted Ernest Jones's 'Papers on Psycho-Analysis' to test whether psychoanalysis is really as full of 'boundless exaggerations' as he (Parkes Weber) had suggested in earlier publications. What he finds, in a chapter on 'Anal-erotic Character Traits', are some 'unexpected allusions to "collectors" and "misers"' (Parkes Weber 1934, 419). He wonders if Jones is joking when he suggests that 'all collectors are anal-erotics, and the objects collected are nearly always typical copro-symbols: thus, money, coins... stamps, eggs, butterflies... books, and even worthless things like pins, old newspapers, etc.' (quoted in Parkes Weber 1934, 419). Parkes Weber confesses that the passage has 'personal interest' for him, since he had formerly 'accumulated a large collection of coins and medals' (Parkes Weber 1934, 419).

Indeed, according to the biographical account of Parkes Weber prepared for the Wellcome, 'he was a great collector' and with the help of his father, had, as a boy, 'built up collections of stamps, butterflies, and moths, mineralogical specimens and fossils' as well as 'coins and medals' in his adulthood (Hall 2001, 525). Jones's linking of a penchant for collecting with anal eroticism must have, therefore, come as an unpleasant affront indeed. If he thought he could escape the 'anal-erotic miserly category' by asserting that he had given his collection away to the British Museum, Parkes Weber is made 'less certain' of this when he reads that 'the opposite of parsimony, namely, extreme generosity and extravagance' are also signs of one's anality. 'Thus,' he says, 'I take him to mean that if black is an "anal-erotic" stigma, white is equally or still more so, the excessive (reactionary) removal of all the black revealing a desire to wipe out all traces of an ingrained "anal-erotic" marking, of which one may perhaps be ashamed' (Parkes Weber 1934, 419). It would seem, then, that if the psychoanalysts have their way, everyone could be considered to be anal-erotic to some degree.

Parkes Weber is willing to admit that we all 'may experience a transient sense of satisfaction on having a sufficient normal action of the bowels' (he compares it to the hen's exultation on laying an egg), but 'this sense of satisfaction ... can hardly be magnified into "libido", "*elan vital*", a joy and mainspring of life, and a reason why one should not commit suicide!' (Parkes Weber 1934, 419). The exclamation point – used rarely in his writing – has that quality again here of the apotropaic amulet, waved in hopes of warding off an imputation that Parkes Weber might find threatening. And indeed, I am struck by the progression here from 'satisfaction' to 'libido' or any of the (perhaps surprising) synonyms for it in Parkes Weber's list: *elan vital* (which he gets from his reading of Bergson's *Creative Evolution*), joy and mainspring of life, and 'reason why one should not commit suicide'. It's not clear where this reference to suicide comes from, since it is not mentioned in any of the quotes on anal eroticism he pulls from the psychoanalytical writings of Jones, Oberndorf, Allendy, Stevens or Winnicott. Parkes Weber had long before decided that libido and *elan vital* could be thought of as the same thing, in his 1919 'Thinking and Dreaming and the Explanation of Dreams', where he had wondered 'how can one support the Freudian claims that nearly all dreams allow of an obvious or latent (cryptic) sexual interpretation?' (Parkes Weber 1919, 272). His answer to this question was that we would have to arbitrarily alter 'the definition of such terms as "love", "libido", etc. so as to make "love" include almost every desire and passion, almost all psychical force, every thought or idea which activates life – in fact to make of it a kind of "joy of life", *elan vital*, a vital influence pervading everything, whatever human beings do or busy themselves about' (Parkes Weber 1919, 276). It was this same *elan vital* that he had decided, in notes jotted after reading Bergson, it was the physician's primary professional aim to 'foster, guard, guide and regulate' during its 'passage through human beings from the commencement of their life (even before their birth) to their [and here he inserted 'body's'] death' (Parkes Weber 1943, n.p.). This image for me recalls Marx's emphasis on how we 'mediate, regulate, and control' our metabolism with Nature. And the resonance of an immaterial *elan vital* with the more palpable substances that make their 'passage through human beings' via the alimentary system is not inconsequential here. In any case, it must have seemed repugnant, indeed, to have to think of oneself as tending toward anal eroticism, most particularly as it might have been connected with his own passion for collection – of stamps, coins, butterflies, medals, unusual medical cases – as the precious vital force that might be enlivening even his own body.

## Notes

1 For a brief discussion of the upper-middle-class clientele treated for neurotic or neurasthenic symptoms by Parkes Weber at his Harley Street Practice, see Shorter (1992). Shorter attributes the large number of female patients who consulted Parkes Weber for nervous conditions to his interest in spas and 'balneology'; 'Parkes Weber ... considered many of his nervous patients "neurasthenic" because they were fatigued, and treated virtually all of them by finding suitable spas for summer and winter' (Shorter 1992, 273). While his bourgeoise clientele were being sent to spas (another term for the kind of sanitaria recommended by Christine Frederick for the household engineer, and frequented by Stekel's patient Louise), Parkes Weber treated his working-class clientele at a public hospital, catering to those who did not have the budget for health tourism.
2 For a suggestive analysis of 'pussy ballistics and the queer appeal of peristalsis' in Korean American comedian Margaret Cho's performances, see Rachel Lee's deployment of Ferenczi's concept of amphimixis. '[A]n amphimixed message laughs,' she writes, 'not via plural heads but from the messy assemblage of bottom orifices – urethra, anus, vagina, and, yes, vomiting mouth – at the demand for a single message: the normative point or straight buildup to the end. . . Cho's giggling peristaltic waves intensify and wane, in waves that overlap,

fold, producing whirlpools that are the wider-environmental (spatial) and durational (temporal) point that mocks the Anthropocene's sense of itself as progressing into a more wealthy, ethical future simply because of the directionality of the arrow of historical time' (Lee 2014, 513).

3 '[There are] young women, who, even whilst they are in their ordinary state of health and quite flourishing in appearance, have a really marvelous facility for vomiting. Not only does the slightest temporary gastric upset cause them to throw up their food, but they have only to look at certain articles of food and think of the associated smells and tastes (for which they happen to have an aversion) in order to be able to vomit. This facility for vomiting may obviously be cultivated by mental processes, and may be temporarily greatly increased by causes which disturb the general health or the mental equilibrium. In fact, one must admit that some persons ... possess the power of voluntarily vomiting, that is to say, they can vomit merely as the result of a psychical condition, which they can themselves induce at will. It is therefore easy to see that great difficulties may arise when one has to deal with hysterical patients gifted with this power of vomiting, and at the same time desirous, as hysterical patients often are, of attracting attention to themselves by malingering if they cannot do so by other means' (Parkes Weber 1904, 193).

4 'Just as sexual selection in the past is responsible for the existence of the tertiary (nervous) sex characters and their abnormal variations of the present day, so sexual selection in the present and future will modify the nervous sex characters, as well as all other instinctive nervous tendencies, of future generations' (Parkes Weber 1912, 138). For more on Parkes Weber as a eugenicist see Schaffer (2012).

8

# Peristaltic Politics of a Suffragette

## From hysteria to suffrage, or the strategic deployment of the gut

After publishing his 1950 follow-up article on Rosa's reversed peristaltic system, Frederick Parkes Weber received an appreciative letter from a fellow doctor wishing to share notes on a patient of his own who claimed to be able to pass air from one end to the other of her peristaltic system in a very short time. 'It is very interesting,' the doctor mused, 'that these cases of anti-peristalsis of such marked degree have disappeared. I have never seen such a case and have never heard of my psychiatric contemporaries mention having seen such a patient' (Scott 1950). Parkes Weber replied in agreement: 'the cases of very violent so-called "hysterical" anti-peristalsis seem to have gone, like the Salpêtrière type of hysterical convulsion with opisthotonus' (FPW 1950). Neither doctor ventured a guess as to why the turn of the twentieth century should have been marked by this peculiar reversal of the alimentary system, except to consign it to the same category occupied by Charcot's hysterics. What both are acknowledging here is that 'anti-peristalsis' was not so much a medical condition that could present at any time or place, but rather a historical phenomenon limited to the conditions of a specific moment, and within a given culture. The reference to 'Salpêtrière', in fact (and the implied reference to Charcot), ties the affliction to institutional practices under the auspices of a particular medical personality: there is no convulsing hysteric without the animator who presents her to his audience. And by extension, no violent faecal vomiter without her partner in peristaltic reversal.

This wasn't the first time Parkes Weber had speculated on the historical specificity of a medical affliction: in February 1944, during the war, a correspondent inquired of the physician as to what might be the reasons 'which led to the disappearance of the condition formerly known as mucous colitis, a psychoneurosis associated with attacks of abdominal pain and the passage of mucous casts, chiefly amongst women, which disappeared about the year 1914?' Could it have had anything to do, he wondered, 'with the suffragette movement and the subsequent more purposeful life adopted by our womenfolk?' (Hardy 1944).

Parkes Weber did not agree with the writer's 'psychoneurotic theory', though he had to admit that many of the sufferers from the condition were 'more or less "neurotic"'. To his mind, the condition was caused by 'a "conservative" bodily reaction towards constipation ... the mucosa of the rectum and often more or less of the colon, got into the habit ... of secreting great excess of mucus in order to facilitate evacuation of faeces, as if of a foreign body'. A constipating diet exacerbated the situation, resulting in a 'vicious circle'. If mucous colitis had subsequently disappeared, it wasn't because suffragettes abandoned their neurotic behaviour and took up useful war work, but rather that 'modern hygienic dietetic methods, and altered general habit of living, have largely "broken" or "cut" the vicious circle' (Parkes Weber 1944). Parkes Weber was alluding here to the work of his colleague, Jamieson B. Hurry, who had made his reputation on the publication of several volumes and articles on the 'vicious circle' in such areas as disease, neurasthenia, sociology and poverty. That a morbid condition could be confined to a given era suggests a sort of historical 'vicious circle' during which ailments symptomatically repeat themselves again and again, *en masse*, until some intervention, or random set of circumstances, jolts the circle back into an unfolding of healthy cycles of repetition. The vicious circle is thus a condition conceived in terms of the pernicious short-circuiting of an otherwise felicitous pattern of organic and behavioural harmony.

That Parkes Weber's correspondent could so blithely consign the suffragette to the same category as the hysteric – as though both were quaint phenomena of a bygone era – will surprise no one familiar with what had become a common practice in public discourse during the heyday of militant feminism: to undermine the legitimacy of the struggle for the vote by depicting it as the ravings of sexually frustrated, and under-occupied, 'womenfolk'.[1] During Marion Wallace Dunlop's inaugural hunger strike at Holloway prison, for example, the prison governor wrote to the Home Office advising that, although it 'would not be easy to certify her as being legally insane', he considered Dunlop to be 'a highly neurotic fanatic', who was likely 'passing through the Climactic Period' (i.e. menstruating) which would 'aggravate her mental condition'. She could not, therefore, be 'credited with a full measure of responsibility for her actions' (quoted in Vernon 2007, 76).

The only feminist response to such a gesture of condescension would seem to require a firm refusal to pathologise the political strategies of the militant feminist movement, and to keep the category of the 'hysteric' well sequestered from that of the 'suffragette'. Having given serious attention in the previous two chapters to the social and political ramifications of the hysteric's dissident peristaltic system, however, I am reluctant now to cordon off the unconscious symptomatology of hysteria from the strategic deployment of the suffragette's gut in the name of politics. What happens, I'm wondering, when we bring the suffragette into the same framework as her contemporary, the hysteric, and ask what their enteric systems had in common? What if we were to consider, for instance, the enteric thinking of the hunger striker along the same lines as the somatic protests of Great War combatants a few years later?[2] If hunger striking did not animate prison medical staff in quite the same way that the symptoms of 'war neurosis' mobilised nerve doctors at institutions like Craiglockhart and Maghull, there is nevertheless some shared territory in the way that diagnostic gestures interacted with declarations of protest. Take the case of Siegfried Sassoon, for instance, whose written 'Soldier's Declaration', read out in parliament, was undermined by his classification as a sufferer of war neurosis. This is not to say that his diagnosis was a sham, that he experienced no symptoms as a result of his experience at the front. But his trauma-induced nightmares and hallucinations served at once to legitimate his admission to Craiglockhart for treatment (thus 'saving' him from a court marshalling that might have drawn attention, and supporters, to his cause), but also to contribute 'neurological' evidence to the argument he had mounted against an unconscionable war that many believed could be ended through negotiation. His was what we might call a hybrid protest, mounted in part through linguistic discourse (his written declaration), in part through the body, or to use suffragette terms, through words *and* deeds, though in this case, we are talking about neurological deeds, taking place at the register of the unconscious, and being 'read' through the interpretive lens of Sassoon's doctor-companion, W.H.R. Rivers.

In this chapter, we turn to the hybrid protest of a suffragette whose story has joined the ranks of the most well-known militants of that period in England – the Pankhursts, Wallace Dunlop, Emmeline Pethick Lawrence, Annie Kenney and Emily Davison. I could focus on the testimony of any of the suffragettes who joined in delegations, were arrested and imprisoned, went on hunger strike, were forcibly fed, and then wrote about it as part of an overarching strategy to acquire for women the right to vote – and indeed, this momentous period in the history of women's suffrage has been extensively treated from manifold perspectives. I want to zero in, however, on a memoir that is rich with implications for an investigation of hunger striking as a specifically *peristaltic* intervention into the interlocking metabolic systems of institutions (both material and symbolic) of urban space, of parliamentary electoral politics and of communications, publicity and commercial consumption: *Prisons and Prisoners: Some Personal Experiences, by Constance Lytton and Jane Warton, Spinster* (1914).

In this reading of Lytton's memoir, I explore how Lytton's professed 'hobbies' of cleaning and prisons (or, more properly, prison reform) reveal a tacit understanding of environmental 'metabolic rift' – a rift that she repurposes, in a different way, at the level of the incarcerated body. I lay stress on the shifting emphasis on internal and external peristaltic movement, and on passivity in the service of political action. Once again, I consider the collaborative aspect of the dissident gut, portrayed as a struggle between patient and physician; indeed, a close reading of Lytton's repeated encounters with the doctor and wardresses who wield the forcible feeding tube will permit me to rework in explicitly metabolic terms Ewa Ziarek's characterisation of the suffragette project as one that wrests what Giorgio Agamben calls 'bare life' from the grip of sovereign power. This will entail revisiting Marx's metabolic model for human labour, but this time through Nicholas de Genova's metabolic reading of Agamben's 'bare life'. Lytton's enteric system offers evidence of what Wilson and Ferenczi term a dynamic rather than flat biology; it is a model of viscerality that asserts an agency in the political realm. Most striking, perhaps, we will find that the self-injury practised by hunger-striking suffragettes was closely observed by Gandhi in the run-up to his own metabolic campaigns for Indian self-rule. If Gandhi deployed what has been termed the 'moral imperfectionism' of a politicised anti-care of the self, it was informed by the passive resistance on the part of the feminist 'satyagrahis' of the suffragette movement.

## Exigencies of the alimentary system

Scholars of the suffragette movement know already that *Prisons and Prisoners* was not co-authored by two separate women, but rather by Lady Constance Lytton, who had been imprisoned twice during the movement before disguising herself as a Plain Jane of the working class and seeking imprisonment a third time to test her suspicion that officials were giving preferential treatment to personages of the upper classes. Incarcerated a total of four times, in three different prisons and cities, she offers a meticulously detailed account not only of the routines of prison life as it pertained to both well-off and working-class women, but also of the condition of her own body (and by extension others) in almost every context associated with the militant movement: country versus city corporeality; the affective quality of circulating in the streets, amidst crowds of other militants, onlookers, hecklers and police; the prison's architectural and disciplinary encroachment on the viscera; the physiology of unaccustomed prison food, unwanted medication, refusal to eat, rubber-tubed forcible feeding and all the rest. But every convolution of the body's implication in this series of motions, counter-motions, ingestions and compressions is accompanied, in her text, by a discursive connecting material – every nuance of the body's formation and deformation is stuck as though by a communicative adhesive to a complex calculus of micro-political advances and retractions.

That Lytton's memoir qualifies, more so than other suffragette accounts, as perfectly suited to our exploration of peristaltic politics is conclusively affirmed by a scathing review of *Prisons and Prisoners* by one of her contemporaries: most likely modernist Dora Marsden.[3] In addition to lambasting the memoir for its sentimentality and emphasis on the 'spirit of service', Marsden shows her greatest disdain for something 'inextricably knitted into the structure and phraseology of [Lytton's] book', something 'far more curious and arresting [than women's mission]', something 'too insistent to be counted as an impression, or as something implied' (Haslam ed. 2008, 335). She finally identifies this 'something' as a 'preoccupation with the exigencies of the alimentary system' (Haslam ed. 2008, 335). By contrast to Wilde's 'vision of souls in pain' in 'The Ballad of Reading Gaol', for instance, Lytton's prison narrative reads like a 'trivial account of sanitary arrangements' (Haslam ed. 2008, 335).

> *Why* this one feature of prison life [exigencies of the alimentary system] should have loomed so importantly in the author's account we do not dare definitely to say, but after conceiving and rejecting various explanations we alighted on one conclusion and give it for what it is worth. It is Lady Constance Lytton's contribution to the 'sex-question'. On the 'touching pitch undefiled', 'to the pure all things are pure' principles she sings on this one note without a tremor and considers it a daring deed done for purity. (Haslam ed. 2008, 335)

While she means to denigrate Lytton by suggesting that the unpleasantness of alimentary concerns has to stand in for sexual concerns (because Lytton can't bring herself to talk about the 'sex question' directly), and thus that Lytton presents herself as not being 'defiled' by the 'pitch' of peristaltic waste (whether it be vomit or shit), Marsden nevertheless reveals a connection between the peristaltic and the libidinal that is worthy of more than just ridicule.[4]

Lytton's memoir takes for granted that her readers already know of her aristocratic family origins, and indeed, the prominent status of her extended family was such that it would have seemed redundant to waste time telling her audience about it, beginning instead with the broad outlines of the 'drift of [her] existence' before she became aware of the women's movement. By this, she means the emergence of a series of undeveloped interests in her youth – a 'yearning to take up music professionally', a longing to 'try my hand at journalism' – accompanied by a chronic invalidism, ameliorated somewhat by the adoption of a vegetarian diet, but also 'an overmastering laziness and a fatalistic submission to events as they befell', until in 1906, she finds herself, at the age of thirty-nine, with 'neither equipment, training nor inclination for an independent life' (Lytton 2008, 51). Today's readers must turn to Lytton's biographer to learn the external trappings of this self-deprecating account of her internal development: the paternal grandfather who was a famous writer and politician,

Edward Bulwer-Lytton, friend of Dickens and Disraeli; the great-grandmother who was an early suffragist and, as a member of the Owenites, a friend of Robert Owen and Jeremy Bentham; the grandmother, Rosina Doyle Wheeler, who was embroiled with her husband, Edward, in a series of public recriminations until he committed her to an asylum, where she (prefiguring her granddaughter's suffragette activity) went on hunger strike before being released through the intervention of friends; the diplomat father, Robert Bulwer-Lytton, who appointed Queen Victoria as Empress of India while he served as Viceroy there (and which meant that Constance spent most of her childhood in India); the mother, Edith Villiers, descendent of a long line of aristocrats, who became lady-in-waiting to Victoria in the last years of the queen's life. In her own generation, Constance, or Con, as she was called by friends and family, befriended Olive Schreiner, already a writer of renown for *Story of an African Farm*; Con's brother-in-law, through marriage to her sister Betty, was Arthur Balfour, Leader of the Conservative Party; and her brother Victor Lytton sat in the House of Lords and was friends with Winston Churchill (Jenkins 2015, xiv, xv, Chapters 1–3). All of this would have been known to the 1914 readership of her memoir, *Prisons and Prisoners*.

So when Lytton entered the fray in 1909, it was as a well-known member of the aristocracy, down on funds, but highly connected. Her distinguished social status was welcomed by the leaders of the Women's Social and Political Union (WSPU), since it was thought that she might have some pull with members of parliament. This turned out not so much to be the case; rather, what she became known for was her undercover investigation of Walton gaol, disguising her body in such a way that it would receive the treatment of a working-class delegate, and serve as the object for Lytton's own experimental observation. Her memoir, as is signalled by its title's focus on 'prison', is as much an investigative report on the conditions of incarceration in England as a testimony of the travails of the movement.

## Hobbies

Lytton's narrative is embedded in an implied understanding of metabolic rift and its implications for the meta-industrial labour involved in provisioning humans from a nature that has been encroached on by industrial capitalism. This can be traced out from apparently innocuous comments she makes about her two 'hobbies': cleaning and prisons. 'Prisons, as you know, have been my hobby', she writes in a letter to her mother, just before joining a delegation that will assuredly result in her arrest and sentencing (Lytton 2008, 73). And elsewhere: 'Washing, the making clean that which had been dirty, and making the crumpled and uncomfortable things smooth, was my hobby' (Lytton 2008, 80–1).

The use of the term 'hobby' to refer to these forms of labour is symptomatic of what she perceives to be the compromised position from which she speaks as a middle-aged woman of the leisured class: compromised because she is not compelled to sell her labour for wages, nor is she qualified to practise a profession, and for this reason she hesitates to assert her authority as one who can militate on behalf of other women who really do engage in work with a (waged) value. Any activity she engages in must, therefore, be couched in the language of hobby or pastime – non-remunerative work done in an 'amateur' fashion, for the love of it. Her affective attachment to these two 'hobbies' in particular move us to ask what the connection is between them; how is a passion for cleaning implicated in or even constitutive of a twinned passion for prison reform? And what is their relation to a third passion not cast as a hobby – that is, the passion for feminist revolutionary politics, carried out through metabolic bodily interventions?

Lytton compares her concern for the plight of prisoners to maternal longing, remarking that her 'yearning after them, turns in me and tugs at me as vitally and irrepressibly as ever a physical child can call upon its mother' (Lytton 2008, 73). This lurking maternity for prisoners is expressed in terms of the 'cruel harm' done to their 'souls and bodies', but even more importantly, the 'exasperating waste of good opportunities in connection with them' (Lytton 2008, 73). As we follow Lytton into the prison, we will witness her persistent vexation in the face of 'waste' on manifold registers. But the visceral pull of the prison is so powerful, so libidinally rooted, as to make her doubt her motives for having joined the suffragettes: 'I have felt from the first that I could not take this woman's movement merely as an excuse for Holloway' (Lytton 2008, 73–4). The first chapters of her book, therefore, cover the process by which she can assure herself that her motives for joining in the fray are not merely to gratify her desire to witness (and take action in) the inside of a penitentiary.

To enter the prison is also to enter a space that represents for her the epitome of an unattainable cleanliness – a space that reeks of the *'puanteur'* that haunts Dostoevsky's account of his imprisonments, 'the smell, as it were, of deadness pervading, I should imagine, every building, however cleanly washed, which is built and used to incarcerate human beings solely for punitive purposes' (Lytton 2008, 68). Moreover, for Lytton, this aspect of the prison is deeply associated with the quality of urban space in general.

Having lived much of her adult life on the centuries-old Knebworth estate, about thirty miles north of London, Lytton counts herself as among those whose 'temperaments cannot acclimatise themselves to town dwelling', and for whom the city appears:

> artificial, repellent from the physical conditions it imposes and the mental outlook resulting from these. Rain, earth and air are better scavengers than any municipal corporation. The ceaseless cleansing, yet never making clean, of town existence has from my childhood fretted my imagination and produced a sense of incarceration. (Lytton 2008, 53)

'Scavengers' refers, of course, to the collectors not only of trash, but of the city's night soil, its human excrement. With its earth 'laid over with tombstones, metalled roads or floors of wood' and its sky limited to 'a mere ceiling' by the 'avenues of bricks and mortar' shutting it out, the town has always seemed to her 'a "deterrent" workhouse at best, and often a punitive prison besides' (Lytton 2008, 53). The two associations, filth and imprisonment, are so entwined with each other that it is hard to tell whether the city's resistance to being made clean transforms it into a place of captivity, or if its impermeable insulation from the 'earth' – its inhabitants held captive by metal, wood, bricks and mortar – makes it perennially dirty. If the 'municipal corporation' can never adequately scavenge the city's waste, this is due in large part to the 'monster of industrialism', to which we have sacrificed both 'the interests of the human beings which should control it' and 'the soil, the land, which alone can produce the raw materials for its task' (Lytton 2008, 53). This is a version, no less, of Marx's metabolic rift, expressed as the gulf between a soil at risk and the city whose waste only pollutes, never replenishes.

Thus, if Lytton's 'hobbies' seem at first unrelated, that is, a preoccupation with the labour of cleaning on the one hand and the conviction about prison reform on the other, we see that they are, in fact, of a piece with one another. The concentration of bodies in a constricted space is inseparable from the vulnerability of these bodies to the industrial degradation of metabolic cycles through which the earth provisions us for survival. Lytton is well aware that it is women who have been primarily responsible for the constant and unending attention to the repair of this degradation through the otherwise unvalued labour of cleaning not only the spaces inhabited by bodies but the apparel that clothes them and protects them from the erosion of day-to-day living.

The two passions, cleaning and prisons, come together in a pivotal scene, when Lytton pauses on the threshold of Caxton Hall, about to step out into the streets for her first deputation designed for the express purpose of being arrested and admitted to Holloway. Threaded through this passage is a conundrum circulating around the suffragette call to action: 'Deeds, not Words!' A resolution has been read out, emphasising that while the 'King's Speech' vitally affects the interests of the female sex (giving women tax-payers a higher financial burden, for instance), 'the Government have not included in the programme for the session a measure to confer the Parliamentary vote upon duly qualified women' (Lytton 2008, 77). The 'Words' of the monarch in this respect function performatively like deeds, while a sector of the population is denied the 'Deed' (the casting of a vote) that would constitute their speech on the matter.

Lytton has been told, however, that when marching in the street, a woman's 'semblance' of making a speech will accomplish the deed of disturbing the peace, and result in the desired arrest. And even as Lytton is well aware that the purpose of the Deputation is not precisely to convey a resolution 'to the Prime Minister at the House of Commons', but merely to *appear* to do so (thus provoking arrest), she nevertheless dreads that 'by some horrible twist of fate the leaders of the Deputation should be refused admittance, and I, if recognized, should have the lonely privilege thrust upon me of being received' (Lytton 2008, 78). Would this constitute admission to the wrong edifice (the right one being the prison), or premature admission to the desired one? Moreover, is it that Lytton is not really prepared to make her words heard in the House of Commons? Or is it rather that she does not yet feel equipped to 'speak' for others, and thus to make her words, like the king's, consequential?

At this juncture, Lytton pauses for a five-page digression on this very question of whether her words would or would not have the power to function as deeds. She asks herself 'for which group of women I should stand, what was my atom's share in this movement if I did not strain after any vicarious office but merely added my own personal weight to the scale?' (Lytton 2008, 78). This 'personal weight' is, she well knows, very slight:

> Without a doubt I myself was one of that numerous gang of upper class leisured class spinsters, unemployed, unpropertied, unendowed, uneducated, without equipment or training for public service, economically dependent entirely upon others, not masters of their own leisure, however oppressively abundant that might seem to the onlooker. (Lytton 2008, 78)

A 'maiming subserviency is so conditional' to the very existence of such spinsters 'that it becomes an aim in itself, an ideal. Driven through life with blinkers on, they are unresentful of the bridle, the rein and the whip' (Lytton 2008, 78). It is hard to tell whether this caustic attack is directed more at herself as a 'single woman, the old maid of later years', or at the 'chain of limitations and restrictions' that produces in her a 'paralysing worship of incapacity' (Lytton 2008, 79). Or is it just that Lytton is unforgiving of herself for not having been one of those who 'by exceptional force of character or ability' have been able to overcome those restrictions, even as she knows that 'freedom, if attained' is too often 'rendered useless by lack of preparation in the competition against trained and privileged beings of the male sex', and amounts to nothing more than 'a distortion, an abnormality, an untidiness of creation' (Lytton 2008, 79).

So even though she could well enough 'stand' for the 'superfluous spinster' (i.e. so much social waste on the modern landscape), she suspects that no one would listen 'to a messenger from this mute array'. After all, 'who cares for the blind, the lamed, the maimed and the dumb? The fearful unnecessity of their disablement awakes no pity, no heart softens at thought of them, no politician would feel his conscience pricked by the narration of their grievances' (Lytton 2008, 79). The metaphorical characterisation of the spinster as 'blind, lamed, maimed, and dumb' plays on the double sense of the term 'disability', understood at once as socially imposed bodily impediments, and the legally imposed obstacle to their access to the franchise. Why would the Prime Minister bother with demands for 'the removal of women's disabilities to the Parliamentary franchise' (Lytton 2008, 72) if such demands come from worshippers of their own 'incapacities'?

Much better, then, if the demand were to come on behalf of 'the working woman, the bread-winning woman', whose situation is 'easily comparable to that of the working class man who quite recently has had himself to fight in order to win his denied claim to freedom' (Lytton 2008, 80). Lytton has whole-hearted sympathy for the 'factory workers ... the sweated home workers ... teachers, nurses, medical women' whose petitions she has read. 'But how could I stand for them when I was not equipped to represent them?' (Lytton 2008, 80).

For Lytton, it is not enough to have read the petitions of the working women; her sympathy and respect for them does not, apparently, 'equip' her to stand for or represent them. Something more, or different, is called for. In this digression in the narration of her first deputation through the streets of London, she brings us to another scene in the street, where something transpires to attach her at a more visceral level to these women for whom she seeks to speak.

Here she recalls an occasion when, 'walking from Holloway to the City in one of our Suffragette processions', she hears, 'for the first time with my own ears the well worn taunt "Go home and do your washing"' (Lytton 2008, 80). This taunt functions like an Althusserian interpellation, awakening in her 'a magic response', while at the same time providing her with a subjectivity that had hitherto eluded her. 'Since the days of my earliest childhood,' she reports, 'washing had held great charm for me, and as a result I had revered the washers exceptionally.' Although in her youth, it is mainly laundry-workers who arouse her passion, she realises as an adult that, with the exception of a 'small proportion of houses where servants are kept', every woman is a laundrymaid, and 'in every house throughout the land, or indeed throughout the world, the cleaning and the washing are done mainly by women' (Lytton 2008, 80).

That the response in her is 'magic' suggests that it works at an unconscious, infantile level; as in a Proustian experience, she is brought back to her 'earliest childhood', proving that the impulse to clean is no deliberately assumed aspect of her personality, a political expediency, but is felt by her as intrinsic to her being. It is her status as 'amateur scrubber and laundry-woman', her passion for washing, cleaning and making 'the crumpled and uncomfortable things smooth' that connects her to women 'throughout the world' (Lytton 2008, 80–1).

If there is 'one single industry highly deserving of recognition ... and of representation under parliamentary systems,' she adds, 'it surely is that of the washers, the renewers week by week, the makers clean' (Lytton 2008, 81). Her own passion for cleaning makes her, too, from 'the moment [she] heard that "washing" taunt in the street', deserving of political representation; it gives her, as an 'untrained spokeswoman', the courage to 'point to the collars and shirt fronts of the gentlemen who received me and claim the freedom of citizenship for the washers' (Lytton 2008, 81).

Only now that her destiny has been definitively linked to that of all women figured *as* the 'renewers week by week' (even as the entrapped filth of the city and the '*puanteur*' of the prison can never be made clean), only now does she conclude her lengthy digression and take us back to Caxton Hall, from whose door she steps out 'through the grime of a foggy February evening', only to catch sight

> of white collars here and there in the crowd, like little flashing code-signals beckoning to us across the darkness. The gnarled hands, the bent backs, the tear-dimmed eyes of those that had washed them white seemed to cry out, 'Remember us. Don't be afraid to speak for us if you get through to the presence of those who know nothing, heed nothing of our toil.' (Lytton 2008, 81)

Strikingly, it is not her childbearing capacity, nor her reproductive organs, that permit Lytton to identify with all women as a political group (and as we recall she is sceptical of her 'maternal longing' for the plight of prisoners, and does not trust it as the right motivation for joining the suffrage movement). Rather, what allows her to speak on behalf of women in general is their relegation, by men, to the reproductive realm of laundering and housework, the 'meta-industrial labour' of repairing and maintaining our metabolic link to the earthly resources necessary for survival, that baseline for the 'productive' labour of industry, commerce and governance. It is as a producer of meta-industrial *value*, in fact, that Lytton finds common cause with the makers clean of the world.

Now begins the Deputation in earnest, that is, the assertion of 'deeds' that will substitute for the 'words' that will not, after all, be spoken by any woman in the House of Commons, whether she has adequately learnt her part or not. To surrender oneself to 'the movement' will prove to entail surrender to literal movement through the streets, in a peristaltic progress that seems to unfold automatically, and requires only that she supply her body to be squeezed along from Caxton Hall, to the House, to the police station, to its cells, to Black Maria, and ultimately to the sought-after belly of Holloway. Having anxiously asked whether she must do something 'to show that I mean business', Lytton is reassured by a companion that she needn't bother about what she'll do: 'It will all be done *to* you' (Lytton 2008, 76). This prompts Lytton to reflect that, though she might encounter physical difficulties, she has 'merely to meet them and endure them, knowing that I could lay no claim to overcome these by physical powers of which I was deficient'. Paradoxically, this acceptance of her passivity makes her 'proud to be one of the active ones at last' (Lytton 2008, 77).

Once in the street, she and her companions are 'hedged in' by a V-shaped avenue of police, until she feels that 'all breath seemed to have been pressed out of my body'; the crowd 'half hindered, half pushed, us along'; at one point she is lifted off her feet and 'relieved of the toil of dragging my body'; if she gains in the direction of the House, it is 'always assisted by the crowd' until eventually she is pinioned by the police and, with her eyes shut, dragged to the police station (Lytton 2008, 81–4). As had been promised, it has all been done *to* her; her journeying after the prison having the quality of being squeezed through a channel of transit made up of the police and masses in the streets, pressing, narrowing, closing in upon her, pulling her back, hindering, pushing, lifting her off her feet, seizing her, squeezing her, throwing her, buffering her, assisting her, leading her away. A long series of contractions and impulsions through which her body passes, in an urban circuit that has by now become, through repetition, a habitual component in the city's overall metabolism.

### Common cause

For a moment, we leave Lytton as she discovers her place within a metabolic commons, allowing her body to be borne along at ground, or should we say street, level among those other politicised toilers in the reproductive realm, and turn to a parallel life that was being lived by one of her exact contemporaries: a barrister, and British subject, who had been born in the same year as Constance and who, like her, spent his childhood in India; who also practised vegetarianism; and who, most notably, was to deploy the cessation of his peristaltic system as a deliberate political weapon, writing about it for the benefit of others who might want to take the same measures in times of extremity. I am referring, of course, to Mohandas Gandhi, whose fasts played a central role not only in the extraordinary social and political changes he brought about, but have come to be (as they are for the suffragettes) central to the legend that surrounds him.[5] It is not just the parallels I see between Lytton and Gandhi that move me to introduce him into our study of peristaltic politics, though I can't resist recounting one anecdote by way of stressing how both fasters participated in what has been called an 'ethics of moral imperfectionism' (L. Gandhi 2014, 5).

In the early twentieth century, Leela Gandhi argues, the concept of ethics had come to signify more than just the determinant of right or wrong, good or bad behaviour. Whether locating themselves within the racist camp of the new imperialism or among its opponents within the discourse of new liberalism, public figures espoused a shared ethic of self-discipline, a 'perfectionism' presumed to distinguish an idealised, disciplined self from the disorganised masses. Through practices of self-restraint and regulation, 'extremists, moderates, and radicals alike . . . projected self-cultivation as an occult work not just upon the self but also upon others'. In this respect 'sympathizers and advocates of antidemocratic programs, especially, extolled an orthodox *askesis* of self-consolidation and perfectionism, distinguishing rare individuals from the common lot' (L. Gandhi 2014, 1–2). The Sorelian socialist, for instance, ostensibly on the side of democracy, expected the working class to practise an ascetic anti-materialism as part of a movement toward a non-consuming democratic norm. But when Gandhi turns to (often non-Western) anticolonial and antifascist practitioners of this period, she finds a concept of democracy 'refashioned as a counter-*askesis*, or spiritual regimen of imperfectionism', which included 'aberrant practices of self-ruination, or an anti-care of the self aimed at making common cause both with the victims and abettors of unjust sociality (by defending the former and reforming the latter)' (L. Gandhi 2014, 2).

M.K. Gandhi is among the 'dramatis personae' of Leela Gandhi's genealogies of 'moral imperfectionism', particularly in the context of the colonial encounter between Britain and India (L. Gandhi 2014, 2). She reminds us of an oft-told tale of Gandhi's composition of *Hind Swaraj*, or *Indian Home Rule*, written in 1909 on the ship that returned him to South Africa after his second fruitless delegation to Parliament in London, where he had failed, through reasonable petitioning, to obtain assurances that the colour bar affecting Indians in South Africa would be reversed. Gandhi had worked on the book for days, according to legend, 'using the ship's stationery and writing with his left hand when the right was tired'. His ambidexterity has been invoked as 'confirmation of his place in the mythic genealogy of the *savyasachi*: a type perfected in the figure of Arguna ... who can wield a bow and shoot fatal arrows equally well with either hand' (L. Gandhi 2014, 18–19). But, as Leela Gandhi points out, it makes no sense to lay stress on the martial qualities of the future Mahatma; better to recast the story as one of 'fluency in the complex technologies of *ahimsa*, or nonviolence. This *ahimsaic* subject,' she writes, 'is not born of prodigious ambidextrous skill so much as from the dissonant commensurability of skill and shortcoming; the insistent partnership, that is, of a proficient right hand and its deficient double' (L. Gandhi 2014, 17–18).

Only three years later, another urgently composed document takes shape in similar conditions of staunch imperfection in the face of immovable parliamentary forces: Constance Lytton writes 'the first personal testimony of a suffragette to be published in a book' (Jenkins 2015, 207). Moreover, like *Hind Swaraj*, *Prisons and Prisoners* is the product of a 'proficient right hand and its deficient double'. Having been partially paralysed by a heart attack in 1912, Lytton taught herself to write with her left hand, and it was thus that she painstakingly composed much of her memoir in hopes of getting 'a reluctant and hostile public to understand the true nature of the militant campaign' (MacKenzie in Lytton 1988, xi). As I move on to the internal peristalsis of Lytton's story, it is with the conviction that any account of the suffragettes' militant campaign in this period, with its 'aberrant practices of self-ruination', must situate it alongside of, if not within, Leela Gandhi's genealogies for moral imperfectionism. After all, it was Gandhi himself who claimed common cause with the suffragettes whose campaign he had been observing during his two delegations from South Africa to London, and of whose struggle for the franchise he kept informed via cablegrams, newspapers and suffragette publications.

I have already mentioned Constance Lytton's vegetarianism, adopted at the suggestion of her aunt T, who had been extolling its health benefits for years.[6] It is possible that Lytton or her aunt knew or at least read the pamphlets and articles of some of London's chief proselytisers for vegetarianism, for example, Henry Salt, author of *A Plea for Vegetarianism* (and, incidentally, a prison reformer himself) and fellow member of the London Vegetarian Society, Josiah Oldfield. You will remember Oldfield's name from a previous chapter, where I examined his evolutionary account of the human body as a tube for processing the world, our similarity to earthworms, with their rhythmic contractions in the interest of motility, and the vexing question of how to treat the widespread malady of modern constipation. Some decades before writing his article on constipation, Oldfield met Gandhi in the late 1880s, and the two shared an apartment in Bayswater while Gandhi studied law at the Inner Temple. Indeed, it was precisely their shared vegetarianism that drew Oldfield and Gandhi together in the first place and that defined their friendship as they 'threw parties where guests were served lentil soup, boiled rice and large raisins', or sallied together out into the world, 'lecturing at clubs and any other public meetings', where they might command an audience for their 'gospel of peace and health' (Guha 2015, 44–5).

Gandhi visited Oldfield on subsequent delegations to London, sent friends to him for vegetarian treatment of their maladies, and sought the doctor's expertise himself on occasion. On the one side, we can think of the shared affective territories of vegetarianism, feminist dissidence, anti-racism and, ultimately, Indian home rule as each of these movements found associations with another, whether specific members met or not. On the other side, it was certainly the case that the most vehement anti-suffrage proponents warned against a sort of domino effect that would take place if you upheld a principle of equality. Such a principle, according to Sir Almroth Wright, for instance,

> consistently followed out, would make of every man and woman *in primis* a socialist; then a woman suffragist; then a philo-native, negrophil, and an advocate of the political rights of natives and negroes; and then, by logical compulsion, an anti-vivisectionist, who accounts

it *unjust* to experiment on an animal; a vegetarian, who accounts it *unjust* to kill animals for food; and finally one who, like the Jains, accounts it *unjust* to take the life of even verminous insects. If we accept this principle of egalitarian equity as of absolute obligation, we shall have to accept along with woman's suffrage all the other 'isms' believed in, and agitated for, by the cranks who are so numerously represented in the ranks of woman suffragists. (Wright 1913, 12)

In this paranoid scenario, to accept someone like a Constance Lytton might lead you right down a spiral that would end at what Wright considers the most preposterous of conclusions, with the very Jainist precepts against doing harm that characterised Gandhi's own outlook. In the middle, of course, is to be found the vegetarianism that links our two protagonists precisely at gut level.

### Eternal negative

Bringing Leela Gandhi's insights about the moral imperfectionism of Gandhi's hunger strikes to bear on the suffrage movement has two effects: to demonstrate the common cause of suffrage with *swaraj*, but also to foreground just what imperfectionism meant at a granular level. Lytton's experience, as she brings our eyes and viscera into the prison, demonstrates how experimental the hunger strike actually was, experimental in the sense that no one could know in advance what, if any, efficacy it would have, nor how destructive of the human body, nor what precisely it would feel like to deprive oneself of food, to subject oneself to or resist the forcible feeding tube, nor the extent to which one's enteric system would obey or rebel, permit consciousness of the first brain, or deprive it of agency, accept the doctor's gruel or spray it back.

Fearing for her daughter's health, Lytton's mother took her abroad in the summer of 1909; this meant that Lytton was not in London during Wallace Dunlop's inauguration of the hunger strike, and its rapid establishment as the prime 'deed' for incarcerated suffragettes. But in the fall of 1909, having visited a girl in a nursing home recuperating from having been forcibly fed, Lytton determined to take her turn in what was becoming a constant stream of suffragettes through the routine of imprisonment, hunger striking and forcible feeding. The tactics of the movement had shifted, and so 'rather than giving onlookers a spectacular activism represented through marches and pageants,' writes Green, 'the discourse of forcible feeding produced a series of uncanny reduplications as woman after woman transcribed her "experience", each narrative constructed by the last and constructing the next' (Green 1997, 86). Lytton's testimony was only one among 'the various documents of bodily invasion' that worked to 'foreground the issue of reduplication by binding together the mode of their own mechanical production and the new feminist strategies of repetition – feeding women into the prison as if on a conveyer belt' (Green 1997, 89). Paradoxically, the speeding up of feminist bodies through the prison system, as if facilitated by the streamlining techniques of rationalised industry, was premised on the slowing down, to the point of stoppage, of the world through the feminist body. As a vegetarian who had shared with Gandhi a heightened sense of the relation between one's own habits of ingestion and what she calls 'the defenceless ones who had no one to speak for their hungry need' (Lytton 2008, 203), Lytton's account of her participation in this aspect of the struggle is notable for its presentation of what Cheryl Jorgensen-Earp calls the first 'political theory of the hunger strike' (Jorgensen-Earp 1999, 105), as well as a highly interesting account of her critical engagement with the doctor whose job it was to start up her peristaltic system by force.

Lytton's first attempt to progress through the entire cycle, from lawbreaking to forcible feeding, went astray because by the time she was arrested in October of 1909 (for having thrown a rock at the car of Sir Walter Runciman, host of Lloyd George during his visit to Newcastle), her identity was known to the authorities. But as with all of her arrests, she took detailed notes of the state of the Central Police station of Newcastle, characteristically focusing on the inadequate provisions for elimination of human waste, i.e. a 'lavatory' whose water 'could only be turned on from the outside'; a men's urinal with a gutter in the floor 'but no water'; no toilet paper nor 'sanitary towels for the women' (Lytton 2008, 199, 201). It is here that she is allowed outside her dark cell long enough to write to the *Times*, laying out the logic of the protest she and her companions are about to take during their incarceration in Newcastle prison:

> We shall put before the Government by means of the hunger-strike four alternatives: To release us in a few days; to inflict violence upon our bodies [via forcible feeding]; to add death to the champions of

our cause by leaving us to starve; or, and this is the best and only wise alternative, to give women the vote. (Lytton 2008, 202–3)

The government is entreated to yield, as she puts it, 'not to the violence of our protest, but to the reasonableness of our demand, and to grant the vote to the duly qualified women of the country' (Lytton 2008, 203).

Via Gandhi, we can layer in a new perspective on the question of passivity and agency in non-violent political struggle; Lytton's presentation of the rationale for their protest is the follow-up to her sense of being 'borne along' by the movement, by the crowd, by the police, as she now develops a calculus of resistance that gradually takes the form of manipulated enteric motility. In this measured rendition of the logic of the hunger strike, there is an element of what Gandhi (and Erik Erikson) has termed the 'eternal negative'.

On his way to London, for instance, Gandhi is repeatedly urged by a friend to eat meat, if only to maintain his strength. 'But I had an eternal negative to face him with,' Gandhi writes. 'The more he argued, the more uncompromising I became' (Gandhi 2018, 116). Finally he says, 'I am helpless. A vow is a vow. It cannot be broken' (Gandhi 2018, 116), and the friend drops his argument. Erikson identifies this as a routine strategy on Gandhi's part; whenever he is presented with a proposal that he must flatly refuse, as for instance when he had faced his caste elders, who objected to his going abroad to England, he replies 'with that "eternal negative" which he so often would express in the nonviolent phrase "I am helpless" – meaning his mind had made itself up, and he had to obey' (Erikson 1969, 158). Erikson describes two other instances of this 'eternal negative': having ordered Gandhi to remove his turban during a court session in Durban, a judge is 'greeted with the "eternal negative". The judge insisted; Gandhi left the court' (Erikson 1969, 164). And when ordered by a conductor to move from a first- to a third-class train car in the Transvaal, 'there followed the "eternal negative", and the arm of the law deposited him and his bags on the station platform' (Erikson 1969, 166).

What Erikson presents here is a rhetorical strategy that has the effect of figuring a wilful refusal on Gandhi's part as a passive resignation to a force more powerful than himself. Even if he wished to eat meat, remove his turban, or give up first-class seating, the choice is completely out of his hands, he is 'helpless'. It is not that he has made up his mind, but that his mind, of its own accord, as though guided by something outside himself (truth? Ahimsa?) has been made up for him. The effect is to abstract the act of refusal from the individual, and to present it to the interlocutor as something that is not a matter of two opposing human wills, but as a flat external fact that will have to be dealt with apart from the desire or agency of either party. In this respect, it comes to have the attributes of an autonomic nervous system, which accomplishes an action independently of the will of the subject.

Thus, when Constance Lytton lays out her list of choices in the letter to the *Times*, she too can be said to engage in a Gandhian 'eternal negative'. She portrays the government not so much as an antagonist locked in a battle of wills with the suffragettes, but as a reasonable entity faced with a number of 'alternatives', only one of which would seem to be the 'best and only wise' one. Ewa Ziarek lays emphasis on the hunger strike's violence ('inflicted on the self as a substitute target for political power') as a paradox of action within refusal, an absence of distinction between active and passive, victim and enemy (Ziarek 2012, 162). If militancy inaugurates revolutionary struggle, it is what Ziarek calls 'a force of invention that exceeds positionality, agency, articulation'. As a transformative act it 'cannot be integrated without a remainder either into the constituted framework of power or into the notion of negation' and thus 'vacillates between activity and passivity' as a 'transitive force that women as much undergo as put into practice' (Ziarek 2012, 34).

Recast via Gandhi's 'eternal negative', we can say that Lytton is not wilfully taking action against the government, but rather acts through an apparently involuntary passivity, as if through an autonomic peristaltic cessation. This resonates with her sense of being propelled by the suffrage movement itself, or by the crowds and police during her participation in deputations through the streets, even as she transforms what Ziarek calls the suffragette's 'impotentiality' into 'a *capacity* for not acting, which is inseparable from the capacity for acting with others' (Ziarek 2012, 110). It is not until she devises a plan to disguise her class privilege that Lytton can finally exercise her '*capacity* for not acting', deployed through the arrested motility of her intestinal tract.

### Jane Warton's metabolism of bare life

Hearing of the ill-treatment of two women on hunger strike in Liverpool's Walton gaol, Lytton determines to gain access to the prison as a woman of the working class, to 'try whether [prison officials] would recognise my need for exceptional favours without my name' (Lytton 2008, 214). To this end, she re-joins the WSPU, but this time in the name of Miss Jane Warton. Her disguise (which she describes in hilarious detail, as well as the elaborate shopping trip she goes on to put it together) is almost so 'unprepossessing' as to appear comical, drawing laughter from boys in the street, and sometimes her fellow suffragettes, thus threatening to give away the show. Now an old hand at minimising any rough treatment she might receive, she speeds up the process of getting arrested by addressing the milling crowd in the streets, urging them to follow her to the prison governor's house and demand the release of mistreated prisoners. 'To my surprise,' she writes, 'the crowd began to follow me.' Finally, worried that she might be roughhoused by the police, she engages in a symbolic infraction, 'limply dropping [stones] over the hedge into the Governor's garden' (Lytton 2008, 220–1). For this she is marched off to the police station, and her adventure as a working-class prisoner begins in earnest.

When, after four days of hunger strike, the Senior Medical Officer gives her one more chance to 'take food voluntarily' before descending on her with his feeding apparatus, he is met with the eternal negative: 'I told him that was absolutely out of the question, that when our legislators ceased to resist enfranchising women then I should cease to resist taking food in prison' (Lytton 2008, 236). She is helpless, in other words, to comply with his request. The ensuing procedure is, as expected, a harrowing one, and although it bears some of the characteristics of Parkes Weber's encounters with the reversed enteric action of Rosa, the fact of its being narrated from the point of view of the 'patient' rather than of the doctor, as well as the plethora of details about what precisely is involved when an arrested peristaltic system is interfered with from the outside, turns Lytton's account into a case study of the doctor's questionable condition as much as a testimony to her own violation. Lytton undergoes several episodes with the rubber tube, documenting along the way a transformation both of herself and of the perpetrator of the violence on her body – 'an anti-care of the self, aimed at making common cause both with the victims and abettors of unjust sociality (by defending the former and reforming the latter)' (Leela Gandhi 2014, 2).

Placing it in the context of Agamben's definition of bare life, Ewa Ziarek characterises forcible feeding as a 'failed attempt to degrade femininity to a life stripped of all political meaning and reduced merely to physical survival' (Ziarek 2012, 162).

> What Agamben's theory allows us to clarify is that the violence of forcible feedings does not represent a juridical punishment but rather a case of the sovereign decision to restore the normal situation of the law's operation. Although all the trappings and the representation of forcible feedings as a 'medical treatment' administered by the prison doctor were meant to mask this sovereign violence by relegating it to medical science, the medicalization of torture most clearly reveals the biopolitical character of sovereignty. (Ziarek 2012, 162)

Like other historians of the suffragette movement, Ziarek analyses the forcible feedings as instances of 'camouflaged sexualized violence of bodily penetration that reenacts rape' (Ziarek 2012, 162), and reminds us that Agamben's 'bare life' is as much about the 'power to inflict torture and rape with impunity' as it is about 'the power to kill without committing homicide' (Ziarek 2012, 162).

But in addition to its status as rape, the forcible feeding should be understood as an instance of the (violent) biopolitics of regularity. If the 'rational authority of the law' is 'haunted by archaic sovereign violence' (Ziarek 2012, 162), it is played out in specifically alimentary and peristaltic terms. First and foremost, in an attempt to 'restore the normal situation of the law's operation', the prison doctor seeks to restore, by mechanical and scientific means, the disrupted motility of the suffragette's intestinal tract, and to reinsert it back into the metabolic workings of the prison house. Constance Lytton counters the doctor's professed scientific methods with some biopolitical knowledge of her own, and indeed, as they argue about how her particular peristaltic system works, she exposes the shortcomings of his medical knowledge, and pulls away the veneer of rationality that masks the passion of his violent impulses. Or rather, she reveals the inherent violence embedded within the rationality of science. Medical knowledge in the hands of the state-appointed doctor here enacts what Agamben calls a 'state of exception',[7] in which what defines one as a political subject (in this case, the apparent right to one's body), is suspended, and the actual relation of the biologically defined human body to sovereign power is revealed.

Let's dig a little deeper into the metabolic workings of 'bare life' and faecal habitus within a biopolitical regime by turning to Nicholas De Genova's take on Marx and metabolism. He reminds us

> that Marx borrows the concept of metabolism to get at the question of what constitutes 'species being', or 'so-called "human nature" from the standpoint of re-situating the figure of the human *within* nature. (De Genova 2016, 131)

'As an objective and natural *living* being,' De Genova writes, 'the human consequently exists in a constant (metabolic) relation to external (objective) nature' (De Genova 2016, 131). Linking metabolic Marx to Agamben's concept of 'bare life', De Genova reminds us of Marx's observation that man, 'through his own action, mediates, regulates, and controls the metabolism between himself and nature ... *as a force of nature*', thereby transforming both his own nature and nature per se. Labour is thus 'a kind of threshold' – to revisit Agamben's phrase, a 'threshold of articulation between [human life as] nature and [human life as] culture' (De Genova 2016, 133). De Genova inserts the bracketed phrases within his quote from Agamben here, in an effort to specify what is meant by the otherwise vague categories of nature and culture, i.e. that it is in particular what we have come to think of as the distinction between natural and cultural 'human life' that is at stake here, particularly as this distinction is continually being crossed, and 'undergoing the practical purposive activity that mediates "the metabolism" between the human species and nature' (De Genova 2016, 133).

Agamben's concept of 'bare life' then is to be understood *not* as natural or biological human life, but

> is only apprehensible in contrast to the plenitude of ways in which human beings really live, namely within and through one or another ensemble of social relations. Bare life is, then, a conceptual foil for all the historically specific and socially particular forms in which human ('biological') life is qualified by its inscription within one or another sociopolitical order. (De Genova 2016, 128)

Bare life is '*what remains* when human existence, while yet alive, is nonetheless stripped of all the encumbrances of social location and juridical identity and thus bereft of all the qualifications for properly political inclusion and belonging' (De Genova 2016, 128). Moreover, in order to authorise its own sovereignty, modern state power 'requires and conjures into being precisely this fictive human beast, this naked figure of life bereft' (De Genova 2016, 128).

We may now rethink De Genova's iteration of Agamben, Marx and this mediated metabolism in the context of faecal habitus. For surely, we must understand that 'bare life' for the human-as-peristaltic-tube is not the figure of pre-historic man whose excretion is as random and frequent as the cow's; rather, it is the contemporary human deprived of the infrastructure and continuous social relations that permit the performance of a specific faecal habitus. Indeed, faecal habitus is nothing other than one of the primary 'forms' that 'qualify biological life' as it is inscribed within a given sociopolitical order; it is one of the 'qualifications for properly political inclusion and belonging'. With this in mind, we must ask, what material connectives facilitate the survival of political man (*bios*) in relation to sovereign power as the state, or the agents of this state, that guarantee this survival? What is the chain of connections through which political man is presumed to be 'rescued' from a life 'bare' of the conventions that allow for a well-managed (in Marx's terms, 'mediated, regulated, and controlled') metabolic existence?

### Rescue operation

We turn now to the harrowing details of Lytton's forcible feeding experiences, as she lies on a plank while a phalanx of wardresses holds down her arms, head and feet. Describing the doctor leaning on her knees and stooping over her chest to get at her mouth, she expresses her trepidation, but not about the forcible feeding itself. 'I had looked forward to this moment with so much anxiety lest my identity should be discovered beforehand, that I felt positively glad when the time had come' (Lytton 2008, 236). Fearful as it is, her goal is finally close at hand, that is, to be able to observe in detail what has been taking place in obscurity, whatever that might entail.

Now a calculated mixture of resistance and submission must be engaged: 'The sense of being overpowered by more force than

I could possibly resist was complete, but I resisted nothing except with my mouth' (Lytton 2008, 236). The doctor begins with a wooden gag, warning that if she doesn't open up, he will have to resort to the more painful steel gag. 'He seemed annoyed at my resistance and he broke into a temper as he plied my teeth with the steel implement' (Lytton 2008, 237). Finally, after pushing painfully on two false molars that can't be removed, he 'got the gag between my teeth, when he proceeded to turn it much more than necessary until my jaws were fastened wide apart, far more than they could go naturally' (Lytton 2008, 237).

> Then he put down my throat a tube which seemed to me much too wide and was something like four feet in length. The irritation of the tube was excessive. I choked the moment it touched my throat until it had got down. Then the food was poured in quickly; it made me sick a few seconds after it was down and the action of the sickness made my body and legs double up, but the wardresses instantly pressed back my head and the doctor leant on my knees. The horror of it was more than I can describe. I was sick over the doctor and the wardresses, and it seemed a long time before they took the tube out. (Lytton 2008, 237)

Let's pull back from the 'horror of it' for a moment to consider how this procedure resonates with what was going on at the German Hospital, where Dr Parkes Weber and his female assistants likewise attended to the anti-peristaltic vomiting of Rosa Strosmann, even facilitating it by inserting suppositories and coloured enemas from behind. In both cases, a woman has found the means to enter a desired institution, and then to come under the attention of its medical experts. What brings them together is a dissenting enteric system. In Strosmann's case, peristaltic reversal would seem, as far as the doctor can ascertain, to be a question of an unconscious hysterical condition, though he must also entertain the possibility that she is malingering, or that at the very least, it is a case of hysterical malingering (willed and unwilled at the same time). In Lytton's case, peristaltic cessation is due to a deliberate act on her part, the hunger strike, and yet even this hunger strike has been presented as something that is beyond her control: she can't 'cease to resist taking food in prison' until legislators have 'ceased to resist enfranchising women' (Lytton 2008, 236). She is helpless, a vow is a vow, it cannot be broken, it is a matter of the 'eternal negative'.

Moreover, in Lytton, we would seem to have a woman who is not among those whose 'gagging capacities of the fauces have borrowed from the pharynx and become more like swallowing' (Wilson 2004a, 81). Lytton gags as soon as the rubber tube touches her throat, and her stomach refuses the food (whose consistency she does not yet know) the moment it exits the tube inside her. Lytton's hunger strike, facilitated by the second brain of her enteric system, is a stubborn one: anything that is forced in by the doctor is immediately returned by the same route, traveling back up her oesophagus and out her widely propped mouth, presumably outside the tube within a tube that has attempted to 'feed' her. It sprays doctor and wardresses alike, and will have to find its way into the city's sewage system without having been 'processed' by Lytton's own metabolism. A local 'metabolic rift' of a different kind is set up here; it presents itself as a conundrum to the doctor and the officials from whom he takes his orders.

That the doctor is not in some respects equipped to handle such a conundrum is signalled by Lytton's report that he seems prone to break out 'into a temper' (as when he can't open her teeth at first), and concludes his encounter by giving his patient 'a slap on the cheek, not violently, but, as it were, to express his contemptuous disapproval, and he seemed to take for granted that my distress was assumed' (Lytton 2008, 237).

Here, I would argue that, aside from hiding her identity as a well-known member of the aristocracy, Lytton's adoption of the Jane Warton persona serves the additional purpose of helping to objectify the specimen under her own study as she investigates the vicissitudes and agential power of peristalsis in captivity. By this I mean that her references to her body and her state of mind as a subject shifts, at key moments, from first to third person as she recounts the sequence of events. The doctor's slapping of her face, so reminiscent of the attitude taken by doctors toward their hysterical patients suspected of malingering (exhibiting not an authentic, but an 'assumed' distress) leads to one of these switch points. At first, she says, 'it seemed such an utterly contemptible thing to have done that I could only laugh in my mind' (Lytton 2008, 237). His impulsive display of contempt arouses her own contempt, as a member of a class equal if not superior to his own, prompting her laughter at the spectacle he has made of himself. But a moment later, as though realising that its status as a contemptible spectacle depends on the relative freedom of the recipient of the slap to witness it as such, she re-evaluates the meaning of the event:

> Then suddenly I saw Jane Warton lying before me, and it seemed as if I were outside of her. She was the most despised, ignorant and helpless prisoner that I had seen. When she had served her time and was out of the prison, no one would believe anything she said, and the doctor when he had fed her by force and tortured her body, struck her on the cheek to show how he despised her! That was Jane Warton, and I had come to help her. (Lytton 2008, 237)

This passage is expressive of Lytton's dissociated state as a reaction to trauma – she leaves her body and observes it as though from the outside, which allows for a defensive preservation of her ego by removing it momentarily from the violence dealt to it. But it is also indicative of how her deliberate disguise as Jane Warton is itself a precaution against trauma, insofar as this, and subsequent shifts to the third person in reference to her 'self', are consciously built into the overall experience of her espionage project. This is and is not a splitting of the psyche as a flight from trauma; or rather, the split has been planned for and then recuperated into a reparative politics in which the one 'saved' is both oneself and all those belonging to one's constituency. Lytton may be understood thus to perform what De Genova calls the 'rescue operation' that sovereign power normally reserves for itself.

'In a sense,' writes De Genova, 'we may understand sovereign power to legitimate itself by means of a kind of rescue operation, recuperating human (properly social) life from this spectral double [bare life] that resides stubbornly within the physical materiality of the human species, but only phantasmagorically, as a putatively "natural" or "animal" (debased) mode of (human) being' (De Genova 2016, 129).

Lytton has already offered an image of the 'bare life' to which women have been consigned by sovereign power in England. In Littlehampton, before she has joined the ranks of the suffragettes, she witnesses a scene in the street that makes a 'great impression upon [her] conscience':

> All kinds of people were forming a ring round a sheep which had escaped as it was being taken to the slaughter-house. It looked old and misshapen. A vision suddenly rose in my mind of what it should have

been on its native mountain-side with all its forces rightly developed, vigorous and independent. There was a hideous contrast between that vision and the thing in the crowd. (Lytton 2008, 59)

Jeered at by the onlookers, the sheep is eventually caught and manhandled by its 'gaolers', and is given a 'cuff in the face'. After lecturing the men, Lytton reflects that the sheep has revealed to her, for the first time, 'the position of women throughout the world'.

> I realized how often women are held in contempt as being outside the pale of human dignity, excluded or confined, laughed at and insulted because of conditions in themselves for which they are not responsible, but which are due to fundamental injustices with regard to them, and to the mistakes of a civilization in the shaping of which they have had no free share. (Lytton 2008, 59)

She realises that she has been 'blind to the sufferings peculiar to women as such' regardless of class, race or nationality (Lytton 2008, 60). 'Designating the passage between the animal and the human,' writes Ziarek, '"the old and misshapen" sheep is the figure of damaged life, deprived of political or religious significance, a life whose biological survival is at risk' (Ziarek 2012, 164). It serves as the figure of 'bare life' not because it is an animal, nor because it naturally occupies the biological realm of pure survival (as it might have done 'on its native mountain-side') but rather because its 'misshapen' quality is precisely the result of what Agamben would call its 'state of exception'. Its status as 'livestock' (rather than as 'wild') has already included it in a grouping of other sheep, all of them 'social animals' governed by the sovereign power of the human farmer; but this particular sheep does not enjoy the 'ensemble of social relations' that would normally characterise the existence of the rest of its flock. This sheep has been 'stripped of all the encumbrances of social location and juridical identity', and is thus 'bereft of all the qualifications for properly political inclusion and belonging' (De Genova 2016, 128). This is the 'state of exception' it has been thrust into, '*banned* or expunged from the political and legal order' of the flock governed by sovereign power.

If Lytton sees the sheep as figuring how women have been 'held in contempt as being outside the pale of human dignity, excluded or confined, laughed at and insulted', it is not because of their intrinsic animal status, but because of their deformity due to 'conditions in themselves for which they are not responsible, but which are due to fundamental injustices with regard to them, and to the mistakes of a civilization in the shaping of which they have had no free share' (Lytton 2008, 59). The sheep, and by extension women, live in a 'state of exception' to the political life otherwise guaranteed the rest of the flock. Or rather, women-as-deformed-sheep have been denied the kind of rescue operation that would normally recuperate 'human (properly social) life from this spectral double' known as 'bare life' (De Genova 2016, 129).

Moreover, Lytton's reference to the 'mistakes of a civilization in the shaping of which [women] have had no free share' resonates with Agamben's remarks on the ambiguity of who counts as a 'citizen'. Agamben turns to Sieyes for an understanding of how women are both included and excluded as citizens. Natural and civil rights are 'those rights *for* whose preservation society is formed' (passive rights), whereas political rights are 'those rights *by* which society is formed' (active rights) (Agamben 1998, 130). Thus women are among those who may enjoy the rights of 'passive citizens' but 'must have no active influence on public matters' (quoted in Agamben 1998, 130). In defining the '*membres du souverain*,' Sieyes continues, women are expressly consigned to the group of those who 'will not be citizens' (Agamben 1998, 131). This describes the status pertaining to women in England at the turn of the century; they possess 'passive' rights, which are in turn 'actively' put in place for them by those who may exercise the right to vote. In this respect, they are starved of the capacity to generate the rights that form the society they must live in. The suffragettes see this clearly, and argue that, as previous rebellions by men were about seizing what Sieyes would call 'active' rights, the women's movement, experienced by Lytton as an amalgam of activity in passivity, passivity in motion, is also about seizing these rights that have been denied to them.

Perhaps most importantly, the particular context in which Lytton takes into her own hands the 'rescue operation' that sovereignty normally reserves for itself is not inconsequential. It happens in the throes of unsuccessful forcible feeding, the autonomic system returning the state's gruel back to it, spraying the agents of sovereign power in the process, and prompting the slap on the cheek, the cuff in the face of retaliation. 'If the torture of forcible feedings is an attempt to recapture bare life as the referent of sovereign power,' Ziarek writes, 'this means that sovereign power over bare life is tenuous and open to contestation' (Ziarek 2012, 163). The materiality of that contestation, of Lytton's extension of 'help' to the Jane Wartons of the world, unfolds in explicitly peristaltic, metabolic terms. Let us return again to the scene of Lytton's repeated confrontations with her opponent.

As the feedings continue, Lytton attempts to intervene, offering advice and suggestions designed to help the doctor carry out his task in a manner that is more satisfactory for all concerned, beginning with the request that 'unless you consider it part of your duty, would you please not strike me when you have finished your odious job?' (Lytton 2008, 239). Oral communications like this are either ignored, or only partially complied with, but never answered directly by the doctor; he seems only inclined to 'reply' when something other than speech reaches him from her mouth. During this feeding, 'the sickness was worse than the time before. As the tube was removed I was unavoidably sick over the doctor. He flew away from me and out of the cell, exclaiming angrily, "If you do that again next time I shall feed you twice"' (Lytton 2008, 239).

During the next feeding, Lytton takes an even more proactive role in how the procedure will unfold, beginning by persuading the doctor to allow her to be fed sitting in a chair rather than lying on the plank. She then shares some information about her enteric system meant to facilitate a more successful feeding experience:

> I told him that I was a small eater, that the capacity of my body was very limited and if only he would give less quantities the result might be better. I also begged that he would not press the tube so far down into my body. (Lytton 2008, 240)

Her advice is unsurprisingly treated with contempt again, the doctor replying that her stomach must be 'longer than his, since I was taller than he was' (Lytton 2008, 240). Thus, she is continually sick as the doctor 'continued to pour food in'. Finally, 'this produced a sort of shivering fit and my teeth chattered when the gag was removed; I suppose that every vestige of colour must have left my face, for the doctor seemed surprised and alarmed' (Lytton 2008, 240–1). Notably, it is a symptom presumed to be impossible to dissimulate (paleness) that causes the doctor to show he is 'sorry for what he had done', and to call a junior medical officer into the cell (Lytton 2008, 241). The colleague listens to her heart through the stethoscope 'for barely the space of a second – he could not have heard two beats – and exclaimed, "Oh, ripping, splendid heart! You can go on with her!"' (Lytton 2008, 241).

With subsequent feedings, she continues to make suggestions for improvement, recommending, for instance, changes in the contents of her meals. It is only after she vomits them back up that she can observe and learn 'what were the ingredients put down my body' (Lytton 2008, 242). Seeing 'Bovril and brandy' in her vomited matter, for instance, she advises the doctor that the brandy warms her at first but then leaves her 'freezing cold after about two hours, and I thought it was no use. As for the Bovril, I had the strongest objection to it of a vegetarian kind, and I begged him not to give it to me again' (Lytton 2008, 242). To this the doctor surprisingly agrees, though she is sick again when given 'milk and plasmon' (Lytton 2008, 277).

Wondering by now if the authorities are starting to suspect that she is not who she appears to be, she decides:

> to take the utmost advantage of any privilege, in order to bring the officials to act reasonably, to check their recklessness as much as possible, and to bring them to strain the regulations so far as might be – not, as heretofore, in the direction of brutality, but in the direction of hygiene, if not of humanity. (Lytton 2008, 243)

She might save them all from being further sprayed by her vomit, if nothing more, and so she pleads 'afresh with the doctor to try the experiment of giving me less quantity of food, of putting less of the tube into the body, of using less glycerine, which greatly irritated my throat the moment the tube touched it' (Lytton 2008, 243). To this, he seems to listen, and though there is 'not much difference in what he did, yet his manner of doing it was different' (Lytton 2008, 243).

At the sixth meal, Lytton attempts to convey something of the state of her intestines, entering directly into the matter of why her peristaltic system remains completely at a standstill, despite repeated attempts to start it up again.

> I complained to the doctor that the processes of digestion were absolutely stagnant. I suggested to him that he should leave out one meal, with a view to allowing the natural forces of the body to readjust

themselves, unhampered by the kind of paralysing cramp and arresting of the natural functions which resulted from fear. I also suggested that instead of brandy – he had given me another meal of Bovril and brandy – fruit juice or the water in which a pear or apple had been stewed should be added to my food. (Lytton 2008, 245)

The state of affairs seems clear enough here; but the doctor turns to his assistant and asks, 'Do you understand her? I don't. Does she mean that she is constipated? If so, you see about it' (Lytton 2008, 245). That she has no doubt trespassed too directly into the territory of his expertise is evident by his reference to her in the third person, thus putting her in her place as object, not subject, of medical discourse. She tries to make her meaning clear to the woman who takes her to the weighing machine, but 'I was never given either a drug [presumably the doctor's intended meaning of 'see about it'] or, so far as I know, the fruit juice in my food' (Lytton 2008, 245).

Moreover, it is not only her enteric system that is kept, through the aid of the doctor and his assistant, in its constipated state of 'paralysing cramp', but, as she points out, her powers of communication as well. This she takes to be the situation for prisoners in general:

> Very likely I had spoken unintelligibly. I seldom had interviewed a doctor on my own behalf, and am not versed in their technical language. Whenever I spoke to this doctor it was either immediately before or after the feeding, so that my nerves were unstrung. Moreover, prisoners are made to feel in the presence of nearly every prison official that they are the scum of the earth, suspected of deceit, prejudged and found wanting; this has a paralysing effect on a prisoner's powers of expression. (Lytton 2008, 245)

If a complete paralysis has set in, both of her peristaltic system and of her 'powers of expression' (which can only be measured by the extent to which her interlocutor receives, and acts upon, the information she has 'expressed' to him), then there is no hope of reconnecting her own metabolic system to the larger circulation and flow of the prison's metabolic system. Or as Lytton puts it, the doctor has 'quite ignored my argument that until I begin to keep down the food I could not profit by it or gain in weight' (Lytton 2008, 245).

This institutionally maintained paralysis threatens to overwhelm Lytton by her sixth night, as she details for us the mechanics by which her body has by now arrived almost entirely at a stand-still. 'Most of my friends had been fed by the doctor standing at the back of the patient,' she begins, 'whereas this doctor adjusted the tube and fed me from the front, a process which he carried out by sitting across my knees' (Lytton 2008, 246). Leaving aside the unwanted intimacy of this front-to-front aggression, Lytton focuses on the effect it has on the circulation in her limbs: 'By this time I could not feel my legs and arms, except just by the joints where I felt the pain of the cold' (Lytton 2008, 246). Normally she would get up at night and walk around, to prevent her limbs from becoming useless.

> But on Thursday night, my sixth in prison, I fell really asleep and when I awoke I had an unexpected feeling of ease and freedom from pain or fear. I was unconscious of my nearly rigid limbs, the beat of my heart was scarcely perceptible; I supposed I had only a little while to live. The prospect of release was inexpressibly welcome. (Lytton 2008, 246)

It is only when she hears, or hallucinates, the words 'no surrender' that she snaps out of it, admonishing herself not to 'abdicate my job in this ease-loving way'. She rubs the life back into her feet and hands, and forces herself to walk up and down her cell, picturing all the 'undefended women' on whose behalf she has been militating, and reflecting:

> How misplaced, unrighteous and unwomanly did non-resistance appear to me then. With every throb of my returning pulses I seemed to feel the rhythm of the world's soul calling to us women to uncramp our powers from the thralldom of long disuse. My whole being responded and I yearned to hand on the message as I myself had in spirit received it – 'Women, you are wanted ... whether or not victory is for your day, at least each one of you make sure that the one course impossible to you is surrender of your share in the struggle.' (Lytton 2008, 246–7)

The forced 'disuse' of her legs and arms, held down by the doctor's bodily weight and the wardress's hands, becomes an analogue for the 'cramp' and thralldom of disuse affecting women in general. Her hunger strike, paradoxically aided and abetted by institutional forcible feeding, results in a correlative to the bodily paralysis observed by the neurologists and psychoanalysts attending to the hysteric's insensible limbs; Lytton's is a communicative paralysis making itself felt at both the organic and the cognitive level at once. Her message goes out to all women who are urged to 'uncramp' their powers 'from the thralldom of long disuse', even as it lays out once more for legislators the absurdity of exerting the pressure that causes the paralysis in the first place.

The resolution to 'resist' is a paradoxical one when it comes to hunger strike and forcible feeding. Refusal to take food amounts to the subtraction of one's body-as-tube (that processor of the world) from the institutional peristaltic system whereby the state, having taken charge of the bodies of its law-breaking citizens, must supply sustenance to them, and then a means of eliminating their waste, even if the conditions for elimination are not in keeping with expectations of a middle-class faecal habitus (privacy, cleanliness, water-borne flush systems in the control of the user of the facility). To resist here means to bring the whole cycle of ingestion and expulsion to a stop, although it would seem (according to Lytton and others) that the prison diet itself can constipate the prisoner and bring on 'stagnation' of its own accord. Whether accomplished by hunger strike or the body's own inability to 'process' the prison food, this non-cooperation burdens the prison system, and by extension the state, with an organism in danger of expiring. Refusing food is only the most extreme among a series of passive renunciations of systemic routine, beginning with the withholding of legal testimony, as when Teresa Billington-Grieg 'refused to testify' in the Magistrates' Court where she was being brought up on charges, 'claiming the Court lacked jurisdiction because women had no part in making the laws she was accused of breaking' (McPhee and Fitzgerald 2001, 6), and when Lytton refuses to change into prison uniform and must be undressed by staff, then refuses to engage in needle-work, and so is ironically punished with a bread and water diet (she is already on hunger strike).

Once forcible feeding begins, a different set of circumstances sets in: for Lytton this means at first the clenching of her teeth – the only place she has a choice to resist or not (her limbs being pinned down by doctor and wardresses); then the unwilled rejection by her peristaltic system itself of the contents of the tube. As if to offer her antagonists a fighting chance to get her metabolic system hooked back up to that of the prison, she begins to offer advice and suggestions, almost as though it is for their benefit. It is the doctor's own fault, then, if he fails to prevent her from losing more weight. Following Lytton's night of paralysis, and her plea for all women to 'uncramp our powers from the thralldom of long disuse', she is subjected to a feeding during which the wardresses have given up holding her, at which point 'the pain of the tube in my body was more than I could bear; I seized hold of it and pulled it up' (Lytton 2008, 248). She is reproved, but the feeding does not continue.

> I was overwhelmed with the horror of the process, and for the first time I was convulsed with sobs. The doctor was kind to me. I said that I only cried from having no strength to resist, but that I meant to live out my sentence if I could. (Lytton 2008, 248)

It seems contradictory that she should think of her crying as due to having 'no strength to resist', given that she has just in fact resisted the forcible feeding by pulling the tube from her mouth. But perhaps what she means is something more like this: that she lacks the strength to go on with the charade that the forcible feeding is doing her any good; given the first opportunity, she has pulled out the tube, rather than resist her body's refusal to 'live out her sentence', tube and all.

Though the authorities eventually do realise who she is, she has by now accomplished the goal she had set for herself: to prove that 'a totally different category of treatment' is 'meted out to one set of people from another' (Lytton 2008, 258). When she was imprisoned as Lady Lytton, her heart was tested and it was determined that she could not withstand forcible feeding; as Jane Warton, she was forcibly fed with no prior medical testing, and only the most fleeting pseudo-examination of her heart was made by the doctor's subordinate. Lytton's reports on the many ordinary women she met, and what seemed to be their unconscionable suffering while at the mercy of the prison system, could now be supplemented by her own testimony as to what a Jane Warton would be subjected to as a ward of the state. And in the end, although she provides an ongoing account of continued betrayals of the Liberal government in its failure to extend the vote, and renewed militant suffrage activity as a result, it would seem that the real value of her account is as a document in the direction of prison reform after all. For by her fourth imprisonment, she and her fellow suffragettes enjoy the benefits of palpable changes in Holloway's routine, though it is not clear the extent to which these changes are enjoyed by the common prisoner, or only by women imprisoned in the line of political action.

## Passive resistance and Satyagraha

Parama Roy argues that the gendered character of Gandhi's fasting 'cannot be understood without invoking a large, inescapably gendered cast, including his mother, his male friends, his wife, his sons, and his female and male disciples' (Roy 2010, 76–7). But surely we must add to this cast the British suffragettes, of whom Gandhi himself was arguably a disciple. For even as Constance Lytton was practising her version of the 'eternal negative', exerting agency through the willed passivity of imperfection and self-ruin, revealing how the militant suffrage movement functioned like a kind of autonomic system of politics, Gandhi was documenting the suffragette campaign with an inspired enthusiasm, publishing regular bulletins about it in *Indian Opinion*.

As early as the autumn of 1906, Gandhi borrows the WSPU slogan, opening a news item for *Indian Opinion* with the 26 October headline: 'DEEDS BETTER THAN WORDS', and praising the petitioners' willingness to go to gaol rather than pay a fine for taking action (attempting to enter the House) when their words fell on deaf ears (Gandhi 1999 Vol. 5, 431–2). In February 1907, news of the latest suffrage delegations having reached him in South Africa from England, Gandhi poses a question to readers of *Indian Opinion*: 'When Women are Manly, will men be effeminate?' He was referring to the 'manly deeds' of the suffragettes: 'The women of England have no franchise. They are fighting for it without minding people's ridicule.' Describing their march on Parliament, he then asks whether Indians in South Africa will be willing to 'go to gaol' if the Asiatic Ordinance is enacted (Gandhi 1999 Vol. 6, 288).

By 1908, he had devised (through the help of a reader's response to a contest) a Gujarati equivalent for what was being called the suffragettes' 'passive resistance': '"Resistance" means determined opposition to anything. The correspondent [winner of the contest Gandhi had announced] has rendered it as *agraha*. *Agraha* in a right cause is *sat* or *satya agraha* ... firmness in a good cause' (Gandhi 1999 Vol. 8, 80). Or as Erik Erikson puts it, 'Satyagraha was the Sanskritic combination Gandhi . . . chose as a name for his way of life and of action – "Truth" and "Force," in literal translation' (Erikson 1969, 198). Erikson adds that Satyagraha can be understood as the 'leverage of truth', where the body is deployed as 'a sensitive instrument' (Erikson 1969, 198), that is, politically instrumentalised.

> Satyagraha did have its origins in a technological imagery in which the body was still part of the tool; and it will be seen that even today the more direct uses of Satyagraha always include the body and the meeting of bodies: the facing of the opponent 'eye to eye', the linking of arms in defensive and advancing phalanxes, the body 'on the line': all these confrontations symbolize the conviction that the solidarity of unarmed bodies remains a leverage and a measure even against the cold and mechanized gadgetry of the modern state. (Erikson 1969, 198)

And so by 11 April 1908, an issue of *Indian Opinion* bears the headline: 'BRITISH WOMEN AS SATYAGRAHIS' and announces that 'We have always compared the Indian satyagraha movement with that of the British suffragettes' (Gandhi 1999 vol. 8, 263).

In early July 1909, when Wallace Dunlop inaugurated the first hunger strike, Gandhi had just arrived for the second of his deputations on behalf of the Indians of South Africa. During this visit, he included substantive reports on suffragette activity in almost every issue of *Indian Opinion*, or in letters to his close associates, describing meetings he had attended, the impressive funds collected, the means of publicity, the admirable willingness of both leaders and rank and file to be arrested and imprisoned (Gandhi 1999 vol. 9, 429, 435, 452–5). His emphasis on details of the incarceration of suffragettes had implications for what was going on in South Africa, where Indian satyagrahis were now indeed submitting to imprisonment rather than accede to unjust registration laws and fingerprinting for non-whites. He meant this emphasis on satyagraha, as an ethos shared by Englishwomen and South African Indians alike, to contrast with the kind of violent resistance that had been demonstrated shortly before his arrival by Madanlal Dhingra's assassination of Sir Curzon Wyllie, a former army officer and civil servant in India. Dhingra had declared that the killing of an Englishman was perfectly justified, given that England was 'responsible for hanging, deporting and starving to death millions of his countrymen, and for draining wealth out of India estimated at £100 million a year' (Guha 2015, 351). If he was sentenced to death, he added, 'the vengeance of my countrymen will be all the more keener' (Guha 2015, 332). The idea of armed struggle against British oppression was always thus an antagonistic force to be contended with in Gandhi's writings in favour of satyagraha. In a long bulletin elaborating on suffragette activity (published in the 28 August issue of *Indian Opinion*), Gandhi included an account of the newest development in militant suffrage strategies. As the government did not concede first class status to suffragette prisoners, Gandhi wrote,

> they resolved collectively to disobey the gaol regulations. They broke the windows of prison cells and refused to submit to any of the regulations. In consequence, they were confined in dark cells ... at last, all the women stopped taking food. One of them ate nothing for six days, some others for five days. In this way, everyone fasted. The Government felt helpless in the end and let them off. (Gandhi 1999 vol. 9, 453)

In August, he describes them as 'putting up a wonderful show', and not letting themselves be 'deterred by any kind of suffering' (Gandhi 1999 vol. 9, 429). They have 'suffered in health, but they do not give up the struggle', showing no 'ordinary courage', but a 'great faith', to the extent that 'a great many women have been ruined, and more are being ruined, in this struggle, but they do not yield.... We can learn quite a few things and draw much inspiration from the suffragettes' example' (Gandhi 1999 vol. 9, 429). Gandhi is clearly impressed at this point by the element of 'self ruin' in the suffragettes' refusal to eat. Their example is nothing less than a practice of imperfection, enacted by disrupting their own peristaltic flow.

It must be clear now that, for Gandhi, the suffragettes were exempla to be followed by the Indians in South Africa; it was the suffragettes' bravery, perseverance, ability to raise funds, willingness to be incarcerated, 'manliness' and, finally, their fasting that Gandhi most often praised in his letters and articles in *Indian Opinion*; and maybe most importantly, it was in response to the suffragettes' 'passive resistance' that Gandhi developed his political philosophy for Indian independence. Even his disapproval of what he saw as suffragettes' violent tactics (stone throwing, window breaking, bothering politicians at their homes) did not prevent him from revisiting the example of women's suffrage throughout the 1900s, 1910s and well into the 1920s, as he worked out the specifics of satyagraha. You could say that satyagraha was born within Gandhi's discursive inhabitation of the suffragette campaign, and that it then slowly distinguished itself from their 'passive resistance' through a process of separation and individuation. If Gandhi always had before him the shifting example of the suffragette struggle as he worked out the precepts of satyagraha, it would suggest that his practice of insistence of truth, including its peristaltic aspects, always contained within it the suffragettes' prior practice of passive resistance.

### Revolt

The central insight of Ziarek's study of the militant suffrage movement is that we must understand the suffragettes' demand for the 'right to vote' as a deeper demand for the 'right to revolt'. Ziarek teases out the political and aesthetic implications of this emphasis on revolt, putting it in the context of Hannah Arendt's distinction between 'constituted' and 'constituting' power:

> The suffragettes' demand for inclusion within the British state and the gendered, class, and imperial power of its institutions – the demand for the vote – challenges and reproduces the *constituted* power of the law. At the same time, the more fundamental political right to revolt reclaims for women *constituting* power and the capacity to create a new beginning that would exceed established power structures. (Ziarek 2012, 32)

She quotes Teresa Billington-Grieg on how emphasis on the vote is exceeded by the women's movement: 'Militancy,' she writes, is not 'the mere expression of an urgent desire for the vote, but . . . an aggressive proclamation of a deeper right – the right of insurrection' (Ziarek 2012, 23). I reproduce Billington-Grieg's words here because she chooses rather a different term to emphasise what lies deeper than the vote: not 'revolt' but 'insurrection'. And in fact, Ziarek could just as easily have chosen one of a number of near synonyms for 'revolt': rebellion, uprising, insurgency, etc. But in her book, it is revolt, associated perhaps with revolution, that serves as the dominant discursive 'beyond' of the vote.

I, too, would place the emphasis on revolt, though not for the same reasons as Ziarek. For no other word in the associational vicinity of revolt carries with it, in addition to the sense of willed political uprising, an unwilled rising up of the gorge. What word can bring together better the political with the biological, the conscious with the autonomic, the overthrow of external power systems with the throwing up of what a stomach refuses to accept? Both Teresa Billington-Grieg and Constance Lytton, the two suffragettes Ziarek reads most closely, use the term 'revolt' in their assessments of the suffragette movement. But it is astonishing to find that, of the six instances in which Lytton uses the term, it applies exclusively to the body's involuntary reactions to that which disgusts or repels it: she finds the crowd's behaviour 'revolting' in their treatment of deputations as spectacle; she wonders whether 'indignation, revolt, dull indifference, remorse, or the harrowingly abject penitence so frequent in suffering beings' is uppermost in the minds of a Black Maria's passengers; her prison shirt and flannel sheet are 'revolting in appearance'; her mind is filled with 'horror and revolt' when she realises a wire netting is meant to catch would-be suicides when they jump; her own 'pent up feelings of indignation and revolt' sometimes make her want to laugh; and when another prisoner is brought in to clean up Lytton's vomit after a forcible feeding, it is 'altogether a revolting business' (Lytton 2008, 87, 93, 110, 173, 181, 239–40). For the realm of the political Lytton uses terms like protest, rebellion, revolution – though (oddly) never insurrection or emancipation.

Billington-Grieg, on the other hand, uses revolt almost entirely in its political sense: pointing out that liberty 'is only won by revolt' (McPhee and Fitzgerald 2001, 114), or that 'where the victims of aggression or custom are ignorant and disunited the opportunities for reasoned and effective revolt are practically reduced to nothing' (McPhee and Fitzgerald 2001, 143); or that 'our revolt itself was of very much greater value than the vote we demanded' (McPhee and Fitzgerald 2001, 148). In a rare passage where the visceral sense of the term emerges, its dual denotation is remarked on explicitly by Billington-Grieg. Describing the earliest years of the WSPU, when its members sought solidarity from their male counterparts in socialist organisations, Billington-Grieg decides in the end that she and her comrades were 'foolish and blind' since 'all around us ... these organized, angry, revolting men – revolting often in both senses – were [either] the evidences of the deeper degradation of women which they ignored or shared in imposing, or, at best, [they] uttered unwillingly a feeble, sentimental and half-dishonest admission of worse injustices than they bore themselves' (McPhee and Fitzgerald 2001, 96).

It is as though Billington-Grieg and Lytton have taken charge each of only one side of this term that in its double-valence indicates the impossibility of marking where biological metabolism ends and social metabolism begins. Read together, the effect of their combined works is to emphasise how political being depends on the sequestering of biological being; insurrectionary revolt in the political realm excluding while relying upon visceral revolt in the realm of peristaltic 'bare life'. If social metabolism under sovereign power relies on the suppressed inclusion of physiological metabolism, then a revolt at the register of the autonomic nervous system undermines the political realm's stability, and assists in the assertion of the right to political revolt.

This splitting of the deployment of 'revolt' between the visceral and the insurrectionary is indicative perhaps of the disparate goals of these two feminists' writings: In *Emancipation in a Hurry*, Billington-Grieg mounts a critical history of the women's militant movement as a whole, and is little interested in an individual's subjective experience in prison, whereas Lytton, though making a political argument, does it through the imagery and rhetoric of subjective experience, observation and affective charge. Forcible feeding, via its direct intervention in the processes of consumption, digestion and excretion, tries to return the female body back to its place in the organic aspect of a state metabolism that is at once political and biological. The political agency of the state is premised on the biological conformity of its female subjects. To hunger strike is to disrupt and expose that relationship. With this in mind, we can see almost all the militant actions by the suffragettes as interventions in various moments of the metabolic circuitry that excludes women at the level of public discourse while including their bodies at the level of private compliance. To immerse one's reader, ad nauseum, in the revolting vicissitudes of the body's peristaltic rebellion under incarceration, all the while insisting on the circuitry that connects and enervates the various registers of metabolic transformations – this is a technique that extends beyond the time and place of the struggle for women's suffrage in Britain.

To gesture toward what I mean by this, I want to return to Leela Gandhi's account of the Mahatma's 'moral imperfectionism'. Gandhi, she reminds us, was engaged in 'politico-spiritual experiments ... to test whether work on the self had a communal effect – not by way of influence and example so much as by a spectral circuit':

> For example, did fasting not just symbolically but alchemically expiate the violence of others? Was there a sympathetic magic whereby acts of personal expropriation or self-reduction actually conjured gifts for the dispossessed? Did the giving up of one's own right to existence yield collateral for life itself? In other words, was the self of *sadhana* contagious? Could you catch the self-work of those around you and, likewise, virally communicate yours across short and long distances? (L. Gandhi 2014, 89)

Gandhi has, I would argue, caught the 'self-work' of the suffragettes by instituting, like them, a metabolic rift at the level of the physiological and social body, and by virally communicating this strategy across short and long distances. This contagion is thus not only something Gandhi wishes to initiate, but also something he has himself been borne along by, through his affective cathection to similar experiments conducted by the likes of Constance Lytton and her comrades. 'The more you develop [non-violence] in your own being,' he writes, 'the more infectious it becomes till it overwhelms your surroundings and by and by might oversweep the whole world' (quoted in L. Gandhi 2014, 90). By slowing to a complete stop the world's passage through his own enteric system, Gandhi seeks, in his common cause with the suffragettes, to 'oversweep' this same world, as though through an autonomic metabolism of political justice.

## Notes

1 For a classic charge of militancy as hysteria, see Sir Almroth Wright (1913, Appendix). For an excellent analysis of Wright's contribution, among a range of other medical authorities, to the 'scientific' argument against extending the franchise to women, see Cheryl R. Jorgensen-Earp and Darwin D. Jorgensen (2016). This includes an illuminating discussion of metabolic theory that posited women as 'anabolic' (conserving energy) and men as 'catabolic' (expending it), and the concomitant (though contradictory) claim that since women lack the physical force to uphold laws, they should therefore be excluded from making them.

2 This would be to return to the argument of Elaine Showalter in *The Female Malady*, whose alignment of shell shock victims during the great war with female hysterics in the same era has been as influential in scholarship on the cultural history of war as it has been in feminist history.
3 'Views and Comments', *The Egoist: An Individualist Review*, 1:10 (15 May 1914), 182–5; reprinted in the 2008 Broadview edition of *Prisons and Prisoners*. Editor Jason Haslam suggests Marsden as the author of the unsigned review.
4 In this respect, Marsden's remark inadvertently draws our twenty-first-century attention to the intersections noted in a recent double issue of *GLQ* on Viscerality: consider this observation in Kyla Wazana Tompkins' introduction:

> Many of the sites in the digestive process – from the mouth to the anus – are linked by the erotic and material economies that emerged from colonialism and slavery. Following this geography of the gut, the essays here return again and again to the moments, texts, and processes in and through which food, flesh, and the alimentary tract are linked to the reproducing of systems of inequality. (Tompkins 2014, 394)

5 For more on the intersection of Gandhi and suffragette hunger strikes, see: Grant 2011, Hunt 2005, and Lennon 2007.
6 For a substantive account of vegetarian restaurants as lively meeting places for suffragettes, see Elsa Richardson (2021): 'Cranks, Clerks, and Suffragettes: The Vegetarian Restaurant in British Culture and Fiction 1880–1914'.
7 '[W]hat characterizes modern politics is not so much the inclusion of zoē in the polis – which is, in itself, absolutely ancient – nor simply the fact that life as such becomes a principal object of the projections and calculations of State power. Instead the decisive fact is that, together with the process by which the exception everywhere becomes the rule, the realm of bare life – which is originally situated at the margins of the political order – gradually begins to coincide with the political realm, and exclusion and inclusion, outside and inside, bios and zoē, right and fact, enter into a zone of irreducible indistinction. At once excluding bare life from and capturing it within the political order, the state of exception actually constituted, in its very separateness, the hidden foundation on which the entire political system rested' (Agamben 1998, 9).

# Conclusion: Faecal Biopolitics in the Twenty-First Century

In the first few chapters of this book, I laid out the theoretical and systemic contexts in which the concept of metabolism, or in particular the peristaltic aspect of metabolism, has provided a model for biological, political, social, economic and affective movement and transformation. The attention drawn by Marx to a consequential 'rift' in the metabolic workings of agriculture, environment and global wellbeing, as well as his understanding of labour as a matter of how humans 'regulate, mediate, and control' the metabolic relation to a nature of which they are also a part, have figured heavily in the macro-picture I have drawn. Embedded within this Marxian metabolic model is Inglis's sociological understanding of one aspect of bodily habitus within classed (raced, gendered and caste-based) contexts, that is, a faecal habitus that emerged (in the West and global North) as a practice by which one group of humans distinguished themselves from other groups deemed subordinate to them. While faecal habitus is defined by Inglis in terms of a clean/dirty binary, I have argued that it is more usefully understood (through a Foucauldian framework) as a matter of the more or less regulated body. Thus a peristaltic norm in any given social or political context is one that entails a tacit or prescribed practice of regulation, a regulation dependent, moreover, on interlocking material supports (such as domestic and public bathrooms, functional waterborne sewage networks, wastewater treatment systems or, in certain times and places, faecal recycling and agricultural replenishing schemes, etc.) and agreed-upon social conventions (such as appropriate times and frequency of evacuation, appropriate places for evacuation, appropriate language around evacuation, etc.).

Agamben and De Genova have helped us to understand that faecal habitus is also one of the forms that qualifies 'biological life' as it is inscribed in a given sociopolitical order; to enjoy the status of being 'human' entails being 'rescued' by the state from the spectre of reduction to 'bare life'. To be deprived of the supports that allow consistent engagement in one's local version of faecal habitus is to be reduced to the 'bare life' of the unregulated excreter. Biopolitics is, among many other things, a matter of the maximisation of humans' metabolic and peristaltic life, deployed through infinite metabolic networks of enhanced motility, regularised enteric systems, available spaces for excreting, adequate sanitation, medical facilities, training clinics, etc.

Bringing Salleh's eco-feminist perspective to bear on Arendt's distinction between labour and work, I show how faecal biopolitics is a gendered affair, in which women are routinely more vigorously targeted for intervention, while also expected to act as the meta-industrial labourers most engaged in humans' metabolic relation to nature. I turn to the science of the human enteric system at the turn of the twentieth century to offer an evolutionary model of the human-as-tube through which a complex nervous system developed for the purpose of processing the world as it passed through us. Neurogastroenterology has characterised the enteric system as functioning like a 'second brain', that is, a gut that takes in stimuli and makes decisions about the proper time to accomplish a movement, semi-autonomously, of the 'first brain' of the cerebral cortex. Moreover, Sándor Ferenczi's biologically inflected psychoanalytic understanding of how the enteric system functions reveals that the gut, like the mind, also proceeds as though it, too, has an unconscious.

In my case-study analyses, I shift away from these more theoretical/structural questions of faecal biopolitics to consider, up close, three women whose peristaltic processes were brought under the 'care' of patriarchal agents of biopolitical enteric management – in the context of psychoanalysis, general medicine and carceral health. Here I examine in detail what happens when deviation, whether conscious or unwilled, from a prevailing faecal habitus is observed by, engaged with and comes into collaboration with medical professionals seeking at once to re-regularise the patient's peristaltic system while also producing knowledge about it – a power/knowledge nexus with multiple implications. To a greater or lesser extent, in each case we might say that a biopower was exercised by the dissident guts of the women in question, as acts of resistance to the biopolitical insistence on peristaltic regularity.

The question remains: what does faecal biopolitics and biopower look like a hundred years later? I opened this book with an instance of state-sponsored biopolitical meddling at the US/Mexico border, where migrants were reduced to the 'bare life' of being deprived of the basic nutritional and sanitary supports necessary to enjoy the 'modern faecal habitus' that has come to define all human social being in the industrialised and post-industrial world. The migrants' desperate response – toilet clogging and hunger strikes – constituted a sort of metabolic rift-as-resistance to the dire straits in which they found themselves. I have no case studies to offer of how any individual migrant has suffered, and expresses her suffering, as much through a deployment of her second brain as through other psychic and bodily distress, though I suspect that psychoanalysts dealing with the trauma of displacement, dislocation, migrancy and incarceration are building mighty archives of contemporary peristaltic disturbance and dissidence.

What I'd like to turn to by way of conclusion are two present-day locales in which populations have been deprived of the kind of plumbing that permits a 'flush and forget' expression of what most people in the developed world have come to enjoy as part of their taken-for-granted modern faecal habitus. Gandhi's attention to the hunger strikes of the British suffragettes a hundred years ago led to his importation, from England to India, of peristaltic cessation as the dominant political tool in the struggle for Indian self-rule. Moreover, his insistence that all individuals take responsibility for their own faecal management, regardless of their caste, became a central component of this self-rule, and thus warrants a consideration of where India finds itself today. What shape does Gandhi's legacy take in how metabolic biopolitics, at least at the level of faecal habitus, plays out in a landscape where open defecation has become a national challenge? I will explore this question in the first half of this conclusion, but lest the reader assume that sanitation problems haunt only 'third world' countries, I will return us, as in the introduction to this book, to the United States, where entire communities (mostly of colour) find themselves living amidst their own excreta. In both India and the US, we will see that social justice activism has deployed a kind of biopower that does not exactly emanate from the gut as a second brain, but shrewdly recognises that to 'count' as a citizen, as a human being, one must first be counted among a general population whose excretory evacuations do not come to haunt them either in terms of their bodily health or their social positioning.

## Faecal *Swaraj*

To address the question of peristaltic biopolitics is to consider the peristaltic process of bodies as they enter the global realm of waste management. The campaign I considered in Chapter 1, to eliminate fat in bodies, sewer systems and cities, is arguably an example of this sort of biopolitical project on a domestic scale; indeed Marvin and Medd warn that their partial account would need to be more fully developed through an examination of 'the global system of oil and fat production, the international movement and distribution of fats and oils, the production and distribution of food chains that incorporate fats and oils, and the social organization of waste oil and fat systems' (Marvin and Medd 2006, 143). My discussion of nineteenth-century sewering and faecal recycling projects in Europe and the UK is also relevant here.

I would now like to consider the contemporary conditions of faecal habitus emerging directly from those nineteenth-century sanitation projects, as well as from my inclusion of Gandhi in a history of peristaltic politics. I am referring to the diverse state- and NGO-led projects that concern themselves with the dangers of open defecation in the global South. Gandhi followers will recall the oft-recounted story in which he caused a commotion at the 1901 Indian National Congress by undertaking to clean the latrine, and to remove excrement left by delegates on the veranda outside their doors.[1] If it was Gandhi's contention that *Swaraj*, or self-rule, must begin with a regard for what goes into the alimentary system, it was equally as important to concern oneself with what came out of it, along with the ever pressing question of how human excreta was to be properly disposed of without relying on the division of labour implicit in the caste system.[2] If one could not entirely take responsibility for one's own excrement, whether in tightly packed urban spaces or in the sparsely populated but often plumbing-free rural realm, then what was to be done with it? And more importantly, if India could not take care of its human waste without relegating it to an untouchable population, then how could it assert its right to self-determination? In other words, *Swaraj* entailed self-determination at every level of the metabolic system, from the inside out and beyond. Gandhi's name is invoked in almost any sanitation campaign in India today.

Two perspectives serve to highlight the tension between competing approaches to 'sanitation' among the poor in India: a critical take on the bourgeois deployment of a war on open defecation (making it a matter of shaming or bribing individuals into a more acceptable faecal habitus); and an activist take on the practicalities of how to intervene in the channelling of one's own shit, through organising and community building. In this latter, 'reparative' approach to shit, we see the coming together of labour and work, of metabolic strategies at the physiological, social and economic levels, an engagement with faeces that forms the basis for the building of international organisations based on one's identity as a 'slum' or 'shack' dweller, seeking rights to the city over and above rights to life.

In 'The Cultural Politics of Shit', Assa Doron and Ira Raja take up the complex challenge of how to 'interpret and explain the spectre of "open defecation" in India's countryside and its booming urban centres' with an end to interrogating 'the idiom of modern sanitation, with its emphasis on cleanliness, progress and dreams of technology, as a constitutive idea and an explanatory force in Indian modernity' (Doron and Raja 2015, 190). They seek to reveal the underlying assumptions of a 'sanitation crisis' that is 'promulgated by international non-governmental organizations (NGOs), in which the practice of "open defecation" is not only a public health concern, but also a violation of human rights for the people "forced" to defecate in the open' (Doran and Raja 2015, 190). Even the expression 'open defecation' poses the problem in such a way that 'ready-made solutions modeled upon ideals of progress, technology, surveillance, and proper civil conduct fly in thick and fast', revealing a 'misguided mirroring of bourgeois values, attitudes and experiences' (Doron and Raja 2015, 195).

Take, for instance, their critique of the 'You Stop, We Stop' campaign in the streets of Mumbai, as depicted in a professionally produced video that went viral on YouTube. To dramatic orchestral music, the video 'features a group of men wearing masks perched on a large yellow fire-truck and touring Mumbai in search of people relieving themselves in the open. When they spot a man urinating in public, they aim the firehoses in his direction, the powerful gush of water from the hose catching him in the act' (Doron and Raja 2015, 202–3). The perpetrators of the crime of pissing, invariably men, are sent running, or are literally knocked over by the powerful jet of water, while inserted shots show passers-by laughing at the spectacle. 'This is a ritual purification of space by the urban bourgeoisie,' write Doron and Raja, 'which wants the city completely for itself, to mirror its ideals and aspirations. Such vigilante acts can be interpreted as the ugly face of middle-class India, frustrated and impatient at the slow pace of progress and development in their country' (Doron and Raja 2015, 204). Or expressed in David Inglis's Bourdieu-inflected terminology, we could say that the 'pissing tanker-approach' to sanitation is a way of asserting middle-class superiority over a subordinate underclass by punishing its unacceptable 'faecal habitus'. Comments on the video either mirror the mirth shown by the passers-by, or castigate the vigilantes, either for wasting water (a precious resource in an environment where it is inadequate to serve the needs of the population as a whole) or for not recognising that the true solution would be to provide more public urinals.[3]

Another shaming technique is used on the outskirts of Pune, where people habitually go to relieve themselves. A local resident interviewed by the authors reports that 'the NGOs tried to stop this and caught whoever was pooping in the open and took pictures of them. They then put these pictures up on a billboard in order to discourage people from doing it. How is that preserving the dignity of the poor that we value so much?' (Doron and Raja 2015, 202).

In rural, and often tribal, areas, a different approach is taken, whereby punishment is replaced with reward for the amelioration of one's faecal habitus. The 'No Toilet, No Bride' campaign entails the relatively inexpensive use of social media and other publicity to advise men to build a latrine in or near their home as a way of attracting a bride (and her dowry). By the same token, marriageable girls (and their families) are exhorted to hold out until a marriage proposal includes the prospect of a toilet in the bride's future home (in these villages, the bride customarily moves from her parents' home to take up residence in her in-laws' house). Often, the family will receive a government-subsidised toilet as part of the 'No Toilet, No Bride' campaign. 'A modern project,' write Doron and Raja, 'it is full of the charisma of the state, practicing clever social engineering to bring in sanitation, liberate women, and intervene in marriages to ensure positive social outcomes – a dream policy' (Doron and Raja 2015, 200). But by presuming that a toilet in the household ensures that a woman is kept safe in the domestic space of her husband's and in-laws' home, the campaign 'runs the risk of intensifying the existing gender inequalities, by closing off the limited access that women have to spaces outside the home where they can meet with, socialize with and befriend other women' (Doron and Raja 2015, 200). The point, they write, is not to neglect provisions for private toilets, but 'rather to draw attention to the unstated assumptions of the campaign, which takes for granted that public spaces belong to men' and focuses on 'keeping women at home as the best way of keeping them from harm's way' (Doron and Raja 2015, 201).

Doron and Raja's emphasis on how the campaign reinforces 'existing gender inequalities' is borne out by other social science studies of this solution to sanitation security. Parimita Routray et al. drill down for a detailed picture of the infrastructural problems, social mores and behavioural patterns that militate against universal adoption of latrine usage in a specific region of rural India, even in villages where many households have built latrines.[4] They lay out a wide range of reasons why residents prefer to go in the open air, rather than use indoor toilets. To use a home-based latrine, one must first walk some distance to a water source and carry back enough water to wash the waste into the tank below, and then to wash one's own body. Most of the men go out into the fields for a full day's work and prefer to defecate at their leisure near an existing water source rather than make an extra trip from home out and back to retrieve water for latrine usage before leaving the house, or after returning at night. Moreover, 'unlike women and girls, [men] do not "schedule" defecation but rather defecate whenever the need arises, either on their way to or returning from their fields' (Routray et al. 2015, 14). In general, 'users of latrines were viewed by study participants to be mainly women, especially the newlywed daughter-in-law', for whose sake, after all, the latrine had been built in the first place (Routray et al. 2015, 14).

For women, while having a latrine at home means that they needn't keep to a 'schedule' to relieve themselves, there are reasons why they choose to go in the open air instead, including the convenience, again, of going near a water source rather than making extra trips back and forth to carry water to the house. But for women with government-subsidised latrines, 'who tended to be of low and middle castes with little outside exposure', the primary reason to go in the open air, even if it means that one's peristaltic system must adhere to a strict morning and evening schedule, is to be granted

> rare daily opportunities to escape the house, the scrutiny of the mother-in-law, and the confines of their hamlet and socialize with women friends and peers. This was most strongly expressed by married women who were daughters-in-law (i.e. not yet mothers-in-law), and a few young ones expressed open regret for having to use the household latrine. (Routray et al. 2015, 14–15)

Moreover, because women are mostly confined to the home all day, running the household, the long walk to meet up with other women for defecation in the open air is considered their time for 'fresh air and exercise' and 'seen as good for health' rather than as an 'inconvenience' (Routray et al. 2015, 11).

A woman's faecal habitus, even across castes, must undergo an adjustment as she moves from unmarried to married status. Routray et al. note that, whether influenced by sanitation campaigns or not, 'male heads of household and future husbands' in their study

> showed more concern for protecting and preserving the dignity, privacy and security of their new daughter-in-law/bride when deciding to install a latrine. They did not want these young women to be seen while they defecated outside because it lowered the prestige of the family. (Routray et al. 2015, 14)

That this same logic was 'not observed in regard to their daughters or other females within the family' suggests that once a woman becomes a daughter-in-law, an additional layer of surveillance attaches to her metabolic function within family and community. For instance, in a family without a (functioning) latrine, the daughter-in-law must get up at 4 or 5 in the morning and be chaperoned by a female family member to an appropriate place for defecation under cover of darkness (Routray et al. 2015, 6). This is not the case for daughters or other female members of a household, who may rise later and go out even in daylight.

Unsurprisingly, there is increased toilet use among both women and men in more financially stable families, since they can afford to design and build latrines that fit their needs. Subsidised latrines are often unfinished, roofless, lack doors or sufficiently high walls, are too small to permit squatting, and lack deep-enough pits, so that 'some feared that if all members [of a family] used the latrine all of the time, the small pit would quickly get filled. So men preferred to defecate outside in the dry season, leaving the latrine for women to use' (Routray et al. 2015, 9). It would seem that the less desirable a latrine is, the more likely there will be a differential between the faecal habitus of men and women; men have more choice about when and where they defecate, while women are constrained to use the facility provided for them, or to correlate their bodily habits with the pre-sunrise hours, when they can defecate under cover of darkness, or to coordinate their forays out with the schedules of their female chaperones, and the like.

Another study throws into stark relief the implications of the 'No Toilet, No Bride' campaign when considered in its full spectrum over different regions of India. In 'No toilet no bride? Intrahousehold bargaining in male-skewed marriage markets in India', Yaniv Stopnitzky seeks to demonstrate, through statistical evidence, whether the campaign really does produce more households with latrine adoption. But he finds that the campaign results in higher rates of latrine ownership only in areas where discrimination against women is especially high, resulting in scarcity of women of marriageable age, due to 'cultural norms that favor sons, which results in a number of common forms of household behavior that combine to cause biased sex ratios' (Stopnitzky 2017, 269). This includes 'differential post-natal care to boys and girls', preferential investment in 'male fetuses' and selective abortion of 'female fetuses', as well as constraints on women's ability to 'travel, seek health care, and work outside of the household' should they manage to survive to adulthood. In areas where women are scarce, in other words, marriageable men (and their families) are more highly motivated to supply a toilet in 'exchange' for a bride. This is borne out by Stopnitzky's statistical analysis: in a woman-scarce locale, the campaign results in as much as a 23 per cent increase in latrine ownership. But 'in marriage markets without this scarcity [of women], the *No Toilet No Bride* treatment effect is statistically indistinguishable from zero' (Stopnitzky 2017, 269–70). A World Bank video singing the praises of the campaign inadvertently points up the irony of the fact that women are more likely to enjoy improved sanitation in those regions where their populations are diminished in other ways. In 'Changing the

Culture of Toilets in India', a nurse seated at her desk describes the range of horrific health conditions seen before the sanitation drive: vomiting, diarrhoea, cholera, insect- and water-borne diseases.[5] Behind her, we see a poster visually exhorting the viewer to attend to another security crisis with the tag line: 'save the girl child'.[6] If the number of toilets increases in inverse ratio to the number of women, then is it the case that saving the girl child will drive down the rate of latrine adoption in rural households? This is a complex calculus of faecal habitus, indeed.

Doron and Raja have usefully addressed the question: 'how do we liberate the conceptual distinction between the "healthy" and the "pathological" body (the latter symbolised by the term "open defecation") from its biomedical (objectivist) overtones' and 'underscore the disciplinary function of such binarism, not to mention its normative influence?' (Doron and Raja 2015, 195). In laying out their critique of bourgeois sanitation projects, they have helpfully turned 'to the subjective experiences of the underclass accused of open defecation' to draw out 'the practical concerns and calculations that constitute this seemingly random practice' (196).

An extraordinary document published by Sheela Patel et al. under the auspices of SPARC of India drives home the implications of mobilising the perspective of an accused underclass. This 100-page booklet titled *Community Toilets: Emergence of Community Toilets as a Public Good* functions as part history, part 'how to' manual, part documentary celebration of the unprecedented triumphs of a grassroots movement that began with the construction of one community toilet in a slum of Mumbai and grew, over decades, into an internationally federated movement propelled by what Arjun Appadurai has called 'anti-governmentality'.[7]

SPARC (Society for the Promotion of Area Resource Centers – founded in 1984) is one of three community-based organisations that together call themselves the Alliance. The other two are NSDF (National Slum Dwellers Federation, founded in the mid 1970s) and Mahila Milan (Hindi for 'Women Together', a group originated by former Mumbai sex workers and pavement dwellers in 1986 to address the demolition of their homes). The remarkable work of the Alliance has been recounted in several contexts, but no one, to my knowledge, has quite brought out the centrality of labour as *metabolic* deployment in their work. By this I mean that an imposed urban 'faecal habitus' (defecation whose 'openness' is only so by default) has been leveraged as the basis for a chain of consequential transformations, material and political.[8]

The Alliance originally came together in the 1980s in recognition that 'issues of land, amenities and a right to the city were deeply political ... and behaving like supplicants expecting the government to give you something was a pipe dream' (Patel et al. 2014, 15). Their immediate goal was to find housing for pavement dwellers facing imminent eviction, to which end they began to explore the most expedient and cost-effective design for structures that would adhere to the 180 square feet permissible for a home on government land (Patel et al. 2014, 15). Research quickly revealed that 'cost of material would go down 25% if they shared toilets', and besides which, they had no running water, making a toilet inside the house a health hazard. Observing that home-based toilets in other state-developed projects had been turned into cupboards or storage spaces, and that most public toilets they visited did not work, or couldn't accommodate children, they decided on 'a community managed city financed toilet with separate and equal seats for men and women and separate spaces for children' (Patel et al. 2014, 15). It was through this organically unfolding process, leading to sanitation as a goal, that 'slum dwellers finally began to dialogue with the city' and undertook to build the first community toilet designed specifically for the use of pavement dwellers (Patel et al. 2014, 15).

The booklet (which is designed for global dissemination among slum dwellers throughout the world) opens with the story of how this first community toilet was built on the P D'Mello Road, which at the time included a sizable population of pavement dwellers who had been forced to relieve themselves behind transport trucks or to pay local businesses for the privilege of using their toilets. Under the supervision of Mahila Milan members (taking time off from a house-building project), the community toilet took shape over a period of three weeks, according to specifications that had been developed by the pavement dwellers themselves: a water tank protected inside the structure, separation of men's and women's toilets, provision for daylight and ventilation, a lockable door controlling access only for local pavement dwellers, etc.

> All the labour – carrying water, mixing cement, soaking bricks, guarding the construction materials at night – was provided by the enthusiastic P D'Mello pavement community, Mahila Milan and street kids

from the Sadak Chaap. Only one skilled mason was involved, and he also lived in the P D'Mello Road pavement community. (Patel et al. 2014, 18)

Images of the construction process show women spreading cement inside a rectangular framing device that looks to be about one-and-a-half by two feet in diameter; these are the slabs or '*laadis*' to be fit into pre-cast beams that form the roof of the structure. The pavement dwellers had decided that the building would require a solid rather than a 'simpler sheet-roofing' since the roof was to offer night shelter for street children (kids on their own, who had left or lost their families).[9] Everyone got in on the act, including 'visitors from federations in Bangalore, Kanpur, Madras and Pune', and even 'delegations of slum dwellers from South Africa and Cambodia'. 'Everyone had a turn with the trowel and the shovel' (Patel et al. 2014 17). The project was novel enough to attract the attention of newspaper and television journalists, as well as an American producer for National Public Radio (Patel et al. 2014, 17–18).

The Alliance brought the idea, as well as the practical strategies, for building community toilets to Pune, and over the subsequent decades, to other Mumbai neighbourhoods, cities across India and (through the international organisation Slum/Shack Dwellers International, or SDI) to other locales across Asia and Africa. The booklet is jam-packed with ideas for toilet design, tips for cost-reducing measures, architectural drawings with statistics and costs per seat, a chart showing 'similarities and differences' between sanitation projects in Mumbai and Pune, a table showing projects 'from the point of view of leveragability and scale', a summary of what to include in a contract between city government and 'Community Development Cells' for city-wide sanitation and an in-depth list of 'Ten Big Ideas' (Patel et al. 2014, 19, 23, 24, 27, 52, 60, 65).[10]

I want to stress two of these big ideas: that there is an important difference between public toilets and community toilets, and that rather than hand-outs, communities need 'space to develop their own commitment to improve the lives of all their members' (Patel et al. 2014, 28–9). The difference between public and community toilets is obvious but crucial: public toilets are 'built for whoever happens to be passing by, and assume transience, anonymity, strangers coming in for a piss' (Patel et al. 2014, 29). Aside from the fact that no one feels responsible for the care and maintenance of a public toilet (which may account for why few of them work), the community toilet, built for an 'informal settlement', changes people's perceptions about the settlement.

> To build a *community toilet* is to acknowledge that a community *does* exist, and that inside that community live women, men and children who have needs that are *legitimate*. A *community toilet* is an asset that belongs to and is controlled by a community – not by the city, and not by the government, and certainly not by a passing stranger. (Patel et al. 2014, 29)

Accordingly, community toilets are usually kept locked, with access available only to those with keys, or whose families have paid a nominal monthly fee (noted on a passbook), or with passes acknowledging their residency in the community. Moreover, a community toilet usually includes living space for its caretaker, or even the caretaker's family. It is thus literally a space whose primary designation as sanitary convenience expands to include accommodation for a body's other physiological functions (sleeping, eating), but also for the social actions of world-making.

That the metabolic space of the toilet opens out into the worldly space of social interaction is emphasised in the other 'big idea' having to do with the rejection of 'handouts' in favour of 'space to develop':

> Toilets are one of the most *communal* improvements and can do a lot to bring communities together – everyone will use them, will have feelings about them. Toilets become central, unignorable facts of people's daily lives. A toilet building project is small enough to be planned and built within a small budget and time frame, but big enough to start many things happening: women get involved, people learn to understand their problems, to work together, to tap skills within the community, to manage money. If you squat along the *nala* (open drain) all your life, it's pretty hard to imagine toilets not being *dirty places*, but when they are clean and well-cared for they become points of congregation! The next step is realizing that slums don't have to be *dirty places* either, but can be beautiful communities in which to live. (Patel et al. 2014, 28).

The community toilet is literally a point of congregation, not only because pavement dwellers gather there for the obvious purpose of depositing their waste, but also because the second floor often includes a community space for people to gather. The toilets in the settlement of Chikhalwadi, for instance, included, along with a room for the caretaker, 'a community space for activities like day care, night classes, etc.' (Patel et al. 2014, 41). Arjun Appadurai has remarked that the slum dwellers of Mumbai have made community toilets sites of 'empowerment and dignity rather than of exclusion and pollution':

> They have done this by making toilets more like community centers (in which the person charged with maintaining a new toilet block lives in a small unit above the community toilet) and have invited government officials and other political figures to launch these community toilets in much the manner of the inauguration of temples and deities in much of India is done, with flowers, coconuts, and public celebrations accompanying these events. This is part of a complex strategy to make defecation a publically [sic] recognised and valid platform for social dignity, in an environment where defecation in public is always a sign of radical dispossession, especially in urban India. (Appadurai 2016, 122).

The booklet includes a link to a video (narrated by Appadurai) depicting such festivals, where the most basic of metabolic activities is presented as the starting place for participatory governance at all levels.[11]

The Alliance's ongoing toilet-building activity is entwined with two other activities crucial to the process of 'social dignity' Appadurai references. The first is a micro-savings and loan practice instituted by Mahila Milan from the very beginning. Community leaders would stop by households in the evening to collect a bit of change leftover from the grocery shopping, or some other small amount. This was a crucial starting point for putting aside communal savings, which would then be used for lending back to whomever needed it. 'This lending is very humble,' Patel writes, 'a few rupees to buy groceries when money is low or to buy a bus pass to go find a job' (Patel 2011, 107).

The second emerged as a necessity when the Alliance sought to 'scale up' to build community toilets across the city. It became obvious that in order to partner in any consistent way with city authorities, a practice of data collection and analysis would have to be instituted, by the pavement dwellers themselves, to keep track of existing sanitary facilities, the condition they were in, repairs needed, the local populations they served, etc. All toilets were 'compiled on a Google Earth image and sanitation data was available on a drop down note that included details of committee members'; data was 'converted into simple EXCEL sheet tables', enabling 'easy creating of lists by ward, by problems, by issues so they could be prioritized' (Patel et al. 2014, 64). Patel observes that surveys (of toilets, but also of pavement dwellers themselves) are valued as both a 'means and an end' in the sense that the Alliance use them not only for their data, but also for the 'relationship' they help to produce among surveyors and surveyed: 'Communities discuss their issues in groups and once they start accepting the presence of other people in their midst as not only data collectors but people who are there to assist them, to help them make connections to the city, "yes-no" answers become discussions and reflections' (Patel et al. 2014, 72). Appadurai comments that this practice of counting and accounting for everyone is not an example of the censuses that are 'salient among the techniques identified by Foucault as lying at the heart of modern governmentality', those 'methods of classification and surveillance' in every state archive, engaging 'highly politicized processes' that are 'always driven from above' (Appadurai 2013, 166). This self-administered system for identifying 'households and families in their own communities' amounts rather to a 'counter-governmentality' (Appadurai 2013, 167).

> The leverage bestowed by such information is particularly acute in places like Mumbai, where a host of local, state-level, and federal entities exist with a mandate to rehabilitate or ameliorate slum life. But none of them knows exactly who the slum dwellers are, where they live, or how they are to be identified. (Appadurai 2013, 166)

From the point of view of the state, these are 'invisible' citizens, 'by definition uncounted and uncountable, except in the most general terms' (Appadurai 2013, 167). The survey techniques render the slum dwellers 'statistically visible to themselves', thus coming into 'control of a central piece of any actual policy process – the knowledge of exactly which individuals live where, how they make their livelihood, how long they have lived there, and so forth' – crucial data in a system that ties 'security of tenure to the date from which occupancy of a piece of land or a structure can be demonstrated' (Appadurai 2013, 167).

If we put these community-building strategies into the same frame of reference as the Marxian model of metabolism, we could say that the Alliance has articulated a system for the channelling of the body's excreta to a concomitant system for political and economic management by and for the pavement-dwelling population – a system of strategic 'hoarding' of money for the purpose of making it available in times of need – think of Marx on the question of social metabolism, that 'there is the practical aspect of hoarding . . . since the "quantity of money in circulation unceasingly ebbs and flows" and must be capable of "expansion and contraction," hoarding creates reserves to "serve as channels through which money may flow in and out of circulation, so that the circulation itself never overflows its banks"' (Marx 1976, 231–2). Moreover, the three-phase process entailing census-taking leads to the exploration of issues requiring interaction between city officials and pavement dwellers, which in turn gives rise to pressure to 'look beyond the sanitation maintenance and to see the engagement between the city and community to address other issues such as solid waste, education, health, locality management and so on' (Patel et al. 2014, 64). One could say that the conditions for world-building grow directly from the infrastructure designed, initially, for managing humans' metabolism with nature/the city. Labour is not so distinguishable from work here (if one thinks back to Arendt's model); both are involved in providing the conditions favourable for participation in the *vita activa* of self-governance.

This is not some easily achieved utopia we are talking about here, but a political process that has by now formally encoded the expectation of pitfalls and stagnations, a strategy of patience and waiting, something akin to Leela Gandhi's counter-askesis of imperfectionism. 'Many mistakes occur while initiating the process,' warns Patel, 'quality management, finances – many things can go wrong. Everyone expects perfection, never assume that is what you seek. The process will improve through monitoring what is being done and learning from your mistakes' (Patel et al. 2014, 61).

Nor, I would argue, is the work of the women of Mahila Milan and the Alliance easily assimilable to India's ongoing *Swachh Bharat* (or Clean India) Mission launched by Prime Minister Narendra Modi in 2014, with the aim of cleaning up India by Gandhi's 150th birthday in October 2019. By 2017, Modi had appropriated Gandhi's term 'satyagraha' (insistence on truth) and refashioned it for the twenty-first century during the 100th anniversary of the first satyagrahi uprising by farmers in Champara in 1917. India's cleanliness campaign, Swachh Bharat, could henceforth be thought of as '*Satyagrah se Swachhagrah*', dispensing with 'truth' (*Satya*) and substituting instead cleanliness (*Swachha*). Indeed, the concluding ceremony celebrating the Champra satyagrahi was attended by '20,000 *Swachhagrahis*', as Modi now called anyone actively devoted to the goal of a sanitary India. 'Swachhagrahis are the ambassadors of cleanliness movement. They are the "foot soldiers" and motivators to implement the Community Approaches to Sanitation at the village level,' proclaims an article on the Bihar ceremony.[12] But I would argue that the campaign of the Alliance is less a matter of narrow adherence to cleanliness, and more an ongoing project of metabolic channelling that deploys the situation of an enforced faecal habitus, with its insistent peristaltic 'truths', for a politics of transformation that extends in consequential ways from the dissident gut right outwards into every social, political and global domain.

## Cesspools on the social justice tour

Most middle-class Americans have only a modicum of awareness of what happens to their bodily effluvia and solids after they flush the toilet. Urban and suburban homeowners may get a little jolt once a month when they pay their sewer bill, though renters might not have even this reminder, if their landlords pick up the tab. Once in a while, if something clogs the waste pipes, and a toilet fails to flush, the plunger must be brought out. Or if some 'flushable wipes' and other products have been sent down the system, one might discover, with horror, that the basement has flooded with sewage, and the roto-rooter guy needs to come to get the system moving again. But these are only periodic reminders of where the 'world' goes after it has passed through our bodies.

In rural areas, there may be no sewer bill at all, since more than a quarter of homes in the US are hooked up, not to municipal or city services, but to onsite wastewater treatment systems, otherwise known in common parlance as septic tanks with leach or drain fields (CDC). When this is the case, your daily faecal habitus might not entail much more awareness of where your excreta goes than that of the city-dweller, depending on how often the tank must be cleaned, and how well it is functioning. But the processing of your liquid and solid wastes takes place completely on your property ('onsite') or on property that you might share, communally, with one or a few others living in your vicinity. This sharing of the outgoing waste pipe can happen in cities, too – though it is usually a blockage or glitch that makes you aware of it – as happened to me a few years ago, when a new neighbour called up to say he had researched our properties and found that his sewer line ran under our house and hooked up with ours before continuing out to the street. Some slight variation in the noise his toilet made sent him in search of a disaster just waiting to happen, and although there was no problem, it conjured for us both the hidden spectacle of our effluvia and solids, joining each other on their way to the city processing plant. Did this mean he had a legal right to unscrew the drain cover in our basement and investigate what was happening under our house, where the unmetabolised remains of his dinner had just met up with the unmetabolised remains of ours in their subterranean journeys? Although it was a strange way to 'meet' our neighbour, it was nevertheless still a minor detail of our shared, middle-class faecal habitus.

And the same is true of the septic tank we share with an uphill neighbour on the mountain where we vacation in a cabin in the Maine woods. He flushes; his shit comes our way and joins our outgoing pipe; and both our stuff winds up in the underground concrete tank on the other side of our house. There, our mutual solids settle, our oils float, and our greywater eventually continues its way through yet another pipe, underneath the road, and into the well-kept, grassy leach field on a third neighbour's property. This is how we share an onsite wastewater treatment system. It all works pretty well, both in the city and on the mountain, and rarely 'comes back to haunt us', as we like to say when human excreta goes astray.

But if you are an African American living in rural Alabama, where the sparse population means that you cannot hook up to centralised municipal wastewater services, you may find that your 'onsite' wastewater treatment makes it impossible for you to be as oblivious to what happens to the contents of your toilet when you've flushed as your white middle-class compatriots. Your daily faecal habitus, whatever its conscious and autonomic routines, will be impinged on by an awareness of what your body produces in ways that at best cause you shame and embarrassment, and at the worst drain your bank account, destroy your health or get you arrested and threatened with imprisonment.

From South Asia, then, I want to shift the focus to another South: that of the United States, where, among other things, Marx's theory of waged factory labour was complicated by slave labour, and the metabolic rift resulting from monoculture was playing out in the clay-rich soil of the profitable cotton industry, and where the relation between the owners of production and the people doing the work could more properly be termed, as Frank Wilderson puts it, a relation of terror than a relation of hegemony (Wilderson 2003, 229–30).[13] I follow the story of social justice activist Catherine Flowers, who grew up in the 1960s in Lowndes County, Alabama, where she and her rural neighbours still used outhouses, or carried out the 'slop jars' they had filled the night before to be emptied in the woods behind their houses. Even as a child she was immersed in political activism, pushing for better educational conditions in her local high school, and following the twists and turns of the civil rights movement as it transformed the lives of her parents, their friends and the country in general. University, teaching opportunities and personal life decisions took her away from the South during her early adulthood. But later in life, Flowers felt called by the 'rich, dark soil' of this part of Alabama's Black Belt, determined to excavate the history of this place where cotton had 'thrived in the fertile earth', where her ancestors, as slaves, had picked it for the profit of their masters, but also where uprisings and resistance had wrought changes, making her home county perfect as a locale for pursuing her social justice objectives in the present day. 'Something about that soil gets in your blood,' she writes, and recalls being determined to help 'hard-working people rise up out of poverty that bogs them down like Alabama mud' (Flowers 3).

But while focusing on economic development and voter empowerment for the rural population of Lowndes County, as well as consciousness-raising about the origin of civil rights gains in the land of the slavery-based cotton industry and Jim Crow, she discovered that, although rural residents now enjoyed indoor plumbing like everyone else in America, they were in some ways worse off than when their faecal habitus involved the use of outhouses and slop jars. The clay-rich soil that had made Alabama perfect for cotton crops turned out to be not so good for the metabolic management of human excreta.

Flowers's story is about how an activist for racial social justice in the tradition of the civil rights movement brought the campaign for equal rights into a specific biopolitical framework. Race biopolitics has been studied for a while now, in the work of Saidiya Hartman, for instance, as well as Sara Smith and Pavithra Vasudevan. But Flowers's swerve from traditional civil rights activism (get-out-the-vote campaigns and local economic development schemes) to a more specific focus on the denial of proper sanitation to communities of colour constitutes nothing less than a race biopolitics that directly addresses the inequities of faecal regulation.

As I research Flowers's story, I am struck by what seems to be a pattern of metabolic overlap of electoral suffrage and peristaltic politics. During the early twentieth century in England, Constance Lytton joins the suffragettes' campaign to extend the franchise to women; her civil disobedience leads to her imprisonment, where a metabolic disruption in the form of hunger strikes met by forcible feeding is played out. The same is true for Gandhi's campaign for self-rule in India. In Lowndes County, Alabama, the story unfolds along different paths, but the historical intersections between access to the franchise, this time for African Americans, and access to adequate sanitation is particularly stark. The events leading up to the assassination of Martin Luther King lays the groundwork for what was to come over subsequent decades.

During Flowers's childhood, criss-crossed by the civil rights movement (her parents' house was a stopover for activists from around the country), Martin Luther King travelled to Memphis to support the sanitation workers' strike, which had unfolded after two trash collectors had been crushed to death by a malfunctioning garbage truck. These meta-industrial labourers, defined by their racial rather than by their gender disenfranchisement, demanded a decent living wage, along with recognition of their union and better safety standards. Martin Luther King's final public address, and arguably his most celebrated – the 'I've been to the Mountaintop' speech – was thus delivered at a rally in support of the racialised labour of trash handlers. In this respect, the civil rights movement was already as much about intervening in the racialised inequities of sanitation as it was about electoral politics, equal access to education, employment, businesses and restaurants, transportation and all the other services taken for granted by white America. In his speech, King evokes the refusal of civil rights activists to be deterred by the obstacles thrown up to stop them: the mace, the dogs and, maybe most strikingly, the water hoses. In Birmingham, for instance, where Bull Connor had ordered that black bodies be met with the brutal force of water shot at high velocity from fire hoses, the protesters persevered. In his address, King emphasises the fact that the streams of water could not extinguish the fire of the activists' righteousness. But we could add that this imagery is also about the deployment by the state of streams of water to 'flush' away the unruly black bodies in the street, as though public space needs to be purified of the bodies that have dared to stray out of place. The fire hoses were Bull Connor's attempt to forcibly sanitise Birmingham, to wash away the protestors like so much waste in need of a water-borne aboveground sanitation system. It was the American South's version of what goes on in Mumbai, where the fire-truck sends jets of water towards public urinators in a 'ritual purification of space by the urban bourgeoisie' (Doron and Raja 2015, 202–3). But the Birmingham protesters were not deterred and refused to be flushed away. The country's most lionised civil rights icon, Martin Luther King, died we might say on the front lines of a battle over who may freely create waste, and who is expected to make it disappear, and expected to remain invisible, ducking under the parapet of the muck-filled trenches.

As Flowers's research reveals, the race biopolitics of sanitation has not only been about how underpaid and endangered black bodies are expected to whisk away everyone's trash; it is also about how these same black bodies are expected to live in constant proximity with the worst of their own waste – which, in turn, marks them as somehow disposable themselves.

Flowers describes her initial discovery of this situation as a story of how she brought prominent politicians and business leaders to her home town in order to shine a light on the barriers to economic growth in rural areas mainly populated by African Americans. Her intention was to forge a sort of pipeline to, or more properly from, Washington, D.C., in hopes of diverting attention and resources to an area suffering from long neglect. It didn't matter whether her contacts were Democrat or Republican, progressive or conservative: everyone was a possible ally in her campaign to bring attention to the rural South.

She started by pressing Alabama Senator Jeff Sessions (during a town hall meeting) on his promises of financial support to communities in need. How could rural counties with no tax base gain access to grants, for instance, if a 25 per cent match was required? Sessions was perplexed by this conundrum.

But Flowers's campaign to lure awareness to the rural South took a decisive turn when she brought conservative African-American leader Bob Woodson to take a look at how his Neighborhood Enterprise program might work in a rural, rather than an urban context. Flowers had already mapped out a tour of sites in need of attention when a county commissioner alerted her to a particularly noteworthy cluster of households with a problem Flowers had not yet fully taken in. It was thus that Woodson and Flowers discovered together the longstanding, unaddressed faecal disaster that haunted any attempt to forge 'public-private partnerships connecting community leaders and organizations with training and funding to uplift their neighborhoods' – ostensibly the goal of Woodson's bootstrap approach to social 'betterment' (Flowers 12).

The discovery went down like this: Flowers and her caravan of cars pulled off onto a rural road, and eventually approached a compound of five mobile homes, with a small country church nearby. As they drove up the incline toward the trailers, they were shocked to see raw sewage streaming alongside the road in the opposite direction. When they got out of their van, the pastor emerged from the church in tears and came over to greet them. He had just been served with an order to shut down his church, and had been threatened with arrest if he did not fix his septic tank. Failure to maintain a permitted septic tank was a criminal misdemeanour in Alabama (Flowers 14). The residents of the trailers were weeping as well, the whole settlement having run afoul of the law because they couldn't afford to properly process their human waste. But what was happening when they flushed their toilets to make the contents run down the road like that? It seemed that they, like an (as yet) untold percentage of rural homes across America, were straight-piping their waste directly out of the building and onto the ground.

Middle-class white Americans might need a brief tutorial here about what 'straight-piping' is all about. Let's back up to Flowers's childhood, when few rural residents had toilets in their bathrooms, and thus had to leave the house, either to use the outdoor privy or to empty their overnight 'honey-buckets' into it. With modernisation, it slowly became possible to enjoy the indoor privileges, that is, the modern faecal habitus, that everyone else seemed to take for granted. You could now, in your trailer or in your house, just walk down the hall into the bathroom and use the toilet. No nineteenth-century indignities, no chilly dashes to the outhouse, no smelly chamber pots under the bed. Just lift your toilet lid, settle down, let go and flush. The septic tank would take care of the rest.

But septic tanks and leach fields function properly only when embedded in favourable soil conditions. The rich, clayey soil that had sustained the cotton industry for so long turns out to be a disaster for the proper functioning of septic systems. Moreover, when rains are heavy, raising the water table, the situation is exacerbated. Septic tanks break down; what has gone into them returns the way it came, in an anti-peristaltic back-flow, and emerges through what were meant to be one-way outlets: toilet, bathtub, shower and sink drains. Repairing the septic system, or more likely, replacing it with one engineered for your soil conditions, far outstrips your yearly salary and is likely more expensive than your whole trailer is worth. So what do you do if you'd prefer to continue to use your toilet without flooding your home with everything you've so diligently flushed?

You rig up a straight-pipe.

A straight-pipe is a piece of plastic PVC pipe that you attach to the plumbing leading out from your toilet, through a hole in the wall behind and onto the ground. The length of your straight-pipe (or additions you've made to extend it) depends on where you want your outflow to end up. For some, just getting it out of the house is enough so it debouches into a puddle in the yard. For others, the pipe extends out into the woods, where its discharge is hidden in the underbrush. Or you might try to disguise the bright white piping, by leading it through some brush on its way to a nearby creek or river, or even dig a shallow trench as far as the ravine, embed the pipe in that, and let the opening poke out at the edge. There are also cases where a straight-pipe leads to a nearby cesspool. By cesspool, I don't mean the kind of cesspool or cesspit professionally designed and engineered to temporarily hold sludge in a sealed underground environment, to be periodically cleaned out when the vacuum truck comes by. I mean an open pool of wastewater, faeces and toilet paper, somewhere nearby, and into which sometimes several PVC straight-pipes are emptying, from a cluster of dwellings.

So, it was straight-pipes that Flowers and her first VIP visitor, Bob Woodson, were seeing on their tour of rural Lowndes County.

Woodson was shocked, to say the least, and vowed (as did wave after wave of subsequent politicians, corporate do-gooders and religious figures) to extend a helping hand to the impoverished residents. Funds were raised to outfit the church and its small community of parishioners with proper septic tanks, more tears were shed, lives were improved. Woodson remarked that the whole situation revealed 'a failure of the civil rights movement'. But Flowers saw it as 'another chapter in a long history of the marginalization of poor minorities and rural residents' (15).

For one thing, when local authorities became aware of a malfunctioning septic tank, their response was not to help the resident resolve the problem, but to issue a court summons, slap them with a fine, and even imprison them if they could not comply with the law. But why would someone want to live in a home where their faecal matter had to be straight-piped out into the yard anyway? Couldn't they just move to a house or trailer with proper sanitation, rather than run afoul of the law?

This was not an option for so many people who had purchased their home, either a modest house or a brand-new mobile home, in hopes of accruing the same kind of wealth, through mortgage payments and equity, that symbolised the American dream. For one thing, trailers begin to lose their value almost as soon as you take ownership (Flowers 10). For another, even if you bought a house, you couldn't trust that the pre-purchase inspection would turn up the bad sanitation problem.

Case in point: Flowers tells the story of a young bank teller who has just bought a recently constructed house, but who has already been threatened with legal action by state health officials. After the new owner had moved in with her children, the neighbours complained that raw sewage from their house was running into their pasture, and their cows were walking through it. When Flowers met health department officials at the house, they discovered that there was no septic tank, and that sewage was being straight-piped out to the yard. Wasn't the house inspected before purchase? Yes, says the health official, but 'All that is necessary is that the inspector flush the toilet. He flushed the toilet' (Flowers 127). But how can you sell a house without disclosing that it lacks a septic tank? According to the health official, there is no state law requiring any such disclosure. The only thing preventing immediate arrest of the new homeowner was Flowers's intervention, buying her time in order to sort out the problem.

Or take the case of a single mother living in a mobile home. She had already scraped together $800 to pay for a perc test to avoid arrest (Flowers 128). A perc test determines the rate at which soil absorbs water; if the absorption rate is too slow (as is the case with the clay-rich soil of Lowndes County bottom land), a highly engineered septic system must be installed. This was the case for this single mother; she was on the verge of being arrested again unless she could install a $10,000 septic tank, which would be an impossibility on her $700 a month salary. Jeff Sessions was called in this time to intervene and avert the imminent arrest. But of course, this did not solve the problem for countless other rural residents in the same situation.

The visit to this woman's home was the occasion on which Flowers was bitten by mosquitoes swarming around the pool of sewage in the backyard. A subsequent rash led her to wonder whether rural residents were suffering from tropical disease and parasites as a result of their sewage problems. Flowers's story takes us through the many discoveries and direct actions, appeals to government and NGO funding sources, long periods of waiting, countless bureaucratic snags and endless rounds of cesspool tours, and the establishment of her organisation. She managed, after an eight-year delay, to implement an EPA grant, not for the purpose of replacing septic tanks, but to fund the first data-gathering efforts to document the percentage of homes without functioning septic tanks, or of town-dwellers whose municipal water-treatment plants weren't working (Flowers 131), or the shocking incidence of hookworm in Alabama, a scourge normally found in underdeveloped 'third world' locales. She founded the Alabama Center for Rural Enterprise, and began serving as the Rural Development Manager at the Equal Justice Initiative founded by Bryan Stevenson in Montgomery. Her consciousness-raising tours were increasingly populated by a who's-who of public policy-makers, climate change activists, left-wing social justice personalities, journalists, National Geographic crews and a UN Special Rapporteur who, when asked by a journalist if he'd seen this before, replied 'not in the first world' (Flowers 155). Bernie Sanders, Elizabeth Warren, Michael Moore, Karenna Gore, Jane Fonda – everyone wanted to jump on the sanitation bandwagon. Cory Booker stated that he wished to become the 'environmental justice senator', which in the context being elaborated by Flowers, might be more explicitly phrased as the 'Fecal Justice Senator' (Flowers 148).

I had opened this story by noting how Catherine Flowers's tours emphasise Lowndes County, and nearby state capital, Montgomery, as distinguished sites for the history of social justice. Because of the area's centrality to the cotton-based exploitation of slave labour, as well as its importance in the unfolding of the civil rights movement, Montgomery and the surrounding county have become a choice destination for anyone wanting to make a pilgrimage to the site of twentieth-century American racial justice history. Ignominy and triumph are intertwined in the tours Flowers gives, starting with the capitol building where George Wallace pronounced that segregation would always prevail in the state. Landmarks of the old South of slavery and Jim Crow have been repurposed as educational sites for the history of resistance: the Greyhound Station (where segregated buses departed and arrived) has now become the Freedom Rides Museum; the street where Rosa Parks was arrested for refusing to sit in the back of a city bus is now the site of a museum in her name; a site on Commerce Street where slaves waited in pens to be auctioned off to the highest bidder now houses the Equal Justice Initiative; behind this is the Legacy Museum, dedicated to understanding the connection between slavery and mass incarceration in the US; and nearby is the first ever lynching memorial, the National Memorial for Peace and Justice (Flowers 5–7). Sites of oppression are reclaimed as monuments to social progress.

From Montgomery, Flowers and her social justice pilgrims drive along Highway 80, the route of the historic march from Selma to Montgomery led by Martin Luther King Jr to campaign on behalf of Black people for the right to vote in 1965. They pass through Lowndes County where, in 1965, no Black person was registered to vote, despite the majority Black population. The Lowndes County Interpretive Center, located mid-route, commemorates the march with, among other displays, bronze statues of the Selma-to-Montgomery civil rights 'foot soldiers'. Here, visitors enjoy interactive 'living museum' installations of the life of the sharecropper, with its replicas of a country store and tenant house. There is also a recreation, complete with iron cot and bedpan, of the Tent City which had housed sharecroppers kicked out by their white landlords for registering to vote.

But the landscape of social oppression fought by social justice is, as I've been suggesting, also a landscape of human waste and parasites; soil that was ideal for slavery-based cotton production is the same soil that defies faecal management; a hopeful pilgrimage to pay homage to the work being done to combat continued racism becomes an unwitting tour of America's as-yet-untreated biopolitics of sewage. Flowers now leads her distinguished visitors to patches of Alabama soil where the oppression takes its most obvious biopolitical shape: yards, cesspools and roads filled with human waste. If her history lesson had begun with the scandal of past genocidal chapters (slavery, Jim Crow) which were then mitigated by the salve of upbeat social justice gains (freedom march sites and commemorative museums), she now subjects her tour members to an experience that immerses everyone's senses in the filth of a present-day scandal: raw sewage, with its overpowering odour, its hideous visuals and its swarms of disease and parasite-bearing mosquitos. No solutions to this problem yet exist, and thus there is no commemorative statue or mural, no museum of odds overcome, to assuage the panic of the visiting do-gooder. The march to Montgomery commemoration has, by this time, become an unremitting slog through sewage.

Let's visit, now, another National Parks-operated interpretive museum, this time in Selma at the foot of the Edmund Pettus Bridge. Here, too, visitors find life-sized statues depicting marchers, learn the story of Bloody Sunday and the passage of the Voting Rights Act of 1965, and interact with exhibits featuring news footage, artifacts and interviews from marchers and police alike. The museum is designed, like the other two interpretive centres devoted to the Selma-to-Montgomery march, to pay tribute to the courage of civil rights activists who refused to give up, despite the continued threat of injury and death.

But what if we were to imagine, some years into the future, what an interpretive centre would look like to commemorate the triumph of rural residents over the outrageous sanitary conditions that had prevailed well into the twenty-first century; what if it were to commemorate an enduring solution to the failure to process human excrement in rural outposts? Because of her persistent efforts as a crusader for functional sanitation in Lowndes County, which has now become the paradigm for understanding faecal biopolitics in the United States, would Catherine Flowers be celebrated with a bronze statue in her image? But would she have to be shown standing next to a bronze replica of a straight-pipe, with outflow spurting into a nearby cesspool? To be truly 'interpretive' as a museum, surely the exhibits would need to include an olfactory element – the synthetically produced odour of raw sewage might be gently puffed from hidden aromatisers where a model trailer is set up, or perhaps the scent would fill the model trailer, as the visitor entered through an off-kilter doorway, gingerly crossed a spongy rug and wandered down the hall, to glimpse a replica of an overflowing toilet through the open door of the bathroom.

But such an interpretive centre exists in the present day, in a way, and is even more realistic than a re-enactment would be. This is because the interpretive centre in Selma, the one at the foot of the Pettus Bridge, marking the starting point of the historical march, this interpretive centre itself suffers from a failed septic system. Its sewage flows onto the property next door, preventing the resident of that house from entering her home through her front door, since she'd have to walk through sewage to get there. Flowers makes the point that no National Park Service site in an urban area would be expected to put up with raw sewage problems, so why is the interpretive centre in Selma left to founder in its own sewage? Policymakers, religious and business leaders, politicians, social justice pilgrims of all kinds are likely oblivious to the fact that if they use the public facilities at the Selma Interpretive Center, their faeces will end up in the neighbour's yard. To alert them to this fact would be to turn this museum commemorating a past into a living museum of the present, and to draw attention to how the faecal habitus of the privileged has, up until the present day, relied on the faecal injustices of the disenfranchised.

Much as I have challenged the disciplinary requirements of a modern faecal habitus, I have come to recognise that, when it comes down to an individual's thriving in the world, regulatory regimes must be considered not only in terms of how to defy them, but also in terms of daily 'access' to them. A certain level of automaticity in one's daily functioning is required before one can marshal the resources needed to transform the very system that allows for this automaticity. What these examples of inadequate sanitary conditions make abundantly clear is how oblivious much of the global population is to the very fact that they engage in a faecal habitus in the first place, and how unaware they are of the sanitary infrastructure, which includes an infrastructure of meta-industrial human labour, that makes their sense of bodily wellbeing possible. It is the impression of 'naturalness' that allows one's habitus to carry one along in that blithe oblivion that is to 'flush and forget'.

# Faecal Biopolitics in the Twenty-First Century 259

To have read this book is to have agreed to forgo, for some time at least, the bliss of peristaltic ignorance that makes your sense of bodily normalcy possible, at least where regularity is concerned. I have occupied your first brain with awareness of the second brain in your gut; I have asked you to contemplate, with either brain, the history of your metabolic existence, whether that includes your implication in the processes of metabolic rift that characterise your urban or rural dwelling, or your reliance on systems of labour that 'clean and make smooth' your movements through the world, or the unconscious ways your body thinks feelingly at every peristaltic turn. Despite what may seem like too much 'preoccupation with the exigencies of the alimentary system', with the 'touching of pitch undefiled', it nevertheless seems to me that I've just barely laid the groundwork for a much larger multi-disciplinary project, which I hope will be taken up by other scholars of the biopolitical dissidence of the gut.

Where there is a faecal habitus, there is also faecal injustice, and the need for faecal activism.

## Notes

1. 'Some of the delegates did not scruple to use the verandahs outside their rooms for calls of nature at night. In the morning I pointed out the spots to the volunteers. No one was ready to undertake the cleaning, and I found no one to share the honour with me of doing it. Conditions have since considerably improved, but even today thoughtless delegates are not wanting who disfigure the Congress camp by committing nuisance wherever they choose, and all the volunteers are not always ready to clean up after them' (Gandhi 2018, 367).
2. 'Self rule, swaraj, was for Gandhi founded upon Indians taking responsibility for their own lives, including responsibility for cleaning up their own mess and not depending upon outcastes to do this for them' (Mattausch 2014, 155). Mattausch discusses Gandhi's 'unfinished struggle' against the backdrop of sanitary reform in Victorian England.
3. See 'You Stop, We Stop: The Pissing Tanker'. Originally posted in 2014 by 'The Clean Indian', the video has been shared and reposted multiple times accruing upwards of 4 million viewers in the process. https://www.youtube.com/watch?v=aaEqZQXmx5M (Accessed 20/2/19)

4 See Routray et al, 2015.
5 See World Bank 2013, 'Changing the Culture of Toilets in India', https://www.youtube.com/watch?v=liBPxiphFoU (Accessed 1/3/2019)
6 For India's Save the Girl Child campaign, see http://savegirlchild.org/ (Accessed 23/2/2019)
7 Patel, Sheela et al. 2014. *Community Toilets: Emergence of Community Toilets as a Public Good: The work of Mahila Milan, NSDF and SPARC in India in the area of Sanitation.* Published by SPARC, INDIA. Available in PDF format at the Environment and Urbanization website: https://www.environmentandurbanization.org/emergence-community-toilets-public-good-sanitation-work-mahila-milan-nsdf-and-sparc-india (Accessed 25/2/2019)
8 See Appadurai's *The Future as Cultural Fact* (2013) and *Banking on Words* (2016), but also Bhan, Gautam, Nik Haynen, Mathew Colman, Sapana Doshi, 2016; Gandy, 2014; Kar, 2018; and Hollis, 2013. Mariangela Veronesi touches on the example set by the Alliance in a specifically metabolic context, that is, drawing on multiple models of city-as-metabolism to analyze the role of informal waste management in the metabolic health of Mumbai. But Veronesi's emphasis is on (non-human) solid waste and recycling strategies. See Veronesi, 2016. In a more popular vein, for a book on the general topic of campaigns and project to address human waste on a global scale, see George, 2008.
9 For more on Sadak Chaap, the organisation formed by Mumbai's street children, see http://www.sadakchaap.org/ (Accessed 1/3/2019)
10 These include a reminder that the poor 'can be involved' in infrastructure decisions; that community-designed, built and managed toilets are good for the whole city ('if soil from half the city's population goes into the river untreated, it's not only bad news for the poor, but for the whole city'); that the poor are 'an enormous and untapped source for solving urban problems' and can be 'catalysts for change'; that while the city must take care of the 'big pipes' of the sewerage and water-supply grids, 'toilets and drainage lines ... are genuine little pipe items and don't really require the city at all'; that the poor are 'best qualified to make decisions about improvements in their own communities', since after all, slums are 'home to those who actually build Indian cities: masons, pipe layers, cement mixers, brick carriers, shuttering designers, stone cutters, trench diggers and metal fabricators'; the importance of 'golden booboos', i.e. errors that become learning experiences; the necessity of receiving visitors and traveling to other communities to share knowledge, and this

includes festivals for the purpose of celebrating newly built toilets (Patel et al. 2014, 27–9).

11 See 'Sandas Mela New Rituals', sponsored by SPARC, https://www.youtube.com/watch?v=CVggpF3651Q (Accessed 2/3/19)

12 'Satyagraha to Swachhagraha', 2018. Interestingly, a respondent to a question about Swachhagraha on Quora claims to have originated the coinage: Kunal Srivastava writes that as an advertising copywriter he had come up with the term while working on a 'cleanliness drive in Gujarat hospitals'. 'It's a play on the word satyagaagrah. Saty-agrah is Insistence on truth. Swach-agraha is Insistence on cleanliness. The point being Gandhi started a movement to rid India of the British, likewise we should rid India of dirt and pollution' (Quora, 'What does Modi's Swachhagraha mean?').

13 '[Capital, and thus] "the socio-political order of the New World" (Spillers, 1987, p. 67) was kick-started by approaching a particular body (a black body) with direct relations of force, not by approaching a white body with variable capital. Thus, one could say that slavery – the "accumulation" of black bodies regardless of their utility as labourers (Hartman; Johnson) through an idiom of despotic power (Patterson) – is closer to capital's primal desire than is waged oppression – the "exploitation" of unraced bodies (Marx, Lenin, Gramsci) that labour through an idiom of rational/symbolic (the wage) power: a Relation of terror as opposed to a relation of hegemony' (Wilderson 2003, 229–30).

# Bibliography

Abraham, Karl. 1954. 'Contributions to the theory of the anal character'. In *Selected Papers of Karl Abraham*. London: Hogarth Press.

Ackerknecht, E.H. 1974. 'The history of the discovery of the vegetative (autonomic) nervous system'. *Medical History*, 18:1, 1–8.

Agamben, Giorgio. 1998. *Homo Sacer: Sovereign Power and Bare Life*. Trans. Daniel Heller-Roazen. Stanford: Stanford University Press.

Alaimo, Stacy. 2010. *Bodily Natures: Science, Environment, and the Material Self*. Bloomington: Indiana University Press.

Anderson, John E. 1933. *Happy childhood; the development and guidance of children and youth*. New York, London: D. Appleton-Century Co. Inc.

Anderson, John E. and Marion L. Faegre. 1929. *Childcare and Training*. Minneapolis: The University of Minnesota Press.

Appadurai, Arjun. 2013. *The Future as Cultural Fact: Essays on the Global Condition*. London: Verso.

Appadurai, Arjun. 2016. *Banking on Words: The Failure of Language in the Age of Derivative Finance*. Chicago: University of Chicago Press.

Arendt, Hannah. 1981. *The Life of the Mind*. NY: Houghton Mifflin Harcourt.

Arendt, Hannah. 1995. *Between Friends: The Correspondence of Hannah Arendt and Mary McCarthy 1949–1975*. Ed. and introduction by Carol Brightman. NY: Harcourt Brace & Company.

Arendt, Hannah. 1958/1998. *The Human Condition*. 2nd Edition. Chicago: University of Chicago Press.

Arendt, Hannah. 2018. *Thinking Without a Banister: Essays in Understanding 1953–1975*. New York: Schocken Books.

Atkinson, V. Sue. 2017. 'Shifting Sands: Professional Advice to Mothers in the First Half of the Twentieth Century'. *Journal of Family History*, 42:2, 128–46.

Barad, Karen. 2007. *Meeting the Universe Halfway: Quantum Physics and the Entanglement of Matter and Meaning.* Durham: Duke University Press.

Benhabib, Seyla. 2020. 'How to Read Hannah Arendt's *The Human Condition*'. *Critique* 13/13, http://blogs.law.columbia.edu/critique131 3kseyla-benhabib-how-to-read-hannah-arendts-the-human-condition -1958/

Bhan, Gautam, Nik Haynen, Mathew Colman and Sapana Doshi. 2016. *In the Public's Interest: Evictions, Citizenship, and Inequality in Contemporary Delhi.* Athens: University of Georgia Press.

Bier, David. 2019. 'Are CBP's Filthy and Inhumane Immigrant Detention Camps Necessary?'. *Cato at Liberty*, https://www.cato.org/blog/are-cbps-filthy-inhumane-immigrant-detention-camps-necessary

Blakeslee, Sandra. 1996. 'Complex and Hidden Brain in Gut Makes Bellyaches and Butterflies'. *New York Times*, 23 January 1996.

Blatz PhD, William E.M.B. and Helen McM. Bott MA. 1928. *Parents and the Pre-school Child.* London and Toronto: J.M. Dent and Sons.

Boyce, Geoffrey. 2014. 'Border Patrol's "Consequence Delivery System" Casts Doubt on President's Immigration Priorities'. Guest blog on *Crimmigration.com.* http://crimmigration.com/2014/02/18/border-patrols-consequence-delivery-system-casts-doubt-on-presidents-immigration-priorities/ (Accessed 27/5/2022)

CDC. 1976, 2006. 'Chapter 10: On-site Wastewater Treatment'. *Healthy Housing Reference Manual,* https://www.cdc.gov/nceh/publications /books/housing/cha10.htm (Accessed 27/5/2022)

Carpenter, Edward. 1921. *From Adam's Peak to Elephanta: Sketches in Ceylon and India.* London: George Allen & Unwin Ltd.

Children's Bureau, US Department of Labor. 1935. Infant Care. Bureau Publication No. 8. Washington: United States Government Printing Office.

Clean Indian, The. 2014. 'You Stop, We Stop: The Pissing Tanker'. YouTube Video, https://www.youtube.com/watch?v=aaEqZQX mx5M (Accessed 27/5/2022)

Cogdell, Christina. 2010. *Eugenic Design: Streamlining America in the 1930s.* Philadelphia: University of Pennsylvania Press.

Costello, Jennifer L. (Acting Inspector General). 2019. 'Management Alert – DHS Needs to Address Dangerous Overcrowding and Prolonged Detention of Children and Adults in the Rio Grande Valley

(Redacted)'. Memo of the Office of the Inspector General, Department of Homeland Security, 2 July 2019. https://www.documentcloud.org/documents/6190486-Costello-IG-DHS-Report.html

Crum, Mason. 1935. 'Next Step – The Child Guidance Clinic'. *Hygeia: The Health Magazine.* 13:10 (October) 912–14.

De Genova, Nicholas. 2016. 'Toward a Marxian anthropology? Bare, abstract, mobile, global'. *Dialectical Anthropology*, 40:125–41.

Deleuze, Gilles and Félix Guattari. 1983. *Anti-Oedipus: Capitalism and Schizophrenia.* Trans. Robert Hurley, Mark Seem, and Helen R. Lane. Minneapolis: U of Minnesota Press.

Des Voeux, Dr H. 1924. 'Constipation: Its Causes, Results and Treatments, from the General Practitioner's Point of View'. *Trans. Med. Soc. Lond*, 47: 33–48.

Dickerson, Caitlin. 2019. '"There is a Stench": Soiled Clothes and No Baths for Migrant Children at a Texas Center'. *New York Times*, 21 June 2019. https://www.nytimes.com/2019/06/21/us/migrant-children-border-soap.html (Accessed 27/5/2022)

Doane, Mary Ann. 2002. *The Emergence of Cinematic Time: Modernity, Contingency, the Archive.* Cambridge and London: Harvard University Press.

Doron, Assa and Ira Raja. 2015. 'The cultural politics of shit: class, gender and public space in India'. *Postcolonial Studies*, 18:2, 189–207, DOI: 10.1080/13688790.2015.1065714.

Douglas, Mary. 1966. *Purity and Danger: An Analysis of Concepts of Pollution and Taboo.* London: Routledge and Kegan Paul.

Emery MD, E. Van Norman. 1925. 'The Child Guidance Clinic'. *The Pacific Coast Journal of Nursing*, 21, 663–7.

Enders, Giulia. 2015. *Gut: The Inside Story of Our Body's Most Underrated Organ.* Trans. David Shaw. Vancouver: Greystone Books Ltd.

Engels, Friedrich. 1935. *The Housing Question.* New York: International Publishers.

Erikson, Erik H. 1969. *Gandhi's Truth: On the Origins of Militant Nonviolence.* New York: W.W. Norton and Co.

Fausto-Sterling, Ann. 2012. *Sex/Gender: Biology in a Social World.* New York: Routledge.

Federici, Silvia. 2004. *Caliban and the Witch: Women, the Body and Primitive Accumulation.* Brooklyn: Autonomedia.

Federici, Silvia. 2017. 'Notes on Gender in Marx's *Capital*'. *Continental Thought and Theory: A Journal of Intellectual Freedom*, 1:4, 19–37.

Ferenczi, Sándor. 1926/1952. *Further Contributions to the theory and Techniques of Psychoanalysis*. Trans. Jane Isabel Suttie. New York: Basic Books.

Ferenczi, Sándor. 1938. *Thalassa: A theory of genitality*. Trans. Henry Alden Bunker. New York: The Psychoanalytic Quarterly, Inc.

Ferenczi, Sándor. 1995. *The Clinical Diary of Sandor Ferenczi*. Ed. Judith Dupont, Trans. Michael Balint and Nicola Zarday Jackson. Cambridge: Harvard UP.

Fischer-Kowalski, Marina. 1997. 'Society's Metabolism'. *International Handbook of Environmental Sociology*. Eds Michael Redclift and Graham Woodgate. Northampton, Mass.: Edward Elgar, 119–37.

Flowers, Catherine Coleman. 2020. *Waste: One Woman's Fight Against America's Dirty Secret*. New York: New Press.

Forth, Christopher E. and Ana Carden-Coyne. 2005. *Cultures of the Abdomen: Diet, Digestion, and Fat in the Modern World*. New York: Palgrave Macmillan.

Foster, John Bellamy. 1999. 'Marx's Theory of Metabolic Rift: Classical Foundations for Environmental Sociology'. *American Journal of Sociology*, 105, no. 2: 366–405.

Foster, John Bellamy and Paul Burkett. 2000. 'The Dialectic of organic/inorganic Relations'. *Organization & Environment*, 13:4, 403–25.

Foster, John Bellamy and Paul Burkett. 2001. 'Marx and the Dialectic of Organic/Inorganic Relations: A Rejoinder to Salleh and Clark'. *Organisation and Environment*, 14:4, 451–62.

Foucault, Michel. 1980. *The History of Sexuality, Vol. I: An Introduction*. Trans. Robert Hurley. New York: Vintage Books.

Foucault, Michel. 1977. *Discipline and Punish: The Birth of the Prison*. Trans. Alan Sheridan. New York: Vintage Books.

Frederick, Christine. 1919. *Household Engineering: Scientific Management in the Home*. Chicago: American School of Home Economics.

Gandhi, Leela. 2014. *The Common Cause: Postcolonial Ethics and the Practice of Democracy, 1900–1955*. Chicago: University of Chicago Press.

Gandhi, M.K. 1999. *The Collected Works of Mahatma Gandhi (Electronic Book)*. New Delhi: Publications Division Government of India, 98 Volumes.

Gandhi, M.K. 2018. *An Autobiography Or The Story of My Experiments with Truth*. Trans. Mahadev Desai. New Haven: Yale University Press.

Gandy, Matthew. 2014. *The Fabric of Space: Water, Modernity, and the Urban Imagination*. Cambridge: MIT Press.

George, Rose. 2008. *The Big Necessity: The Unmentionable World of Human Waste and Why it Matters*. New York: Henry Holt and Co.

Gershon, MD, Michael. 1998. *The Second Brain: A Groundbreaking New Understanding of Nervous Disorders of the Stomach and Intestine*. New York: HarperCollins.

Gottlieb, Alma. 2014. 'First Acts of Small Violence: Reflections on Breastfeeding and Enemas in West Africa'. *Childhood, Youth, and Violence in Global Contexts: Research and Practice in Dialogue*. Eds K. Wells, E. Burman, H. Montgomery, A. Watson. New York: Palgrave Macmillan. Kindle Edition.

Grant, Kevin. 2011. 'British Suffragettes and the Russian Method of Hunger Strike'. *Comparative Studies in Society and History*, 53:1, 113–43.

Green, Barbara. 1997. *Spectacular Confessions: Autobiography, Performative Activism, and the Sites of Suffrage 1905–1938*. New York: St Martin's Press.

Grosz, Elizabeth. 1994. *Volatile Bodies: Toward a Corporeal Feminism*. Bloomington: Indiana University Press.

Guha, Ramachandra. 2015. *Gandhi Before India*. New York: Vintage Books.

Hall, Lesley. 2001. 'A "remarkable collection": The Papers of Frederick Parkes Weber FRCP (1863–1962)'. *Medical History*, October 45:4, 523–32.

Hamlin, Christopher. 1985. 'Providence and Putrefaction: Victorian Sanitarians and the Natural Theology of Health and Disease'. *Victorian Studies*, 28: 381–411.

Haraway, Donna. 2016. *Staying with the Trouble: Making Kin in the Chthulucene*. Durham: Duke University Press.

Hardy, T.L. 1944. Letter to Frederick Parkes Weber (4 February) PP/FPW/B67/1/1. Frederick Parkes Weber Papers, Wellcome Library.

Hartman, Saidiya. 2020. *Wayward Lives, Beautiful Experiments: Intimate Histories of Riotous Black Girls, Troublesome Women, and Queer Radicals*. W.W. Norton & Company.

Haug, Timothée. 2018. 'The Capitalist Metabolism: An Unachieved Subsumption of Life Under the Value-form'. *Journal for Cultural Research*, 22:2. 191–203.

Hird, Myra J. 2012. 'Digesting Difference: Metabolism and the Question of Sexual Difference'. *Configurations*, 20:3. 213–37.

Hollis, Leo. 2013. *Cities are Good for You: The Genius of the Metropolis*. New York: Bloomsbury.

Holt, L. Emmett. 1894. *The Care and Feeding of Children.* New: York: Appleton & Co.
Honig, Bonnie, ed. 1995. *Feminist Interpretations of Hannah Arendt.* University Park: Penn State University Press.
Hunt, James D. 2005. *An American Looks at Gandhi.* New Delhi: Promilla & Co.
Inglis, David. 2001. *A Sociological History of Excretory Experience: Defecatory Manners and Toiletry Technologies.* Lewiston, NY: The Edwin Mellen Press.
Inglis, David. 2002. 'Dirt and denigration: the faecal imagery and rhetorics of abuse'. *Postcolonial Studies*, 5:2. 207–21.
Inglis, David and Mary Holmes. 2000. 'Toiletry Time: Defecation, Temporal Strategies and the Dilemmas of Modernity'. *Time Society*, 9:2/3, 223–45.
Jenkins, Lyndsey. 2015. *Lady Constance Lytton: Aristocrat, Suffragette, Martyr.* London: Biteback Publishing.
Jorgensen-Earp, Cheryl R., ed. 1999. *Speeches and Trials of the Militant Suffrage Campaign, 1907–1914.* London: Associated University Presses.
Jorgensen-Earp, Cheryl R. and Darwin D. Jorgensen. 2016. 'Physiology and Physical Force: The Effect of Edwardian Science on Women's Suffrage'. *Southern Communication Journal*, 81:3, 136–55.
Kar, Snehendu B. 2018. *Empowerment of Women for Promoting Global Health and Quality of Life.* Oxford: Oxford University Press.
Keller, Evelyn Fox. 2003. *Making Sense of Life: Explaining Biological Development with Models, Metaphors, and Machines.* Cambridge: Harvard University Press.
Kirsch, Adam. 2009. 'Beware of Pity: Hannah Arendt and the power of the impersonal'. *New Yorker*, 12 January 2009. (Accessed 27/5/2022) https://www.newyorker.com/magazine/2009/01/12/beware-of-pity
Landecker, Hannah. 2011. 'Food as Exposure: Nutritional Epigenetics and the New Metabolism'. *BioSocieties*, 6:2 (June), 167–94.
Landecker, Hannah. 2013. 'The Metabolism of Philosophy, in Three Parts'. In *Dialectic and Paradox: Configurations of the Third in Modernity.* Eds Berhard Malkmus and Ian Cooper. Bern: Peter Lang, 193–224.
Landecker, Hannah. 2014. 'Postindustrial Metabolism: Fat Knowledge'. *Public Culture*, 25, no. 3: 495–522.
Laporte, Dominique. 2002. *The History of Shit.* Trans. Rodolphe el-Khoury. Cambridge: MIT Press.
Lee, Rachel. 2014. 'Pussy Ballistics and the Queer Appeal of Peristalsis, or Belly Dancing with Margaret Cho'. *GLQ*, 20:4, 491–520.

Lennon, Joseph. 2007. 'Fasting for the public: Irish and Indian sources of Marion Wallace Dunlop's 1909 hunger strike'. *Enemies of Empire: New perspectives on imperialism, literature and historiography*. Portland, OR: Four Courts Press.

Liebig, Justus von. 1863. *The Natural Laws of Husbandry*. Ed. John Blyth MD. London: Walton and Maberly.

Long, Clara [Guest]. 2019. 'Trump Admin Moves 100 Migrant Kids Back to "Child Jail" Despite Concern over Inhumane Conditions'. Interviewed by Amy Goodman and Juan Gonzalez. *Democracy Now*, 26 June 2019. https://www.democracynow.org/2019/6/26/child_jail _facilities_at_us_border (Accessed 27/5/2022)

Lupton, Ellen and J. Abbott Miller. 1992a. *The Bathroom, the Kitchen, and the Aesthetics of Waste: A Process of Elimination*. New York: Kiosk.

Lupton, Ellen and J. Abbott Miller. 1992b. 'Hygiene, Cuisine and the Product World of Early Twentieth-Century America'. In *Incorporations*. Eds Jonathan Crary and Sanford Kwinter. New York: Zone, 497–515.

Lytton, Constance. 1988. *Prisons and Prisoners: The Stirring Testimony of a Suffragette*. Midge MacKenzie, Intro. London: Virago Press (first published as *Prisons & Prisoners: Some Personal Experiences, by Constance Lytton and Jane Warton, Spinster*. London: William Heinemann, 1914).

Lytton, Constance. 2008. *Prisons and Prisoners: Some Personal Experiences*. Ed. and introduction by Jason Haslam. Peterborough, ON: Broadview Press.

Marald, Erland. 2002. 'Everything Circulates: Agricultural Chemistry and Recycling Theories in the Second Half of the Nineteenth Century'. *Environment and History*, 8, no. 1 (February), 65–84.

Marvin, Simon and Will Medd. 2006. 'Metabolisms of Obe-city: flows of fat through bodies, cities and sewers'. In *In the Nature of Cities: Urban Political Ecology and the Politics of Urban Metabolism*. Eds Nik Heynen, Maria Kalka and Erik Swyngedouw. NY: Routledge, 137–49.

Marx, Karl. 1976. *Capital: A Critique of Political Economy*. Vol. 1. Trans. Ben Fowkes. New York: Penguin.

Marx, Karl. 1981. *Capital: A Critique of Political Economy*. Vol. 3. Trans. David Fernbach. New York: Penguin.

Marx, Karl. 1988. *Economic and Philosophical Manuscripts of 1844*. Trans. M. Milligan. Amherst, NY: Prometheus Books.

Massumi, Brian. 2002. *Parables for the Virtual: Movement, Affect, Sensation*. Durham: Duke University Press.

Mathias, Manon and Alison M. Moore, eds. 2018. *Gut Feeling and Digestive Health in Nineteenth-Century Literature, History and Culture*. Palgrave Macmillan.

Mattausch, John. 2014. 'Gandhi's Prescription: Health and Hygiene in the Unfinished Struggle for *Swaraj*'. *South Asia Research*, 34:2, 155–69.

Mayhall, Laura E. Nym. 2003. *The Militant Suffrage Movement: Citizenship and Resistance in Britain, 1860–1930*. New York: Oxford University Press.

McPhee, Carol and Ann Fitzgerald, eds. 2001. *The Non-Violent Militant: Selected Writings of Teresa Billington-Greig*. New York: Routledge.

Montes, Aaron. 2019. 'Indian Asylum Seekers on Hunger Strike Transferred to El Paso ICE Detention Facility'. *El Paso Times*, 18 July 2019. https://www.elpasotimes.com/story/news/2019/07/18/asylum-seekers-hunger-strike-transferred-el-paso-ice-detention-facility/1773475001/ (Accessed 27/5/2022)

Mullens, Esther Elizabeth. 1911. 'Letter to the Editor'. *T.P'.s Weekly*, 27 October 1911, 538.

Office of Inspector General (OIG). 2019a. *FY 2019 CBP Spot Inspections*. Project #19-039-SRE-CBP (5/13/2019 – 5/15/2019) (https://www.documentcloud.org/documents/6178541-Final DocumentsRedacted.html (Accessed 27/5/2022)

Office of Inspector General (OIG). 2019b. *FY 2019 CBP Spot Inspections*. Project #19-039-SRE-CBP (5/14/2019–5/16/2019) (https://www.documentcloud.org/documents/6178541-FinalDocumentsRedacted.html (Accessed 27/5/2022)

Oldfield, Josiah. 1943. 'The Elimination of Constipation in Man'. *The Medical Press and Circular*, Vol. 210, 15 December, 381–5.

Owens, Patricia. 2012. 'Human Security and the rise of the social'. *Review of International Studies*, 38, 547–67.

Parkes Weber, Frederick. Nd. 'A dream of neurotics in past ages' from PP/FPW/B.267 Psychoneuroses, malingering, etc. 1910–1949.

Parkes Weber, Frederick. 1904. 'Faecal Vomiting and Reversed Peristalsis in Functional Nervous (Cerebral) Disease: A Summary of Cases and Conclusions', Reprinted from *Brain: A Journal of Neurology*. Vol. 27 (Summer), 170–98.

Parkes Weber, Frederick. 1904–1951. Faecal Vomiting and Anti-Peristalsis PP/FPW/B114/1. Wellcome Library.

Parkes Weber, Frederick. 1911. 'On the Association of Hysteria with Malingering, and on the Phylogenetic Aspect of Hysteria as

Pathological Exaggeration (or Disorder) of Tertiary (Nervous) Sex Characters'. *Proceedings of the Royal Society of Medicine.* Vol. 5, 26–32.

Parkes Weber, Frederick. 1912. 'Two Strange Cases of Functional Disorder, with Remarks on the Association of Hysteria and Malingering'. *International Clinics,* Vol. 1, 22nd Series, 125–38.

Parkes Weber, Frederick. 1919. 'Thinking and Dreaming and the Explanation of Dreams' (reprinted from *Contributions to Medical and Biological Research, dedicated to Sir William Osler, in Honour of his Seventieth Birthday, July 12, 1919, by his Pupils and Co-workers.*) New York: Paul B. Hoeber, 269–79.

Parkes Weber, Frederick. 1932. 'The Storming of the New Jerusalem: A Dream', reprinted from *The Medical Press and Circular,* London, Vol. 184, 217.

Parkes Weber, Frederick. 1934. 'Extravagance in Freudian Teaching and Freudian Explanations'. *The Medical Press and Circular,* London, 7 November, Vol. 189, 419–20.

Parkes Weber, Frederick. 1943. 'Bergson's "Vital Force" (Elan Vital), etc.'. Handwritten Notes, 1 June 1943. PP/FPW B.96/2. Wellcome Library.

Parkes Weber, Frederick. 1944. Letter to T.L. Hardy. (4 February) PP/FPW/B67/1/1. Frederick Parkes Weber Papers, Wellcome Library.

Parkes Weber, Frederick. 1950a. 'Retrograde Peristalsis and Vomiting of Faeces, Enemata and Suppositories in Functional Nervous Conditions; Remarks on the Tonic Leiomyospasms'. *The Medical Press,* No. 5779, 8 February, 120–6.

Parkes Weber, Frederick. 1950b. Letter to Dr W. Clifford M. Scott. (9 May) PP/FPW/B 114/2. Frederick Parkes Weber Papers, Wellcome Library.

Patel, Sheela et al. 2014. *Community Toilets: Emergence of Community Toilets as a Public Good: The work of Mahila Milan, NSDF and SPARC in India in the area of Sanitation.* Published by SPARC, INDIA. Available in PDF format at the *Environment and Urbanization* website: https://www.environmentandurbanization.org/emergence-community-toilets-public-good-sanitation-work-mahila-milan-nsdf-and-sparc-india (Accessed 27/5/2022)

Penner, Barbara. 2001. 'A World of Unmentionable Suffering: Women's Public Conveniences in Victorian London'. *Journal of Design History,* 14.1, 35–52.

Probyn, Elspeth. 2000. *Carnal Appetites: FoodSexIdentities.* New York: Routledge.

Raitt, Suzanne. 2003. 'Psychic Waste: Freud, Fechner, and the Principle of Constancy'. In *Culture and Waste: The Creation and Destruction of Value*. Edited by Gay Hawkins and Stephen Muecke. Lanham, MD: Rowman and Littlefield, 73-4.

'Report of the Conference of Jewish Women: Held at Portman Rooms, Baker Street, London' (13-14 May 1902). https://archive.org/stream/reportofconferen00confiala/reportofconferen00confiala_djvu.txt (Accessed 27/5/2022)

Richardson, Elsa. 'Cranks, Clerks, and Suffragettes: The Vegetarian Restaurant in British Culture and Fiction 1880-1914. 2021'. *Literature and Medicine*, 39:1. 133-53.

Ring, Jennifer. 1989. 'On Needing Both Marx and Arendt: Alienation and the Flight from Inwardness'. *Political Theory*, 17:3, 432-48.

Roach, Mary. 2014. *Gulp: Adventures on the Alimentary Canal*. New York: W.W. Norton and Co.

Ronell, Avital. 2009. *Examined Life: Excursions with Contemporary Thinkers*. Ed. Astra Taylor. New York: The New Press.

Routray, Parimita, Wolf-Peter Schmidt, Sophie Boisson, Thomas Clasen and Marion W. Jenkins. 2015. 'Socio-cultural and behavioural factors constraining latrine adoption in rural coastal Odisha: an exploratory qualitative study'. *BMC Public Health*, 15: 880ff.

Roy, Parama. 2010. *Alimentary Tracts: Appetites, Aversions, and the Postcolonial*. Durham: Duke University Press.

*Sadak Chaap*. http://www.sadakchaap.org/ (Accessed 27/5/2022)

Saito, Kohei. 2017. *Karl Marx's Ecosocialism: Capital, Nature, and the Unfinished Critique of Political Economy*. New York: NYU Press/Monthly Review Press.

Salleh, Ariel. 1997. *Ecofeminism as politics: Nature, Marx and the postmodern*. London: Zed.

Salleh, Ariel. 2001. 'Sustaining Marx or Sustaining Nature?: An Ecofeminist Response to Foster and Burkett'. *Organization and Environment*, 14:4, 443-50.

Salleh, Ariel. 2004. 'Sustainability and Meta-Industrial Labour: Building a Synergistic Politics'. *The Commoner* (N.9) https://base.socioeco.org/docs/synergisticariel_salleh.pdf (Accessed 27/5/2022)

Salleh, Ariel. 2010. 'From Metabolic Rift to "Metabolic Value": Reflections on Environmental Sociology and the Alternative Globalization Movement'. *Organization & Environment*, 23:2, 205-19.

Salisbury, Laura. 2011. 'Bulimic Beckett: Food for Thought and the Archive of Analysis'. *Critical Inquiry*, 53:3, 60-80.

'Satyagraha to Swachhagraha: Narendra Modi addresses rally in Champaran'. 2018. *Business Standard*, 10 April. https://www.business-standard.com/article/current-affairs/champaran-satyagraha-118041000379_1.html (Accessed 27/5/2022).

*Save Girl Child*. Website. http://savegirlchild.org/ (Accessed 27/5/2022)

Schaffer, Gavin. (2012) 'Unmasking the "muscle Jew": the Jewish soldier in British war service, 1899–1945'. *Patterns of Prejudice*, 46:3–4, 375–96. DOI: 10.1080/0031322X.2012.701809 (Accessed 1/10/2020)

Schmidt, Alfred. 1971. *The Concept of Nature in Marx*. Trans. Ben Fowkes, London: New Left Books.

Scholz, Roswitha. 2011. *Das Geschlecht des Kapitalismus: Feministische Theorien und die postmoderne Metamorphose des Patriarchats*. Bad Honnef: Horlemann.

Scott, Dr W. Clifford. 1950. Letter to Frederick Parkes Weber. (3 May 1950) PP/FPW/B 114/2. Frederick Parkes Weber Papers. Wellcome Library.

Shorter, Edward. 1992. *From Paralysis to Fatigue: A History of Psychosomatic Illness in the Modern Era*. New York: The Free Press.

Showalter, Elaine. 1987. *The Female Malady: Women, Madness and English Culture*. London: Virago.

Simmel, Georg. 1950. 'The Metropolis and Mental Life'. (1903) in K. H. Wolff (trans. and ed.), *The Sociology of Georg Simmel*. New York: Free Press, 409–24.

Simmons, Dana. 2006. 'Waste Not, Want Not: Excrement and Economy in Nineteenth-Century France'. *Representations*, 96, no. 1: 73–89.

Smith, Sara and Pavithra Vasudevan. 2017. 'Race, biopolitics, and the future: Introduction to the special section'. *Government and Planning D: Society and Space*, 35:2, 210–21.

Solomon, Harris. 2016. *Metabolic Living: Food, Fat, and the Absorption of Illness in India*. Durham: Duke University Press.

SPARC. 2012. 'Sandas Mela New Rituals'. YouTube video. https://www.youtube.com/watch?v=CVggpF3651Q (Accessed 27/5/2022)

Stekel, Wilhelm. 1967. *Frigidity in Woman in Relation to Her Love Life: A Scientific Investigation of the Genesis, Dynamics, and Physical Symptoms of the Psychic Disorders of Love in Woman*. Trans. James S. Van Teslaar. New York: Washington Square. Trans. of *Die Geschlectskälte der Frau (Eine Psychopathologie des Weiblichen Liebeslebens)*. Berlin: Urban und Schwarzenberg, 1927.

Stopnitzky, Yaniv. 2017. 'No toilet no bride? Intrahousehold bargaining in male-skewed marriage markets in India'. *Journal of Development Economics*, 127, 269–82.

Styan, J.L. 1982. *Max Reinhardt*. Cambridge: Cambridge University Press.

Swyngedouw, Erik. 2006. 'Metabolic urbanization: the making of cyborg cities'. In *In the Nature of Cities: Urban Political Ecology and the Politics of Urban Metabolism*. Eds Nik Heynen, Maria Kalka and Erik Swyngedouw. New York: Routledge, 20–39.

Tavernise, Sabrina. 2016. 'A Toilet but No Proper Plumbing: A Reality in 500,000 US Homes'. *New York Times*, 26 September 2016, https://www.nytimes.com/2016/09/27/health/plumbing-united-states-poverty.html

Taylor, Astra, ed. 2009. *Examined Life: Excursions with Contemporary Thinkers*. New York: The New Press.

Thom MD, D.A. 1974. 1923, 1938. *Habit Clinics for Child Guidance*. Bureau Publication No. 135 (first published in 1923 as *Habit Clinics for the Child of Preschool Age*). Reprinted in Children's Bureau Studies, William M. Schmidt, ed. NY: Arno Press.

Tompkins, Kyla Wazana. 2014. 'On the Visceral'. *GLQ: A Journal of Lesbian and Gay Studies*, 20:4 and 21:1.

US Border Patrol. 2012. *2012–2016 Border Patrol Strategic Plan*. Washington, D.C.: Customs and Border Patrol. https://www.cbp.gov/sites/default/files/documents/bp_strategic_plan.pdf (Accessed 27/5/2022)

Vernon, James. 2007. *Hunger: A Modern History*. Cambridge, MA: Harvard University Press.

Veronesi, Mariangela. 2016. 'Mumbai's urban metabolism and the role of waste management through informality', DPU Working Paper 183, Bartlett Development Planning Unit, https://www.ucl.ac.uk/bartlett/development/sites/bartlett/files/migrated-files/WP183_Mariangela_Veronesi__0.pdf (Accessed 27/5/2022).

Walker, Alice. *You Can't Keep a Good Woman Down*. Harcourt, Brace, Jovanovich. 1981.

Walton, Jean. 2001. *Fair Sex, Savage Dreams: Race, Psychoanalysis, Sexual Difference*. Durham: Duke University Press.

Walton, Jean. 2002. 'Female Peristalsis'. *differences: A Journal of Feminist Cultural Studies*, 13, no. 2 (Summer): 57–89.

Walton, Jean. 2010. 'Modernity and the Peristaltic Subject'. In *Neurology and Modernity: A Cultural History of Nervous Systems, 1800–1950*. Eds Laura Salisbury and Andrew Shail. London: Palgrave Macmillan, 245–66.

Weinberg, Martin S. and Colin J. Williams (2005). 'Fecal Matters: Habitus, Embodiments, and Deviance'. *Social Problems*, 52:3, 315–36.

'What does Modi's Swachhagraha mean?'. 2017. *Quora.* https://www.quora.com/What-does-Modis-Swachhagraha-mean (Accessed 27/5/2022)

Whorton, James C. 2000. *Inner Hygiene: Constipation and the Pursuit of Health in Modern Society.* Oxford: Oxford UP.

Wilderson III, Frank. 2003. 'Gramsci's Black Marx: Whither the Slave in Civil Society?'. *Social Identities: Journal for the Study of Race, Nation and Culture,* 9:2, 225–40.

Wilson, Elizabeth. 2004a. 'Gut Feminism'. *Differences: A Journal of Feminist Cultural Studies,* 15:3. 66–94.

Wilson, Elizabeth. 2004b. *Psychosomatic: Feminism and the Neurological Body.* Durham: Duke University Press.

Wishart, Ryan, R. Jamil Jonna and Jordan Besek. 2020. 'Metabolic Rift: A Selected Bibliography', *Monthly Review,* https://monthlyreview.org/commentary/metabolic-rift/ (Accessed 27/5/2022)

World Bank. 2013. 'Changing the Culture of Toilets in India'. YouTube video. https://www.youtube.com/watch?v=liBPxiphFoU (Accessed 27/5/2022)

Wright, Sir Almroth. 1913. 'Letter on Militant Hysteria', *Times,* March 28, 1912, in *The Unexpurgated Case against Woman Suffrage.* London: Constable and Company, Ltd.

Ziarek, Ewa Plonowska. 2012. *Feminist Aesthetics and the Politics of Modernism.* New York: Columbia University Press.

# Index

abdominal woman
  as new species of individual,
    117, 127–8n
accumulation, 16, 86, 93, 96, 149,
    150–1, 261n
  accumulation hierarchy, 40,
    42
  of faeces, 94, 114
  of fat, 34–6
  of time in the body (Foucault),
    16, 92–3
advertising as laxative, 118
affect/affective, 2, 10, 12, 17, 78,
    92, 94, 100, 131, 143, 164,
    167 169, 191, 194, 203,
    228–9, 231
  autonomy of affect, 16, 94–8
Agamben, G., 1–6, 9, 190,
    208–11, 214–17, 230n,
    232–3
agency, 11, 13, 16, 18, 20, 31, 67,
    94, 102–3, 190, 204, 206–7,
    223, 228
alimentary tract, canal, tube, or
    system, 2, 11, 20, 84, 86,
    101, 113, 117, 124, 162,
    164, 168, 173, 181–2, 185,
    187, 191–3, 230n, 234, 259
Althusserian interpellation, 90,
    129, 198

ambidexterity (of Gandhi and
    Lytton), 202
amphimixis, 166, 185n
anabolic (women) vs catabolic
    (men), 229n
'Anal-erotic Character Traits'
    (Jones), 183
anality/anal function, 90–1, 105,
    119, 136, 166
  anal sadistic patricide, 148–9
  collectors as anal-erotics,
    183–5
Appadurai, A., 240, 244–5
architectural design, 18, 110, 122,
    129, 191
  and economics/aesthetics of
    waste (Lupton and Miller),
    110–27
  and process of elimination,
    117–18
  kitchen and bathroom as
    erotogenic zones of domestic
    body, 117–19
  of community toilets in urban
    India, 241–2
architectural space(s)
  as appropriate for defecation,
    95
  as conditioning the gut, 169
  boarding school, 136, 142

276     Dissident Gut

architectural space(s) (*cont.*)
  boardinghouse, 132–3, 136, 138, 142
  domestic space, 40–1, 110, 113, 117, 118–27, 129, 142–3, 170, 237
  hospital, 179–82, 185n
  housing for pavement dwellers, 241–3
  prison, 191–2, 195, 196, 204–5, 209, 221, 225
  public lavatories in London, 151–5
  sanitarium, 127, 132, 133, 142
  segregation of depending on genitalia or race, 95, 256
Arendt, H., 58, 59, 78n
  feminist critique of, 79n
  on introspection, 68–9, 102–4
  on labour vs work, 15, 63–71
  on metabolism in Marx, 64–71
  on the shapelessness of inner organs, 102–4
  on world-making, 15, 16, 66, 71, 103–4
autointoxication (due to intestinal stasis), 112–13, 114, 119, 132, 135
  as catchall diagnosis, 112, 114
  as making women unmarriageable, 115
autonomic function, process(es), or nervous system, 2, 16, 18, 40, 78, 80, 81, 82, 91, 93, 104, 105, 110, 167–8, 172, 207, 216, 223, 228–9; *see also* enteric nervous system, peristaltic system

bare life, 1, 4–6, 9, 190, 208–11, 214–17, 228, 230n, 232–3
becoming, 142
Bergson, H., 68–9, 102, 184–5
Billington-Grieg, T., 221, 226–8

biology/biological, 2, 5, 7, 10, 20, 64–5, 68–9, 83, 92, 103–4, 118, 143, 210–11, 215, 227–8, 231–2
  biological unconscious, 105, 146, 165, 170
  dynamicism of biology of enteric system, 162–70
  biological substrate of the body, 146, 162, 163
  as capable of pleasure and wishes, 165
  as interested broker of psychosomatic events, 164, 167
Bion, W., 87
biopolitics, biopolitical, 104, 109
  biopolitical enteric management, 232
  faecal biopolitics, 210, 231–59
  metabolic or peristaltic biopolitics, 1–56, 209, 233–4
  race biopolitics, 250–1
biopower, as exercised by women's dissident guts, 11, 232–3
body, 4, 5, 11, 12, 13, 19, 25, 31, 35, 58, 80, 104, 112, 128n, 131–42, 146, 148, 151, 158, 162–3, 166, 173, 181–2, 185, 188, 237
  and affect, 12, 16, 165, 259
  and autointoxication, 112–17
  and biopolitics, 7, 54, 210
  and city, 33, 152, 154–5, 200, 234
  and faecal habitus, 46–56, 231, 248
  and metabolic rift, 27, 30, 35–6, 39–40, 42, 52, 229
  and temporality, 11, 16, 18, 50, 80, 87, 91–4, 152, 155
  Arendt on, 64–71, 103, 104
  as tube, 81–6, 88–9, 91, 221

disciplinary training of, 92–101, 102
evolutionary account of, 81, 85, 86, 88, 203
female body as site of expulsion/faecal production, 109–10, 154, 158, 163, 188
household as, 119–27
incarcerated body, 7–9, 90, 191, 193, 204, 205, 208, 212–14, 217–18, 220, 222, 228
Marx on, 60–2, 64, 72–3, 75, 77, 78, 102
of homemaker or household engineer, 122–7
raced body, 144, 251, 261n
visceral training of as processor of world, 88, 102, 247
Bourdieu, P., 10, 15, 46, 51, 56, 236
Boussingault, J.-B., 38–9
bowel(s), 18, 55, 82, 84, 88, 89, 91, 93–4, 113–14, 124, 131, 156, 166, 173
bowel habits, 10, 12, 51, 55, 93, 96, 98, 99, 102, 109–10, 111, 112, 113, 115, 125, 130
and sexual desire, 17, 130, 131, 133–5, 140–2, 146
as form of discourse, 131, 168
bowel movement, 106n, 114, 132–5
as never unconditioned, 169
brain (first), 61, 80–4, 89–91, 95, 101, 103, 146, 168–9, 172, 204, 232, 259
role in faecal vomiting, 161–2
see also second brain
bulimia, 109, 166–7
Burkett, P., 61–2, 78n

*Capital, vol.1 and 3.* (Marx), 26, 30, 59, 72; *see also* capitalism, commodities, Marx, money
capitalism, 26, 81, 50
and commodities, 71–8
and domestic design, 111, 118, 142–3
and metabolic rift, 14, 26–8, 30, 31, 38–40, 41, 52, 193
and social metabolism, 11, 60, 71–8
and women, 13–14, 41, 50, 70, 141, 142–3
Carpenter, E., on Indian fakirs who reverse peristaltic system, 173
cesspool(s), 100, 113, 253, 257
social justice tours of, 247, 255, 257
chamber pot or bedpan, 50, 153, 253, 256; *see also* honey-bucket or slop jar
'Changing the Culture of Toilets in India', 239–40
Charcot, J.-M., 147, 160, 175, 187
childcare practices, 1, 3, 6, 7, 10, 17, 41, 96, 100, 102, 125, 168; *see also* habit clinics
circulation, 35, 136, 153, 220
economic, 15, 71–7, 117, 246
of metabolic systems, 32, 38, 59, 72, 117, 219
citizenship/citizen, 4, 41, 48, 51, 154–5, 216, 221, 233, 245
and tax on public lavatories, 75
and toilet training, 18
as fashioned in the home, 96, 100, 102
passive vs active citizenship, 216
women as denied citizenship, 199

citizenship/citizen (*cont.*)
city, 6, 14, 15, 26, 29, 31, 42, 49, 51, 147–8, 152, 155, 191, 195, 198, 199 236, 242–8, 260, 260n
    city-as-metabolism/waste management, 6, 15, 25–6, 32–8, 43n, 47, 153, 234, 248, 260n
    contrasted with country living, 28, 191, 195
    right to the city, 235, 241
circulus, 39, 42; see also faecal recycling, metabolic rift
civil rights movement, 249–51, 254, 256–7
civilisation, 50, 53, 132
    as detrimental to bowel health, 113
class, 11, 17, 26, 41, 58, 70, 119, 143, 146, 151, 153–6, 171, 176, 185n, 191, 193, 194, 197, 198, 201, 206, 207–8, 213, 215, 225, 226, 231, 247, 252
    and bodily habitus, 12, 15, 18, 46–56, 110, 221, 236, 248
cloaca, 147–8, 183
colectomy, or 'short circuit operation' (Lane), 114–16
    as more frequently performed on women, 114
colonialism, 12, 56n, 173, 176, 178, 202, 230n
commodities, 15, 25, 26, 31, 34, 70–9, 92, 101, 118; see also *Capital*, capitalism, circulation
common cause (L. Gandhi), 199, 200–4
community toilets in urban India, 240–7
    advantages over public toilets, 242–3
    as community centres, 244
    linked to micro-savings and loan practice, 244
*Community Toilets: Emergence of Community Toilets as a Public Good*, 240–7
conditioning, 99, 104, 168–9
Consequence Delivery System, or CDS (as border security), 7–8
constipation, 1, 6, 35, 39, 56, 81, 84, 91, 92, 99, 113–15, 128n, 131, 135, 151, 156, 168, 188, 203
    and amphimixis, 166
    and colectomies, 114–16
    and hoarding, 77
    as source of (mental) fatigue in homemaker, 124–7
    caused by prison diet, 219
    treatments for, 109, 111
'Constipation: the Universal Malady' (Oldfield), 84–8
consumption, 14, 28, 36, 39, 40, 59, 63, 65, 66, 68, 70, 74–5, 79, 99, 101, 109–11, 118–19, 120, 129, 135, 143, 190, 228
counter-governmentality (Appadurai), 244–5
'Cultural Politics of Shit, The' (Doron and Raja), 235–7, 240, 251

defecation, 35, 50, 86, 90–1, 95, 99, 144, 233–47
    and bourgeois body, 47, 48, 51, 53–5
    and inner sphincter, 91, 110, 131, 143–4, 168–9
    and 'push button mechanism', 86, 88–90
    as valid platform for social dignity, 244

De Genova, N.
  on Agamben's 'bare life', 5, 190, 210–11, 214, 215, 216, 232
  on Marx and metabolism, 210–11
deputation(s) and procession(s) (suffragette), 196, 198, 200, 207, 224, 227; *see also* street(s)
desiring machine/production (Deleuze), 110, 129, 130, 135, 140, 141, 142, 144–5n
digestion/digestive, 1, 2, 17, 32, 39, 66, 68, 80, 87, 92, 102, 106n, 111, 113, 114, 118, 150, 151, 163, 166, 167, 169, 218; *see also* alimentary tract, enteric nervous system
discipline/disciplinary techniques/structures, 11, 16, 34, 48–50, 109–10, 129, 155, 191, 201, 240, 258, 259
  of large intestine/metabolic system, 2, 13, 52, 92–105, 110
disguise
  as working-class woman, 207–8, 214
  of straight-pipe, 253
dissident gut, 1, 2, 9, 11, 17, 20, 110, 190; *see also* fasting, faecal vomiting, hunger strike
doctor–patient relation, 11
  as collaboration, 152, 160, 190, 232
  as libidinally charged, 160
  Lane and multiple patients, 16, 113–17, 143, 146
  Parkes Weber and Rosa Strosmann, 146–86, 152, 160
  prison physician and Constance Lytton/Jane Warton, 187–30
  Stekel and Louise K, 129–45

  W. H. R. Rivers and Siegfried Sassoon, 189–90
domestic engineers, 17, 111, 120–6, 142, 185n
domestic space, 40–1, 93, 94, 110, 111, 113, 119, 124, 142, 143, 170, 237
  and planned obsolescence/streamlining, 117–21
  *see also* architectural design, architectural space(s), Frederick, C.
Doron, A. and Raja, I., 235–40, 251
Douglas, M., 7, 31, 36
dream, 19, 164, 235, 236, 241
  'A dream of neurotics in past ages', 174–8
  American, 254
  sexual daydreams of Louise K, 131
  'The Storming of the New Jerusalem: A Dream', 147–9, 183
Dumas, J.-B., 38–9
Dunlop, M. W., 189, 190, 204, 224

efficiency, 35, 38, 54, 143
  and domestic space, 80, 111
  and peristaltic system, 80, 94, 101, 122, 125
  efficient homemaker, 80, 120–7, 128n
  efficient scientific research, 151
elimination, 39, 84, 116, 176, 179
  of faeces or waste, 1–2, 6, 15, 25, 33–4, 42, 47, 51, 52, 75, 79n, 84, 90, 92, 96–101, 123, 124, 125, 155–6, 205, 221, 234
  of objects in household, 117–20, 124, 126

elimination (*cont.*)
  of unnecessary movements, 17, 36, 120, 124
embodiedness, 12, 74, 81, 154; see also body
enema, 105–6, 112, 114
  to guard against imposture, 157–60, 212
  vomited enemata, 158–60, 171
Engels, F. 26, 31–2, 51, 61
enteric nervous system, 17, 56, 58, 68, 87, 146, 163, 181, 189, 204, 206, 217, 219, 229, 232
  and governmentality in the body, 89–92
  and neurology, 81, 232
  and world-making, 101–4
  autonomy of, 82–3, 94–5, 190, 212–13, 232
  targeting of, 5, 93, 232
Erikson, E., on Gandhi, 223–4, 206
eroticism/erotic, 109, 130, 131, 136, 137, 139, 140, 144
  anal, 136, 166, 183–5
  intestinal, 138, 146, 230n
'eternal negative' (Gandhi, Lytton), 204–8, 212, 223
eugenics, 128n, 176, 179, 186n
evacuation of bowels, 45, 87, 93, 125, 110, 188, 231, 234
evolution, 16, 61, 62, 81, 85–7, 147, 164, 173, 176, 178, 183–4, 203, 232
  and kinked colon, 113
excrement, 14, 19, 33, 41–2, 45–6, 75, 195, 234, 257
  as fertiliser, 14, 28–32, 36–40, 42, 53
  as symbolic capital/morally dirty, 45–50
  as waste vs resource, 15, 25–32, 36–40, 51, 53, 120

'Extravagance in Freudian Teaching and Freudian Explanations' (Parkes Weber), 183–5

faecal habitus, 15, 18–19, 45–56, 56n, 92, 233
  and bare life, 210–11, 232, 258–9
  and euphemistic language, 47–8
  and metabolic rift, 51
  and the prison, 221
  and toilet training, 93–105, 110, 167
  as a matter of perfecting regularity, 52–6, 89, 231
  as tool for class distinction, 45, 48, 231
  as tool for gender distinction, 49–50, 105, 132, 238–40
  as tool for race-based distinction, 56n, 144
  binary vs metabolic model of, 52–6, 231
  bourgeois, 46–8, 52, 153–4, 248
  deviation in, at level of the individual, 143, 146, 232
  in India, 233–47
  in Southern US, 247–59
  modern, 11–12, 48, 52, 233, 252
  proletarian, 46–8
faecal management, 233, 257
faecal recycling, 15, 26, 31, 36–45; see also metabolic rift
faecal vomiting, 17, 156, 158, 161, 183, 187
  cure/treatment, 161–2, 166, 179–82
  feigned, 157, 171–2
  hysterical faecal vomiting, 157, 171–2

fasting, 109, 201, 223, 225, 229; see also hunger strike
fat, 52, 121
  as actant in urban metabolism, 15, 26, 33–5, 43n
  as like savings in the bank, 122
  as model for waste elimination, 15, 34, 36, 78, 224
  circulation of, 33–5
  money as, 77
female body, 49, 228
  as evoking spectre of sexuality, 154
  as site of faecal production and management, 110
*Female Malady, The* (Showalter), 230n
feminism, 9, 10, 109, 189, 203, 230n
  as failing to understand biology as dynamic (Wilson), 12, 13, 166–7
  environmental/eco-, 40, 232
  Marxist, 14, 40
  materialist, 12, 40–1, 66, 70–1
  militant, 188–9, 191, 194, 205, 228
Ferenczi on biological substrate of hysteria, 146, 163–9, 185n, 190, 232
fire hoses
  used on protesters in Birmingham, 251
  used on public urinators in Mumbai, 235–6
Flowers, C., 249–59
'flush and forget', 233, 258; see also toilet(s), straight piping
forcible feeding, 9, 190–1, 204, 205, 211, 221, 250
  as causing vomiting, 212–13, 216–18, 221, 227
  as instance of (violent) biopolitics of regularity, 209–10, 216
  sovereign violence masked as medical treatment, 18, 209, 216, 228
Foster, J. B., 6, 12, 14, 28–32, 50–2, 61–2, 78n
Foucault, M., 54–6, 80, 109–10, 117, 127n, 245
  on accumulation and capitalisation of time in the body, 16, 92–3
Frederick, C., 111, 120–9, 132, 185n
Freud, S., 25, 79n, 147, 157, 163–4, 183–4
*Frigidity in Woman* (Stekel), 129–44, 146, 169, 185n

gag reflex, 166–7, 213
Gandhi, Leela, 201–2, 209, 229
Gandhi, Mohandas
  and *ahimsa*, 202
  and eternal negative, 206–7
  and hunger striking, 201, 224–6, 229
  and satyagraha, 19, 223–6
  and suffragettes, 191, 202–3, 223–6, 229, 230n
  and *swaraj*, 234, 259n, 261n
  vegetarianism of, 203, 205
German Hospital, Dalston, 151, 156, 170, 178, 180–2, 212
  as metabolic system, 181–2
  Kosher kitchen, 179–81
Gershon, M., 80–5, 88–92, 95, 105–6n, 168
Gilbreth, Frank and Lillian, 120
Global North, 11, 17, 19, 41, 59, 231

gut
  as having an unconscious, 104–5, 143, 146, 165, 170, 232
  as social, 84
  as thinking, 143
  communicative agency of, 84, 103
  gut pathology as form of perturbed relations to others (Wilson), 106n, 169
*Gut Feminism* (Wilson), 13

habit clinics
  as essential to modulating child's bodily economy for maximum productivity, 101
  proliferation of in early 20th century, 99
habits of eating, sleeping, and elimination in childcare literature, 92, 96–8, 100, 243
Hall, L., on Parkes Weber archives, 149–50, 183
Hamlin, C., 38, 42–3, 52–4
*Happy Childhood* (Anderson), on training of habit of elimination, 96–7
Harris, S., 12, 19
Haug, T., 14, 70
heteronormativity, 18, 110
heterosexualisation-gone-wrong, 138–41
*Hind Swaraj* (Gandhi) or *Indian Home Rule*, 202
Hird, M., 12, 127n
hobbies
  Arendt's disdain for, 68
  Lytton's hobbies of cleaning and prison reform, 190, 193–6, 198–9
  Parkes Weber's hobby of collecting, 183–5
Holmes, M., 50, 94

home
  and fabrication of future citizen, 96
  as emotional cesspool vs workshop where child personality developed, 100
homoerotic desire/homosexuality, 129–30, 136–7, 139, 141, 142
honey-bucket or slop jar, 249, 252; *see also* chamber pot or bedpan
household engineer, 111, 120–27, 142, 185n
*Household Engineering: Scientific Management in the Home* (Frederick), 111, 120–7, 129
Hugo, V., 25–6, 36–7
*Human Condition, The* (Arendt), 15, 64–5, 78n, 79n
hunger strike, 9, 19, 189–90, 193, 204–9, 212–29, 233, 250
  as experimental, 204
  as peristaltic intervention in larger metabolic systems, 18, 228
  as practice of imperfectionism or self-ruin, 190–1, 201–2, 204, 223, 225, 228–9
  first political theory of, 205–6
hysteria, 17, 147, 161, 177–8, 187
  peristaltic, 147, 157–62, 186n, 187
  vs malingering, 17, 170–2, 173–6, 179, 183, 212
hysteric(s), 10, 127n, 144, 146, 177, 187, 230
  and psychoanalysis, 110
  and suffragettes, 183, 188–90, 212–13, 221, 229n
hysterical conversion, ideation vs biological substrate as cause, 163–4, 169

hysterical vomiting, 163, 170, 172, 175

ideational content, 105, 106n, 157–8, 162–3
  that hijacks bodily function, 164
ileo-caecal valve and anti-peristalsis, 159, 160–1
incarceration, 9, 233, 256
  and forcible feeding, 191–229
  and suffragettes, 18, 19, 190–229
*Indian Opinion*, 223–5
industrialisation, 11, 13, 40–1, 49, 195, 233
  and metabolism, 13–15, 26–8, 31, 40, 52, 118
Inglis, D., 12, 15, 18, 45–56, 56n, 57n, 89, 94, 231, 236
inner hygiene, 110, 111–17, 122, 135; *see also* autointoxication, intestinal stasis
interoceptive perceptual apparatus (Massumi), 16, 94–6; *see also* second brain
intestine(s), 2, 6, 16, 25, 37, 39, 55, 82, 85, 87, 89, 90, 92, 93, 97, 122, 128n, 130, 133, 134, 136, 144, 156–7, 159–64, 168, 218
  intestinal erotics, 129, 138–9, 140, 141, 142
intestinal stasis, 2, 16, 17, 35, 78, 88, 110, 113–17, 119, 124, 128n, 131, 135, 146, 158, 207, 209
  and household stasis, 121–3, 125–6
  as root cause of illness, 111–12

Jewish body/bodies, 4, 179, 181–2
  antisemitic figure of, 39
Jim Crow, 249, 256–7

Jones, E., 183–4
Jorgensen-Earp, C., 205, 229n

King, Martin Luther, 256
  and sanitation workers' strike, 250–1
kinked or blocked colon, 113–17, 120, 128n, 146; *see also* autointoxication, Lane, Sir Arbuthnot

labour, 2, 14, 15, 39–40, 48, 52, 79n, 80, 119, 180, 234, 235, 241, 259
  and Augean stable (Hercules), 67, 79n
  as outsourced to women, 69–71
  as threshold between [human life as] nature and [human life as] culture, 210
  in Marx, 11, 26, 27, 30, 31, 52, 56, 58, 60–3, 72–8, 79n, 190, 231, 249
  meta-industrial, 10, 16, 17, 19, 26, 39–41, 44n, 50, 93, 96, 105, 110, 119, 154, 193, 199, 232, 240, 250, 258
  racialised, 250, 261n
  reproductive or women's, 11, 13, 40–1, 44n, 49, 52, 116, 125–6, 182, 194–6, 232, 240
  slave, 249, 256, 261n
  vs work in Arendt, 15, 63–9, 78n, 103–4, 232, 246
Landecker, H., 12–13, 43n, 68, 79n, 127n
Lane, Sir Arbuthnot, on 'kinked' colon, 16, 112–17, 119–20, 124, 143, 146, 177
Langley, J. N., 58, 82, 105n
laundrymaid/laundry-workers, 198
  as deserving of representation by parliament, 199

laundrymaid/laundry-workers (*cont.*)
  Lytton's identification as, 198–9
leach or drain field, 247–8, 253; see also septic tank, straight piping, toilets
lesbianism, 136, 139, 140
libido, 136–9, 164, 192, 194
  and *elan vital*, 184
  and medical knowledge production, 151, 160, 183
Liebig, Justus von, 26, 28–31, 35–7, 51–2, 62, 79n
London, 19, 113, 127n, 146, 147, 149, 156, 170, 179
  debate about public lavatories for women in, 17, 18–19, 152–5
  faecal recycling plan for, 54
  Gandhi in, 202–4, 206
  suffragette deputation(s) through the streets of, 196–200, 204–5
  working class women in, 151–3, 155, 180
London Vegetarian Society, 203; see also vegetarianism
Louise K, 129–45, 185
Lowndes County, 249–50, 253, 255, 256–7
Lupton and Miller, 111, 117–20, 128n, 129
Lytton, Constance, 190–223, 227–9, 250

Mahila Milan (Women Together), 240–1, 244, 246; see also community toilets
malingering, 17, 157, 170–6, 178–9, 186, 212–13; see also faecal vomiting, hysterical vomiting
Marald, E., 12, 25, 36–8, 42, 43–4n

Marsden, D., 191–2, 230n
Marvin and Medd, 33–5, 43, 52, 234
Marx, Karl/Marxism, 9, 61, 249, 261n
  and metabolic model of economics, 10, 11, 14, 56, 58, 71–8, 104, 117, 246
  and metabolic rift, 6, 11, 12, 14, 16, 26–32, 35, 51, 59, 143, 195, 231
  and metabolism, 10, 12, 15, 17, 56, 60–5, 68, 70–1, 79, 88, 89, 99, 102, 104, 118, 124, 185, 190, 210–11, 231, 246
  discovery of a law of movement (Arendt), 58, 111
  and feminism, 14, 40–1
Marxist environmentalism, 6, 10, 14, 26, 43n, 45, 51
Massumi, B., 12
  on interoceptive sense of the viscera, 16, 94–5
  on thinking with pure feeling, 95
masturbation, 127n, 137–9, 143–4
maternal longing for plight of prisoners (Lytton), 194, 199
menstruation, 154, 189
metabolic biopolitics, 1–9, 10, 56, 233; see also biopolitics
metabolic life, 2, 10, 11
metabolic rift, 6, 10, 11, 12, 14–15, 25–32, 35–43, 45, 50–6, 59, 66, 124, 143, 146, 190, 193, 195, 213, 229, 231, 233, 249, 259; see also Marx/Marxism, nature
metabolism, 1–9, 12–16, 19–20, 25–6, 59, 68, 81, 92, 103, 179, 181, 190, 213, 231–4, 235, 246–7

as model for urban systems, 15, 31, 32–6, 43n
as model of labour (Marx), 62–4, 67, 190
as requiring human mediation, regulation and control (Marx), 7, 10, 13, 16, 31, 51, 58–63, 71, 78, 88, 102, 119, 124, 185, 210–11, 231–2
feminisation of metabolic labour (Salleh), 16–17, 40–2, 69–71, 110–11, 124, 142, 181, 228, 240
metabolic infrastructure of London, 152–6, 200
of bare life, 9, 190, 208–11, 214, 216, 228, 232–3
of humans with nature (Marx), 10, 59–65, 67, 119, 143, 185, 209–11
of political justice, 229, 250
of scientific research, 149–51
social metabolism (Marx), 10, 15, 71–8, 89, 99, 101, 117–18, 228
two registers of in Marx, 59–60, 72, 118
meta-industrial labour (Salleh), 19, 40–2, 105, 193, 250
and the resourcing of capitalist markets (Haug), 40–2, 70, 96
as producing value, 16, 41, 110, 199
as women's reproductive labour, 17, 40–2, 44n, 50, 59, 70, 93, 119, 154, 232
metropolis, 16, 28, 105, 151–2, 155, 170; see also Simmel, temporality
'Metropolis and Mental Life, The' (Simmel), 152, 155
militancy, 207, 226, 229
modern metabolic or peristaltic subject, 6, 93, 110, 152; see also abdominal women, subject
Moleschott, J., 62, 72, 79n
money, 71, 74, 92, 183, 243
as fat of Body Politick, 77
as fibre of metabolic motility, 72–3
as having no smell, 75
as like shit, 25, 79n
catabolic function of, 77
hoarding of as peristaltic stasis, 76–7, 246
moral imperfectionism (L. Gandhi), 191, 201–2, 204, 228; see also Gandhi, Leela
motherhood
and maternal maintenance, 119, 143
as in need of state intervention for proper toilet training, 96
at border detention centres, 6–7
motility, 34, 232
hunger strike as arrested motility, 206–7, 209
of bureaucratic systems, 6, 9
of economic circulation, 39, 72, 76–7
of human intestines, 2, 13, 78, 81, 203
movement, 10, 19, 26, 32, 36, 43n, 93, 259
and time and motion studies, 120
civil rights movement, 249–50, 254, 256
law of (in architectural design), 111, 120, 124–6, 143
law of (in Marx), 10, 13, 14, 58–9, 60, 63, 65, 72–3, 111
peristaltic, 5, 33, 35, 38–9, 58–9, 63, 73, 78, 84–5, 88, 92, 97–8, 109, 125, 161–2, 190

286    Dissident Gut

movement (*cont.*)
   sanitation movements, 240, 247, 261n
   'the movement' (suffragette), 18, 19, 188–9, 191–200, 203–4, 207, 209, 216, 223–4, 226–8
   through the streets, 200, 206–7
Mumbai, 19, 235, 240, 242, 244, 245, 251, 260

nature, 2, 33, 92, 102, 104, 193
   as man's inorganic body, 61–2, 78n, 89, 102
   metabolic relation to, 10, 13–17, 26, 31, 38–41, 51, 60–1, 63–72, 78, 79n, 88, 96, 102, 118–19, 143, 185, 210, 231, 232, 246
nerves, 81–3, 85–9, 94, 105n, 125, 164, 189, 219
nervous system, 81–6, 89–95, 105n, 127, 155, 161, 172, 174, 181, 207, 228, 232
   enteric, 81–3, 89–95, 181
neurogastroenterology, 10, 80, 105n, 168, 232; *see also* enteric nervous system, gut, intestine
neurosis, 130, 140, 147, 181, 188–9; *see also* faecal vomiting, vomiting
night-soil, 37, 43–4n, 195
'No Toilet, No Bride' campaign, 236, 239–40
'No toilet no bride? Intrahousehold bargaining in male-skewed marriage markets in India', 239
*non olet* (it has no smell), 75

Oedipus complex, 139, 141, 144–5n, 148

oesophagus, 134, 159, 163, 213
Oldfield, J.
   on constipation, 81, 84–90, 92, 111
   shared apartment and vegetarianism with Gandhi, 203
olfactory-intestinal principle, 133–4, 140, 141
'On the Association of Hysteria with Malingering, etc.' (Parkes Weber), 173–6
'open defecation', 233
   'openness' by default, 240–1
   preference for open air defecation over latrines, 237–8
   shaming techniques to curb, 235
organ(s), 16, 49, 81–3, 97, 112, 115, 126, 132, 155, 174, 199
   and amphimixis, 166
   as grown-on or grown-in tools, 61–3, 102
   internal (peristaltic) vs sexual, 136, 138, 141–3, 166
   language of organs (Ferenczi), 165–70
   purifying organs of psychic cathexis, 164–6, 170
   shapelessness of (Arendt), 102–4
organism, 15, 28, 65, 221
   as both conscious and unconscious, 165
   as having 'urge to appear'(Arendt), 103
   as thinking, 165–70
   evolution and, 85–94
outhouse or privy, 75, 119, 249, 252–3; *see also* community toilets, toilet(s)

Index  287

paralysis, 197, 202
   and communication, 221–2, 219
   hysterical, 162, 174
Parkes Weber, Frederick, 146
   on eugenics, 176, 179, 186n
   on reverse or anti-peristalsis, 146–85, 187–8, 208, 212
   on tertiary sex characters, 17, 144, 147, 174–9, 183
passive resistance, 191
   contest to find Gujarati equivalent for (satyagraha), 223–4
passivity and agency in non-violent political struggle, 190, 200, 206–7, 216, 223
Patel, S., et al., 240–6, 260–1n
pathology, 42, 106n, 112, 135, 141, 149, 157, 162, 169, 172–3, 178, 240
Pavlov's experiments and peristaltic movement, 162
Penner, B., 153–5
perc test (soil absorption rate), 255
peristalsis, 5, 33, 35
   and biopolitics, 5–9, 207–9, 211, 232, 234
   and faecal habitus, 45, 51, 54–6, 231, 238, 247
   and temporality, 18, 76–8, 80, 94, 101, 122, 125
   as psycho-social phenomenon, 13, 81, 110
   human within larger systems of, 2, 5, 12, 20, 25, 27, 33, 51–2, 88, 109, 110, 136, 141, 152–5, 231
   modern peristaltic subject, 6, 93, 129, 152
   peristaltic movement through streets, 200
   regulation of, 9–13, 52, 92–105, 111, 143, 231, 238
   reverse or anti-peristalsis, 17, 146, 156–73, 176, 179, 181–3, 187–8, 212, 253
   women's peristaltic systems, 17–19, 109–10, 111, 114–17, 130–44, 146–9, 152–5, 156–73, 176, 179, 181–3, 185n, 187–8, 189–92, 207–9, 211, 217–23, 225–6, 226–9, 232
peristaltic system/process, 25, 80–92
   and domestic engineering, 117–27, 129
   and economic system, 73, 76–8, 141
   as second brain, 16, 58–9, 80–4, 89, 91, 94–5, 101, 105–6n, 146, 168–9, 213, 232–3, 259
   libidinal and peristaltic, 130–44
   scientific pursuit as peristaltic, 149–51
phylogenetic aspect of hysteria, 164, 166, 167, 173, 178, 183
politics, peristaltic, 189–92, 201–2, 207–9, 211, 217–23, 225–9, 233–4, 250; see also biopolitics
power
   biopolitical power, 3–6, 11, 209, 230n, 232–3
   constituted vs constituting (Arendt), 226
   despotic, 261n
   faecal habitus and, 46, 52, 55
   labour, 66, 79n
   of passivity, 207, 211, 213, 219
   peristaltic power, 172–3, 186n, 227
   power and pleasure, 11, 109

power (*cont.*)
  sovereign, 60, 190, 210–11, 214–17, 228
prison(s), 189, 191–206, 208–9, 211–14, 217–29
  Holloway, 189, 194, 196, 198, 200, 223
  Newcastle, 205
  Walton gaol, 193, 208
prisoner(s), 9, 18, 194, 199, 208, 214, 219, 221, 223, 225, 227; *see also* suffragette(s)
*Prisons and Prisoners: Some Personal Experiences* (Lytton and Warton), 190, 191, 193, 202
prostitute(s), 140, 142, 154
protopsychic state and body's substrata (Ferenczi), 164
psychoanalysis, 13, 17, 104–5, 115, 141, 143, 146, 148, 162, 167, 183, 232
'Psychology of the Frigid Woman, The' (Stekel), 129
public toilets/lavatories/conveniences, 17, 19, 75, 152–5, 182, 205, 241–2
purgative(s), 112, 132–3
  anxiety as, 133
  nearby person as, 133, 142
  sexual excitation as, 135, 138

rationality, 16, 31, 165, 261n
  inherent violence in rationality of science, 209–10
  rationalisation of agriculture, 29–30
  rationalisation of housework, 17–18, 36
  rationalisation of industry, 50, 58, 205
  rationalisation of second brain, 101
regularisation of movement, 109–27

regularity, 9–11, 36, 80, 109, 158, 168, 259
  and erotic desire, 129–44
  as like 'sexuality' in Foucault, 54–6
  as technique for maximising life, 10, 55–6, 209, 231–2
  cultural obsession with bowel regularity, 110–13
regulation
  as capitalising time in the body (Foucault), 92–3
  of faecal habitus, 48, 51–6, 94, 231–2
  of metabolism, 7, 8, 10–11, 12–18, 31, 36, 51, 58–78, 81, 84, 86–9, 91–4, 96–102, 104, 185, 210–11, 231, 233
  social inequities of faecal regulation, 10, 231–2, 250, 258
  women as regulating domestic peristaltic health, 17, 50, 52, 109, 119–27, 143
  women as targets of peristaltic regulation, 111–17, 209–10
regulatory regimes, 10, 15, 18, 104, 258
reparative approach to shit, 235
reproductive labour, 40–1, 44n, 66, 70, 199, 201; *see also* meta-industrial labour
rescue operation ('bare life'), 211–17, 232
resistance, 59, 91, 109, 191, 204, 206, 208, 211–12, 220–6, 233, 249, 256; *see also* dissident gut
reverse or anti-peristalsis, 17, 88, 146, 156–73, 187, 208, 212, 253
  and phylogenetic regression, 166
  as historical phenomenon, 187–8

cure(s) for, 162-3, 179-82
  see also faecal vomiting
revolt, 9, 18, 226-9
  as unwilled rising up of the gorge, 227
  as willed political uprising, 227
  right to vote as right to revolt, 226
'Rosa' bundles at Wellcome archives, 150, 181; see also Parkes Weber, Frederick
Routray, P. et al., 237-9
Roy, P., 12, 223

Salisbury, L., 87
Salleh, A., 17, 21n, 40-2, 44n
Salpêtrière, 147, 160, 187
sanitarium, 132-3, 142
  for fine-tuning of household engineer, 127
sanitation, 45, 113
  and biopolitics, 232
  and faecal habitus, 48, 52
  and septic systems, 247-59
  critique of bourgeois sanitation projects in India, 19, 234-40
  in Rural Southern US, 233, 247-59
  sanitary arrangements of prison, 192
Sassoon, S., hybrid protest of, 189-90
*Satyagrah se Swachhagrah*, as substituting 'cleanliness' for 'truth', 247, 261n
satyagraha/satyagrahis (British women as), 19, 191, 223-6; see also suffragette(s)
Schmidt, A., 62-3, 72
second brain (or brain in the gut), 16, 58-9, 80-105, 105n, 143, 146, 168-9, 213, 232-3, 259
  disciplining of, 94, 101
*Second Brain, The*, (Gershon), 80
self-ruination, self-injury, 190, 201-2; see also moral imperfectionism
self-rule, Indian, 191, 233-4, 250, 259n; see also *swaraj*
septic tank(s), 247-8, 252-5; see also leach or drain field, straight pipe, toilets, sanitation, sewage
sexuality, 109, 129, 144, 154
  and regularity, 54-6, 110
  relation to bowel habits, 56n, 130, 136
sewage, 119, 247
  as fertiliser, 29, 30, 31, 37-8, 42-3, 53-4
  raw sewage in rural Alabama, 252-8
sewer(s) or sewage system, 2, 20, 25, 29, 33-5, 113, 155, 213, 231, 234, 260
Shaw, G. B., 154-5
Simmel, G., 152, 155
Simmons, D., 12, 38-9
simulation
  hysterical or neurotic, 171, 174
  malingering, 157, 171, 172
  mythomania and pathomimia, 175
  of faecal vomiting, 157, 171
  women's instinct to deceive, 176
slavery-based cotton industry, 249, 256
'slum' or 'shack' dweller, 235, 240-5, 260n
social justice tour, 247, 251-2, 255-9
social metabolism, 73, 77, 78, 246
  and human peristaltic system, 76, 89, 99, 101
  as prescribed by metabolism with nature, 15, 30, 59-60, 63, 71-2, 118, 228
*Sociological History of Excretory Experience, A*, (Inglis), 45, 49

soil
  and metabolic rift, 6, 14, 26–31, 36–42, 51–3, 59, 79n, 195, 260
  clay-based as inappropriate for septic systems, 19, 249, 253, 255–7
soma/somatisation, 150, 157, 162, 164, 167, 169, 171, 189
sovereign power, 6, 60, 190, 210, 211, 214–17, 228; *see also* biopolitics, power
'species being' and metabolism, 81, 210; *see also* labour
sphincter, 55, 62, 161
  as target of disciplinary training, 93, 97, 110
  internal/external, 90–2, 95, 131, 143, 144, 168–9
state of exception, 209, 215–16, 230n; *see also* bare life, sovereign power
Stekel, W., 17, 129–44, 146, 169, 185n
*Stoffwechsel*, 62, 76; *see also* metabolism
stomach, 62, 89, 95, 113, 134, 156–7, 159, 164, 213, 217, 227
Stopnitzky, Y., 239–40
straight-piping, 252–4, 257; *see also* sanitation, septic tank(s), sewage, toilets
streamlining, 8, 205
  and eugenics, 128n
  and metabolic capitalist circulation and transformation, 117–18
  as excretory aesthetic, 118
  domestic space, 109, 117–18, 129
  of food packaging to increase velocity of consumption, 117–18
  of household objects, 18, 118
  of kitchen and bathroom, 117, 118–19
  peristaltic nature of, 120–7
street(s), 153–6, 191, 196, 198–200, 207–8, 214, 235, 241–2, 251, 256; *see also* suffragette(s)
Strosmann, Rosa aka Rosa Jackson, 146–52, 156–71, 177, 179, 183, 187
  and faecal vomiting, 156–72
  consultations with Parkes Weber, 149, 156, 178–9, 208, 212
  hired as cook at Kosher kitchen of German Hospital, 179–82
subject, 8, 43, 47–8, 81, 84, 87, 210, 207, 228
  *ahimsaic*, 202
  and social realm, 81, 112–13
  anoedipal, 141
  modern (peristaltic) subject, 6, 18, 110, 115, 129, 135, 142, 152, 155
  of peristaltic training, 93, 97
suffrage movement, 18, 199, 204, 207, 223, 226, 250
suffragette(s), 9, 18, 187–229, 250
  and war neurotics, 189
  as sharing dissident gut with hysterics, 189–90
  Gandhi's study of and reports on, 19, 190–1, 200–4, 207, 223–6, 228–9, 233
suppository, 97, 98
vomited, 158–60, 212
*Swachh Bharat* (Clean India), 246–7
*Swaraj* (self-rule), 19, 204, 259n
  faecal, 234–47, 259n
Swyngedouw, E., 12, 32–3

Taylorism of household management, 120–7
temporality, 16, 43n, 58, 62, 147, 150–1, 185–6n
  and accumulation and capitalisation of time in the body (Foucault), 11, 16, 92–3
  and peristalsis, 13, 18, 50, 55, 80, 84–8, 90–4, 96–102, 135
  evolutionary time, 16, 58, 61–2, 81, 85–7, 113, 147, 165, 174
  natural vs cultural time of excretion, 170
  of commodity transformations, 13, 76, 246
  of metropolitan life (Simmel), 152, 155
  of the housewife under patriarchy, 50, 111, 120–7
  reverse peristalsis as contradiction of time's peristaltic arrow, 170
  uni-directionality of time, 80, 94, 170
terror vs hegemony of slave labour, 249, 261n
tertiary sex characters, 174–7, 179, 186n
  hysteria as exaggeration of female tertiary sex traits, 174
*Thalassa* (Ferenczi) and phylogenetic longing for piscine era, 165–7
time and motion studies, 80, 111, 120, 123, 127
toilets, 152–6
  and straight-piping, 252–5, 257
  community, 240–7
  water-based, 15, 42, 45, 48
toilet training, 19, 92–105, 110, 132, 167
  and bodily regulation of time, 92–4
  and coordination of child's habits of elimination with social metabolism, 96–7, 99, 102
  and meta-industrial labor, 16, 17, 50
  as essential to happiness, 92, 100
  as re-enactment of the civilisation process in miniature (Inglis), 94
  as technique for capitalising time in the body, 11, 16, 92–3
  denied in detention centre, 7
  state intervention in, 96, 101–2
  use of suppository to facilitate, 97

US border detention, 3; *see also* bare life

value, 55, 86
  and commodities, 26, 62, 73–6, 79n
  labour, 26, 64
  metabolic, 16, 41, 70–1, 110, 199
  meta-industrial, 16, 41, 70–1, 110, 199
  of faeces, 51
vegetarianism, 112, 192, 218
  as linking Lytton and Gandhi at gut level, 201, 203–4, 205
vomiting
  during forcible feeding, 212–13, 216–18, 221, 227
  facility for vomiting on cue, 172, 173, 186n
  functional nervous vomiting, 161
  of faeces, 17, 156, 158, 161, 183, 187
  prison doctor sprayed by, 217–18

vote, 188, 190, 196, 206, 216, 222, 226–7, 249–50, 256

wardresses, 190, 211–13, 220, 222
Warton, Jane (Lytton's disguise as), 190, 208, 213–14, 217, 222
waste
  American obsession with, 118
  and faecal habitus, 47, 49, 52
  and metabolic cycles, 32, 36–43, 43–4n, 52, 53, 67, 75, 85, 119, 121–2, 143, 170, 195
  and planned obsolescence, 36, 118
  and toilet training, 93, 94, 99, 110
  as cessation of useless motions, 17, 36, 80
  as what fails to leave the body, 35–6, 77–8, 135
  creative waste/aesthetics of waste, 119–20, 123
  definition of, 15, 26, 27, 34, 36
  elimination of, 99, 111, 113,114, 118, 125, 155–6, 205, 221, 252
  humans as, 7, 10, 56, 197, 251
  who gets to create vs who must clean waste, 251
waste management, 2, 12, 14, 17, 34, 50, 122, 231, 234, 247–8, 260n; *see also* faecal recycling
water borne sewer system
  accessibility of, 35
  and bourgeois denial of defecation, 47, 231
  as replacing fecal recycling, 36, 45
Whorton, J., 110–17, 119, 127–8n, 132, 135

Wilson, E., 10, 13–14, 106n, 127n, 146, 163–9, 190, 213
women's bowel habits 109, 130–1, 135, 140, 146
Women's Social and Political Union (WSPU), 193, 208, 223, 227
Woodson, B., 252–4
work
  Arendt on, 63–71, 78n, 79n, 104, 232
  as world-making, 15–16, 64, 66, 71
  vs labour, 15, 63–71, 78n, 104, 232, 235, 246
working woman/women, 151, 153, 156, 191, 198
  Lytton's desire to represent them, 198–9
world
  as created by work, 15–16, 65–7, 71, 103, 243, 246
  as moving through us, 2, 16, 19, 34, 39, 55, 63, 84–90, 92, 94–5, 101–2, 104, 155, 168, 203, 205, 221, 229, 232
  our metabolic positioning within, 2, 6, 63, 101, 104, 168, 259
worldliness vs worldlessness (Arendt), 64, 68–9, 71, 104
Wright, A., on domino effect of suffragism leading to Jainism, 203–4, 229n

'You Stop, We Stop' campaign, 235–6

Ziarek, E., 190, 207, 209, 215, 217, 226–7
zoē/bios and state of exception (Agamben), 230n

EU representative:
Easy Access System Europe
Mustamäe tee 50, 10621 Tallinn, Estonia
Gpsr.requests@easproject.com